THE ALEXANDER SHAKESPEARE

Text edited by Peter Alexander

General Editor
R. B. Kennedy

Study notes and introduction by Noel Cassidy

Consultant editor: Dr Saadiqa Khan

Twelfth Night

CSEC® Edition

Collins

William Collins' dream of knowledge for all began with the publication of his first book in 1819. A self-educated mill worker, he not only enriched millions of lives, but also founded a flourishing publishing house. Today, staying true to this spirit, Collins books are packed with inspiration, innovation and practical expertise. They place you at the centre of a world of possibility and give you exactly what you need to explore it.

Collins. Freedom to teach.

Published by Collins
An imprint of HarperCollins*Publishers*
The News Building
1 London Bridge Street
London
SE1 9GF

HarperCollins*Publishers*
Macken House, 39/40 Mayor Street Upper,
Dublin 1, D01 C9W8, Ireland

Browse the complete Collins catalogue at www.collins.co.uk

© HarperCollins*Publishers* Limited 2020

10 9 8 7 6 5 4

ISBN 978-0-00-839962-7

All rights reserved. No part of this publication may be reproduced, stored in a retrieval system, or transmitted in any form or by any means, electronic, mechanical, photocopying, recording or otherwise, without the prior written permission of the Publisher or a licence permitting restricted copying in the United Kingdom issued by the Copyright Licensing Agency Ltd., 5th Floor, Shackleton House, 4 Battle Bridge Lane, London SE1 2HX.

British Library Cataloguing in Publication Data
A catalogue record for this publication is available from the British Library.

Text edited by Professor Peter Alexander
Study notes author and introduction:
    Noel Cassidy
General Editor: R.B. Kennedy
Consultant editor: Dr Saadiqa Khan
Publisher: Elaine Higgleton
Product manager: Catherine Martin
Development editor: Lucy Hobbs
Copy editor: Sue Chapple
Proofreader: Sonya Newland
Cover designer: Kevin Robbins
Cover illustrations: Jef Thompson/Shutterstock
    and Meranna/Shutterstock
Internal designer: 2Hoots Publishing Services Ltd
Illustrator: Martin Bustamente
    (Beehive Illustration)
Production controller: Katharine Willard
Printed in India by Multivista Global Pvt. Ltd.

With many thanks to Sandra Morton for reviewing the study notes.

This book contains FSC™ certified paper and other controlled sources to ensure responsible forest management.

For more information visit: www.harpercollins.co.uk/green

CONTENTS

TIMELINE OF SHAKESPEARE'S LIFE AND TIMES	4
THE CONTEXTS OF THE PLAY	7
WHO'S WHO? A GUIDE TO THE MAIN CHARACTERS IN *TWELFTH NIGHT*	15
ACT AND SCENE NOTES	17
A GUIDE TO THE PLAY'S THEMES	72
EXAM PRACTICE FOR CSEC® ENGLISH B	85
TWELFTH NIGHT	95

TIMELINE OF SHAKESPEARE'S LIFE AND TIMES

1558 Queen Elizabeth I is crowned.
1564 William Shakespeare is born in Stratford-upon-Avon, England.
1567 Mary, Queen of Scots, is deposed. James VI (later James I of England) is crowned King of Scotland.
1571 Shakespeare's father John is made Chief Alderman of Stratford.
1576 James Burbage builds the first public playhouse, The Theatre, at Shoreditch, outside the walls of the City of London. At this time, Shakespeare's father's fortunes decline and Shakespeare probably has to leave Grammar School.
1577 Francis Drake begins his voyage around the world, completed in 1580. The idea of sea journeys and their dangers is to feature in a number of Shakespeare's plays, including *Twelfth Night*.
1582 Shakespeare marries Anne Hathaway. Their daughter Susanna is born six months later.
1585 Their twins, Hamnet and Judith, are born. Twins appear in *The Comedy of Errors* and *Twelfth Night*.
1585–92 Shakespeare leaves Stratford for London.
1592 Robert Greene, the London theatre critic and a rival playwright, calls Shakespeare 'an upstart crow'. His early plays – comedies like *The Comedy of Errors* and *The Taming of the Shrew* and corpse-laden histories/tragedies like *Henry VI* and *Richard III* – obviously ruffled feathers among the established writers, who were university educated.
1593 Shakespeare's friend Christopher Marlowe, the best dramatist of the day, is killed in a London tavern. He was bold, brilliant and experimental, and a good role model for Shakespeare.
1593–4 Shakespeare writes 'Venus and Adonis' and 'The Rape of Lucrece', poems for an upper-class audience. The established acting company the Lord Chamberlain's Men accepts him as a resident writer as well as an actor at The Theatre.

TIMELINE OF SHAKESPEARE'S LIFE AND TIMES

An Elizabethan playhouse. Note the apron stage protruding into the auditorium, the space below it, the inner room at the rear of the stage, the gallery above the inner stage, the canopy over the main stage, and the absence of a roof over the audience.

1594–8 Shakespeare writes two plays a year on average, including the comedy *A Midsummer Night's Dream*, the tragedy *Romeo and Juliet* and the histories *Henry IV Part 1* and *Part 2*.

1596 He applies successfully for a coat of arms, showing he wishes to be seen as a rich gentleman. Hamnet, his only son, dies. (Hamnet's twin sister lives until 1662.)

1597 Shakespeare buys New Place, one of the finest houses in Stratford, and moves his family there while he remains in London for much of the year.

1598 The Lord Chamberlain's Men move The Theatre timber by timber over the River Thames and re-erect it at Bankside to form The Globe.

1598–1608 During this period, Shakespeare writes his greatest plays: mature comedies like *Twelfth Night*; problem plays like *Measure for Measure*; and the great tragedies *Julius Caesar, Hamlet, Othello, King Lear, Macbeth, Antony and Cleopatra* and *Coriolanus*. He moves to Southwark but keeps his money interests in Stratford.

1603 Queen Elizabeth I dies. The new King James I honours the Lord Chamberlain's Men by renaming them the King's Men. Fashions change and the King's Men invest in an indoor playhouse, Blackfriars Theatre, built in 1596.

1605 The Gunpowder Plot is stopped: this is an attempt by a group of Catholics to blow up the Houses of Parliament.

1609 Shakespeare publishes *The Sonnets* (probably written many years before). Poetry is the 'high' literary art of the time and these works confirm his genius with a highly educated audience.

1610 *Cymbeline* is produced.

1611 *The Winter's Tale* and *The Tempest* are produced. Shakespeare's last plays follow some aspects of the new fashion for more spectacle, magic and make-believe, and the greater scenic scope allowed by the indoor theatre.

1613 The Globe theatre burns down during a performance of *Henry VIII* (Shakespeare's last play). Around this time, Shakespeare returns to Stratford.

1614 The Globe is rebuilt in 'far finer manner than before', according to Edmund Howes's contemporary account in *The Annals or General Chronicle of England*.

1616 Shakespeare dies in Stratford on his birthday, 23 April.

1623 *The First Folio*, the first collected edition of Shakespeare's plays, is published. It is a large and expensive book, showing the prestige in which Shakespeare is already held.

THE CONTEXTS OF THE PLAY

Elizabethan England at war

The first recorded performance of *Twelfth Night* was in 1602, in the last year of the reign of Queen Elizabeth I. She died in March 1603, after 45 years on the throne. While those years at the height of the English Renaissance saw art, literature and science flourish, England itself was far from stable politically. The Wars of the Roses, a century of civil wars fought for the right to rule England, had ended in 1485. The effects of that turmoil were still felt a little over a century later. Shakespeare wrote about these wars in the three parts of *Henry VI* and *Richard III*. He also showed the continuing significance of earlier English wars of royal succession by writing another sequence of plays about them: *Richard II*, *Henry IV Part 1* and *Part 2*, and *Henry V*, culminating with the Battle of Agincourt. Elizabeth I was very aware of the country's history of war and rebellion, and used powerful advisers to help maintain her position on the throne. She was constantly suspicious, believing that conspirators were attempting to overthrow her – and with good reason. One such plan, the Babington Plot, aimed to replace Elizabeth I with the Catholic Mary Stuart, Queen of Scots. Elizabeth's Principal Secretary, Francis Walsingham, who ran a tight network of spies on the Queen's behalf, infiltrated the plot, resulting in Mary's arrest, imprisonment and execution.

England was also involved in international war, with a conflict against Catholic Spain lasting from 1585 to 1604. That war included the famous defeat of the Spanish Armada, a fleet of 132 ships, by the English naval force of 34 warships and 163 armed merchant ships in the English Channel in 1588. In addition, there was frequent military action against rebellions in Ireland, which was under English control.

Shakespeare was not, therefore, writing in peaceful times, which is perhaps why he so frequently explored England's turbulent past in his history plays. It may also be the reason why he wrote comedies, to provide his audiences with a distraction from more worrying issues.

The power of Queen Elizabeth

Elizabeth I was, of course, the most powerful person in the country, and she was represented in poetry and art almost as a goddess. She actively encouraged this mythologising and would appear in public wearing sumptuous gowns and jewels. She was usually carried above the heads of the people. The image of the queen was presented as an object of devotion. In some early portraits she was associated with classical goddesses, while as the Virgin Queen (she never married) her image to some extent came to replace the Catholic image of the Virgin Mary. Such imagery made her seem all-powerful and remote, impossible to challenge, thus promoting social order and discouraging rebellion.

Although Elizabeth was a powerful and very well-educated woman, her reign did very little to advance the cause of women in England more generally. Women were still denied the same rights to property, wealth and political power as men.

> **Activity 1**
> Discuss in groups what similarities you can see between Queen Elizabeth I and the characterisation of Olivia. Consider how Olivia's position contrasts with the position of most women in England in Shakespeare's time. How do you think Shakespeare's audience might have responded to Olivia?

Courtly love

Courtiers' attitudes to Elizabeth I were very reminiscent of the medieval traditions of courtly love. This was a set of rituals between men and women which were popularised in poetry and art in the Middle Ages, particularly in the poetry of the Italian poet Petrarch (1304–74). Typically, the lady who was the object of love was of high rank and a remote presence. To win her attention, the knight who wished to woo her had to demonstrate the qualities of chivalry, such as devotion, duty and honour. Traditionally, this love was unrequited, usually outside marriage, and the lover's tone was one of suffering, as seen in these lines from a poem by Petrarch, translated by the English poet, Geoffrey Chaucer:

> If no love is, O God, what feel I so?
> And if love is, what thing and which is he?
> If love be good, from whence comes my woe?

The ideas of courtly love were largely artistic, not concerned with defining how relationships actually formed. Marriage among men and women of the court was usually governed by family, power and business interests, rather than love. A key aspect of the tradition is the combination of romantic love with respect for the lady, which is why some of its traditions were also used in Catholic devotional poetry in praise of the Virgin Mary.

> **Activity 2**
> To develop your understanding of how the traditions of courtly love were used in Elizabethan poetry, research in books or online to find examples of love poems by Christopher Marlowe, Sir Walter Raleigh, Ben Jonson, Sir Philip Sidney and Shakespeare himself. Choose a favourite poem and share it with the class. You might want to start with Shakespeare's famous Sonnet XVIII.

As Elizabeth I was of the highest rank in the country, and was unmarried, she became a suitable subject for such service and devotion from her courtiers. The language of love and of service can be very similar. This is reflected in the dialogue of *Twelfth Night*, for instance in the lines between Antonio and Sebastian. More prominently, Shakespeare uses the ideas of courtly love to characterise Orsino's unrequited devotion to Olivia.

Shakespeare's most productive period

Born in Stratford-upon-Avon in central England in 1564, Shakespeare came to London at some point in the 1580s and initially worked as an actor before he turned to writing plays. By the time he retired and returned to Stratford, he had written 37 plays. He was widely admired and highly successful in his own time, and he is now probably the most famous playwright in the world. *Twelfth Night* was written at the most productive period of his writing career, when he was at the peak of his powers. In the period between 1598 and 1601, he wrote seven plays, including *Henry V*, the Roman history *Julius Caesar* and *Hamlet*, perhaps his most famous play. It was also when he wrote his three great mature comedies, *Much Ado About Nothing*, *As You Like It* and *Twelfth Night*.

Shakespeare's theatre

The theatre world of Elizabethan England was a vibrant one. William Shakespeare himself was rooted in theatre. He began his career as an actor, so he had an actor's sense of which speeches would be effective on stage and how plays could be delivered with maximum impact for an audience. When writing his plays he worked directly with his company, the Lord Chamberlain's Men. It is therefore likely that he valued feedback from the actors as rehearsals progressed. However, a permanent theatre building was still a new idea, as the first one was only built in London in 1576. The Globe, where most of Shakespeare's plays were first performed, was built in 1599, only three years before *Twelfth Night* reached the stage.

This was an unprecedented period of theatrical inventiveness, with many playwrights providing material for performance. Some are now forgotten, but Shakespeare worked alongside writers such as Thomas Kyd, Ben Jonson, Christopher Marlowe, Thomas Middleton and John Fletcher. These men were both rivals and friends, and he probably collaborated with some of them at various points in his career. Plays at this time were largely written in verse, prose being used for casual conversations and dialogue between comic or lower-status characters. In *Twelfth Night*, most of the dialogue between the main characters is in verse, while the comic scenes involving Sir Toby Belch, Sir Andrew Aguecheek, Fabian and Maria are written in prose.

Christopher Marlowe was credited with establishing iambic pentameter as the favoured rhythm of verse drama, and Shakespeare developed its use. The iambic pentameter line has five units known as feet (*penta* means five in Greek, and *meter* is a measure). Each foot has two syllables, with the emphasis on

THE CONTEXTS OF THE PLAY

the second syllable. For example, look at Viola's line here (Act 1 Scene 4 line 42). The stressed syllables are in bold so that you can see iambic pentameter in action:

> Whoe'**er** I **woo**, my**self** would **be** his **wife**.

This is a flexible rhythm that fits the patterns of English speech naturally, making it perfectly suited to dramatic dialogue and monologue. One thing to look for in Shakespeare's verse is where he makes changes within the rhythm to create a different emphasis. Look at the following line, where Olivia emphasises the promise she seeks from Sebastian, thinking he is Cesario:

> **Plight** me the **full** assu**rance of** your **faith**. (Act 4 Scene 3 line 26)

The words of plays were very important – Shakespeare's audiences would speak of going to *hear* a play rather than to see one. The Latin root of the word *audience* means 'to hear' and the visual elements of the theatre were relatively simple. On Shakespeare's open-air stage at The Globe, there was little set compared with what we would expect in a theatre today. While many audience members attending the theatre would not have been able to read or write, there was a long tradition of oral storytelling. Listeners loved words and paid careful attention to them, which is why the plays of Shakespeare and his contemporaries are full of rich verbal imagery and extensive word play.

The Globe Theatre was a circular building, referred to as a 'wooden O' in Shakespeare's *Henry V*. The actors performed on a raised **apron stage** at about an adult's chest height. As can be seen in the illustration on page 5, this stage stuck out into the circular yard, known as the **Pit**, surrounded on three sides by the audience. The pillars, shown in the illustration, could have been used as hiding places in Act 2 Scene 5 as Malvolio reads the letter. There was a curtained-off area to the rear of the stage, allowing for dramatic reveals. This could have been used for the cell where Malvolio is imprisoned in Act 4 Scene 2, for instance. A **gallery** above this area was used by musicians, perhaps including those that Orsino asks to play for him at the beginning of *Twelfth Night*. (The now famous balcony scene in *Romeo and Juliet* would have made use of this gallery too.)

A thatched roof covered the seating areas and the stage, but the central Pit was open to the weather. There was no artificial lighting, so performances usually started in the early afternoon. The atmosphere was probably quite rowdy at times; the standing audience in the Pit would form a lively crowd, eating and drinking during performances and voicing their opinions about the events of the play. We can imagine their comments at the sight of Cesario and Sir Andrew Aguecheek facing each other in their terrified duel in Act 3 Scene 4.

> **Activity 3**
> Discuss in groups how the comic scenes, the soliloquies and asides in the play would be performed with members of the audience in such close proximity to the actors. For example, when Viola takes the audience into her confidence at the end of Act 2 Scene 4, or when Sebastian shares his confusion at the beginning of Act 4 Scene 3.

Ordinary working people could afford to attend the theatre, as a ticket to stand in the Pit cost very little. Audience members in the Pit were known as **groundlings** and a number of characters in Shakespeare's plays make disparaging comments about them. Around the Pit, forming the walls of the theatre, were more expensive seats on three levels. Access to these seats cost at least double the entrance to the Pit, and a box in a prime position cost considerably more. Shakespeare's audiences therefore represented a full cross-section of Elizabethan society.

Women were not allowed to act in Shakespeare's time. This meant that boys played the female parts, which perhaps explains why women characters dressing up as young men to disguise themselves is a key part of two of Shakespeare's comedies, *Twelfth Night* and *As You Like It*. Viola's role, disguised as Cesario for most of the action, is central to *Twelfth Night*. This makes the role easier for a boy actor to maintain, while the layers of pretence add to the comedy of the performance.

Shakespeare's comedies

Love is the central subject matter of Shakespeare's comedies, but in these plays relationships do not go to plan and are tested by circumstances. There are confusions and challenges, but the relationships are eventually affirmed at the plays' endings. In this way, Shakespeare's comedies conform to the traditions of the **comic genre**: these plays start with characters being separated, but after a sequence of confusions and difficulties, challenges and tests, they move towards reunion, marriage and a happy ending. In many of Shakespeare's comedies, though, the completeness of the happy ending can be questioned. For example, at the end of *Much Ado About Nothing*, Hero marries the man who has previously cruelly rejected her. Even the marriages at the end of *Love's Labours Lost* are postponed by bad news. As Berowne, one of the characters in that play says, 'Our wooing doth not end like an old play'. *Twelfth Night* ends with a number of weddings, but Antonio stands alone, while crucially Malvolio departs swearing revenge on 'the whole pack of you' (Act 5 Scene 1 line 381). The play ends happily for the higher-ranking characters, but those lower on the social scale do not entirely share the joy.

The play in performance

When *Twelfth Night* was first performed, the famous comic actor Robert Armin played the part of Feste. As the play was written at a similar time to *As You Like It*, it seems likely that the Lord Chamberlain's Men had two talented boy actors who were able to play subtle romantic women's roles. More recently, there have been a few significant performances of the play, some of which can be viewed on DVD recordings or the internet.

Kenneth Branagh's 1987 Renaissance Theatre production was set at Christmas time, and the melancholy of Orsino's scenes was accentuated by blue lighting. The comic scenes, particularly Malvolio's discovery of the letter, used clever stage business to great effect, with the conspirators hiding behind garden shrubs in mobile plant pots, allowing them to move around Malvolio. Richard Briers gave a masterful performance in the role, beginning the play as a repellent, sneering figure, but transforming into a horrifically broken man by the end.

A reproduction of the Elizabethan Globe Theatre has been built close to where Shakespeare's theatre once stood on the south bank of the Thames in London. The company based there staged a production of *Twelfth Night* with an all-male cast in 2012, with Mark Rylance as Olivia and Stephen Fry as Malvolio. Although men, rather than boys, played the female parts, this production experimented with the effects of Shakespeare's style of theatre for a modern audience. While a 'cross-dressing' production might seem a strange affectation today, Shakespeare's audience knew nothing else.

Simon Godwin's 2017 production at the Royal National Theatre also experimented with the play, casting Tamsin Greig as Malvolia (a female Malvolio). This unusual interpretation was very successful and, interestingly, created a much greater sympathy for the character. In the theatre, audiences cheered for Malvolia at various stages of the action and were devastated by the character's eventual fate.

Activity 4
Research performances of the play online, if possible, and find reviews of different productions. Discuss ways in which seeing different performances or reading about different interpretations increases your understanding of the play.

Task
The first recorded performance of *Twelfth Night* took place in the hall of the Middle Temple, one of London's law schools, but it was performed at The Globe as well. Consider how indoor and outdoor performances might have differed.
- Choose two examples where the features of The Globe stage, described above, could have been used effectively in performance of the play.
- Give an example of where the quieter atmosphere and candlelight might have been effective in an indoor performance.
- If you were staging the play today and had the option of an indoor or an outdoor space, which would you choose, and why?

WHO'S WHO? A GUIDE TO THE MAIN CHARACTERS IN *TWELFTH NIGHT*

Orsino is the Duke of Illyria, who has fallen in love with Countess Olivia. When she rejects him, he is sorrowful and wallows in his rejection. He forms a strong friendship with the character he knows as Cesario, and sends him to win Olivia for him.

Viola is shipwrecked on the coast of Illyria and decides to dress as a young man in order to serve in the court of Duke Orsino. There, she is known as **Cesario** and is employed as Orsino's messenger to Olivia. However, she falls in love with Orsino herself.

Sebastian is Viola's twin brother, shipwrecked in the same storm, but separated from her. He is helped by a sailor, Antonio. He makes his way into Illyria where he is mistaken for Cesario, his twin sister's male personality. Olivia, initially believing that he is Cesario, marries him.

Olivia is a countess, a woman of high society, who is in grieving for her dead brother and has sworn never to marry. She therefore refuses to see Orsino, but when his messenger Cesario arrives, she falls in love with him, not realising that Cesario is in fact a woman in disguise.

Malvolio is Olivia's chief servant; he is pompous and self-important, which leads to conflict with other members of Olivia's household. He is also secretly in love with Olivia himself, which makes him the object of other characters' jokes and mockery.

TWELFTH NIGHT

Feste is a clown, or jester, who entertains at both Orsino's court and Olivia's household. He is always keen to earn money by his singing and jokes, but often also seems to know more about what is going on than he admits. He takes a central role in the mocking of Malvolio.

Sir Toby Belch, Olivia's uncle, enjoys drinking alcohol and making jokes. While he is the life and soul of the party, he also takes advantage of Sir Andrew Aguecheek and behaves cruelly towards Malvolio. He is happy to make other people uncomfortable for his own amusement.

Sir Andrew Aguecheek has fallen in love with Olivia and hopes to marry her. He is, however, a bumbling fool who has no chance of success. His foolishness provides a great deal of humour, but at the end he gains sympathy because he is so badly treated by Sir Toby.

Maria is one of Olivia's servants, who is quick-witted and mischievous. She invents the plan to deceive Malvolio, and at the end of the play we hear she has married Sir Toby.

Fabian is another servant in Olivia's household, who takes part in the jokes and tricks created by Sir Tony and Maria. He admits the truth of what has been happening to Olivia at the end of the play.

Antonio is a faithful sailor, who helps Sebastian in Illyria. This causes problems, as he is a wanted man in Illyria because of his role in sea battles against Orsino's navy, but he takes the risk because of his devotion to Sebastian.

Activity 5
Now that you know a little about each character, what else would you like to find out about them? For each character, write down one or two questions that you plan to find answers to as you gain more understanding of *Twelfth Night*.

ACT AND SCENE NOTES

Twelfth Night is 5 January – the twelfth night after Christmas, the night before the Epiphany in the Christian calendar. In Europe, in Shakespeare's time, this end of the Christmas period was the excuse for a final party. Traditionally, it was quite an energetic celebration, with much eating and drinking. It was a time of 'misrule', where practical jokes were played and the normal standards of behaviour were abandoned for a night: masters waited on their servants and sometimes men would dress as women. Although it is not certain why Shakespeare called his play *Twelfth Night*, its subtitle *What You Will* reflects some of this anarchic spirit. It is a play of confusions, costumes, practical jokes and misunderstandings, where the world is turned topsy-turvy. In the Caribbean, 'twelfth night' refers to a sudden and unexpected change at a key moment; many such moments can be recognised in the play's action.

A law student, John Manningham, recorded in his diary that he saw *Twelfth Night* performed on 2 February 1602, which is the earliest reference to the play. He saw it not at The Globe, but in Middle Temple Hall, part of the Inns of Court in London. He was an experienced playgoer and compared the play with Shakespeare's other comedy involving twins, *The Comedy of Errors*, and to an Italian play, *Gl'Ingannati*, which translates into English as *The Deceived*. Although there is no direct evidence that Shakespeare knew this play, there are clear similarities with *Twelfth Night*, as both involve a plot of confusions with a pair of girl/boy twins at the centre. In Shakespeare's theatre, the confusions and comedy would have been pushed further because boy actors played the female roles.

Act 1

Summary
Shakespeare's plays are divided into five acts. When performed in a theatre like The Globe, the action would have been continuous, but in an indoor theatre like Middle Temple Hall, breaks between acts would have allowed the candles used to illuminate the stage to be trimmed. The first act of the play is

often known as the **exposition**, as it introduces key characters and establishes the foundations for the action to follow. Tension and conflicts are created in Act 1, which are then developed throughout the play until they are resolved at the end. In this play, the concern with love is swiftly introduced and the audience has met nearly all the main characters by the end of the act.

Act 1 Scene 1

Lines 1–15 Orsino demonstrates the changeable moods of someone in love, asking for music to play and then stopping it according to his feelings.

Lines 16–24 Curio tries to distract Orsino by suggesting other activities, like hunting. Orsino reveals that the object of his love is Olivia.

Lines 25–42 Valentine returns from Olivia's house and confirms that Olivia has refused to see anyone for seven years because she is mourning her dead brother. Paradoxically, Orsino takes this as an encouraging sign: it seems contradictory that he should be encouraged by Olivia's refusal to see anyone.

What happens

Orsino's first speech sets the initial mood of the play, presenting the audience with a version of love which might remind you of a self-absorbed, love-struck teenager. The speech is all about how Orsino feels; he doesn't even mention the person with whom he is in love. Olivia is only named when Curio suggests hunting as a diversion – in line 17, Shakespeare puns on the word 'hart' (a female deer) and 'heart' (the source of love). Orsino's view of her is full of **hyperbole** (exaggeration) – he states that she 'purg'd the air of pestilence' (line 20). The audience finds out more about Olivia from Valentine. He reports that she will not see Orsino, or indeed any person, but will live like a nun ('like a cloistress she will veiled walk', line 29) and will cry in her rooms in tribute to 'A brother's dead love' (line 32). Orsino is encouraged that any woman who has such love for a brother might eventually have even deeper love for him. He goes off to dream of love while lying among flowers, another comic version of his romantic ideas.

ACT AND SCENE NOTES

The characters
Orsino dominates this scene, giving the audience a comically exaggerated characterisation of romantic love. In his character, Shakespeare is satirising the conventions of courtly love (for more on this, see pages 8–9). He is clearly a rich man, too, with servants and musicians in attendance to do his bidding.

Curio and **Valentine** are two young gentlemen who serve in Duke Orsino's court.

> **Activity 6**
> Take some of Orsino's romantic ideas of love and develop them into a love letter from him to Olivia. Try to imitate some of the language he uses in the scene. To take it further, you could try to write the love letter in the form of a poem. Compare your version with others in the class.

Dramatic techniques
The scene begins with a **monologue** of 15 lines. This substantial speech by a single character gives an insight into Orsino's feelings before the audience knows who he is. It is likely that the set, and perhaps more specifically in Shakespeare's time, Orsino's costume, would indicate his wealth and status. Wealthy patrons of the Elizabethan theatre sometimes handed down grand clothes for productions, and occasionally theatre companies spent considerable sums on resplendent robes that could have been used for noblemen such as Orsino. His status, but not his name, is revealed when Curio addresses him as 'my lord' (line 16) and he finally names Olivia in line 19. Rather than giving out all the information straight away, Shakespeare feeds the audience a little at a time in this scene, creating curiosity and laying down threads for the audience to pick up in later scenes.

Language
Shakespeare shows Orsino's preoccupation with his own feelings in a speech full of rich **imagery** – 'music' is compared to a 'food' (line 1) to consume and there are references to 'excess', 'surfeiting' and 'appetite' (lines 2–3). Orsino then equates the beauty of music's sound with the beauty of the scent of flowers. Note how Shakespeare uses the **caesura**, a break in a line of verse, in line 7 to show Orsino's shift of thought, when he has

had 'Enough' of music. He suggests love is as changeable as the sea and in line 14 links love with 'fancy', or the imagination.

The playfulness of the language about love continues with the hart/heart **pun** (lines 17 and 21), shared between Curio and Orsino, while Orsino uses the exaggerated **simile** of 'cruel hounds' to describe his 'desires' (line 22), suggesting he is hunted down by his own feelings of love for Olivia.

> **Activity 7**
> What is your reaction to Orsino? Do you sympathise with him, or find him ridiculous? Can you think of any similar characters in films or people who are characterised in a song? What are the connections?

Valentine's description of Olivia presents her voluntary removal from the world in a similarly hyperbolic way. She will cut herself off for 'seven years' (line 27), be 'veiled' like 'a cloistress' (line 29) and weep 'eye-offending brine' (line 31) for her brother. Shakespeare balances Orsino's excessive expressions of love with Olivia's exaggerated mourning for her brother. The audience might find something false in both of them.

Act 1 Scene 2

Lines 1–21 Finding herself on the shores of Illyria after a shipwreck, Viola's first concern is for her brother. The Captain thinks he also may have survived the shipwreck, since he saw him swimming while clinging to a mast.

Lines 22–64 Viola learns that Illyria is governed by Duke Orsino and decides to seek employment with him as a servant.

What happens

A young woman, whom the audience later discovers to be Viola, has been rescued from a shipwreck by sailors and finds herself on the coast of a country called Illyria. She fears that her brother drowned in the shipwreck, but the Captain gives her hope that he managed to survive. She decides she will try to get a job with Duke Orsino, of whom she has previously heard, but for that, she needs to be disguised as a man. The Captain agrees to help her.

ACT AND SCENE NOTES

The characters
Viola is established as one of the play's central characters, though she is unnamed on this first appearance – and indeed is not named until the final scene of the play. Here, she is distraught over the possible loss of her bother, but plucky enough to come up with a plan which will help her survive in a strange country.

Captain is one of a number of humble characters who have an important role in the action. He has helped save Viola from the shipwreck and immediately agrees to assist in her plan.

> **Activity 8**
> What is the first impression you gain of Viola? Consider carefully what she says about herself, her brother, the Captain and Orsino.

Dramatic techniques
The setting of Illyria is important. Shakespeare sets a number of his plays in locations outside the normal confines of society. Illyria was an ancient region in Europe, on the eastern coast of the Adriatic Sea, but Shakespeare is less interested in the geography than in creating the impression of a far-distant place where strange events can happen. This technique is similar to the wood outside Athens in *A Midsummer Night's Dream*, where the lovers can escape the rules of the city, and Prospero's island in *The Tempest*, where magic can occur. In *As You Like It*, characters discover more about themselves in the Forest of Arden outside the city.

> **Activity 9**
> In pairs, discuss whether you think it is important for the set design to suggest that Illyria is a place where strange things can happen, or whether it should be more realistic. Make a few suggestions for the design for this scene.

Language
Viola's brother, Sebastian, does not appear until the beginning of Act 2, but it is important to establish his character early, so Shakespeare devotes the first section of the scene to him. Though he is not named, the word 'brother' is used three

times and the Captain creates a vivid image of his survival, showing 'Courage and hope' and clinging to a 'strong mast' (lines 13–14). The simile 'like Arion on the dolphin's back' (line 15) emphasises his ease in the stormy waters.

Rank is emphasised in this scene: the Captain tells Viola that Illyria is governed by a 'noble duke' (line 25) and that Olivia is 'the daughter of a count' (line 36), lower in status than a duke but still among the higher social classes. The Captain emphasises this by observing that 'What great ones do the less will prattle of' (line 33). The verb 'prattle' suggests idle gossip and implies that ordinary people ('the less') will always be fascinated by those higher in society – like the rich and famous today. Viola announces her intention to 'serve this duke' (line 55) as a 'eunuch' (line 56). While this particular identity would help account for the pitch of her voice and her femininity, it is one to which Shakespeare does not refer again.

> **Activity 10**
> This is the scene in which disguise is introduced into the play, and this idea features prominently in the language. Look carefully at Viola's speech between lines 47 and 55 to see how many references she makes to different kinds of disguise and appearance. Discuss their significance with a partner.

Act 1 Scene 3

Lines 1–41 Maria reprimands Sir Toby Belch for his excessive drinking.

Lines 41–129 Sir Andrew Aguecheek enters. His unsuitability as a match for Olivia is soon made plain as both Maria and Sir Toby make jokes at his expense and he shows himself to be a gullible fool.

What happens

This is the first scene set at Olivia's house, but Olivia herself does not yet appear. Instead, Shakespeare introduces the audience to other members of her household: Maria, her waiting woman; Sir Toby, her uncle; and Sir Andrew, a dim-witted young gentleman who hopes to win Olivia's favour and marry her. These characters form the basis of the comic **subplot** of the play. We learn quickly that Sir Toby is known for 'quaffing and drinking' (line 13) and Sir Andrew is 'a foolish knight' (line 14). The rest of the scene develops Sir Andrew's foolishness, as Sir Toby and Maria take advantage of him by making fun of him, playing on his misunderstandings. For example, he is beginning to realise that his quest for Olivia is hopeless, but Sir Toby encourages him to persevere and to demonstrate his skills, one of which, Sir Andrew claims, is dancing. It is likely that Sir Andrew's dancing is as undeveloped as his verbal wit.

> **Activity 11**
> Compare the ways in which Shakespeare presents Orsino's court and Olivia's household. Think about the mood of the scenes and the characters the audience sees. What do you think might be the effect on the audience of this contrast? How does it contribute to the development of the comedy?

The characters
Maria is Olivia's personal servant; it is on Olivia's behalf that she reprimands Sir Toby for drinking late. However, she is clearly on very good terms with Sir Toby and shares the mockery of Sir Andrew with him.

Sir Toby Belch is appropriately named for a drinker, and though he is the uncle of a count's daughter, he does not behave like a nobleman, enjoying unrestrained drinking, parties and practical jokes.

Sir Andrew Aguecheek is a gentleman of some wealth ('three thousand ducats a year', line 20), but is physically unattractive, with lank hair that 'hangs like flax on a distaff' (line 93). He is also slow-witted, the butt of other people's humour.

Dramatic techniques
Many of Shakespeare's plays have a subplot, but that is in some ways a misleading term, particularly for *Twelfth Night*. It implies that this part of the narrative is of secondary importance to the main plot, but the two plots in this play are very closely intertwined. The subplot presents a distorted reflection of the main plot, and in this scene Sir Andrew is a comic parallel to

Orsino – where Orsino is sophisticated and romantic, Sir Andrew is naively hopeful but foolish.

> **Activity 12**
> Produce imaginary dating profiles for Orsino and Sir Andrew Aguecheek. Think about how they might present their age, social position, attractive qualities, hobbies. Try to match the characters as Shakespeare presents them. How do they compare, and how might Olivia respond to them?

From his appearance to his inability to keep pace with verbal humour, Sir Andrew is portrayed comically for the amusement of other characters and the audience. He is an unconscious clown, unlike the professional clown Feste, whom the audience meets later. As well as **verbal comedy** in this scene, Shakespeare includes **physical comedy**. While Sir Andrew claims he can dance well – 'cut a caper' and 'have the backtrick' (lines 111 and 113) – it is clear that Shakespeare does not intend him to dance well at all. The scene ends with Sir Toby directing Sir Andrew in a ludicrous dance: 'Let me see thee caper. Ha, higher! Ha, ha, excellent!' (lines 128–9).

Language
Much of the humour in this scene is verbal, playing on different meanings or misunderstandings. The first is in line 46, when Sir Andrew misinterprets Sir Toby's imperative 'Accost' (meaning to address someone) as Maria's name. When Sir Toby explains, in rather colourful terms (lines 52–3), Sir Andrew misinterprets again, taking Sir Toby too literally. When Maria joins in, she keeps changing the meaning of the words 'hand' and 'dry' (lines 60–73) and Sir Andrew consistently fails to catch up. This kind of wordplay was very popular in Elizabethan poetry and drama.

> **Activity 13**
> Sir Andrew admits in lines 77–8 that he lacks 'wit', a moment of self-knowledge amid the humour. With a partner, discuss how far Shakespeare presents Sir Andrew as a complete fool, or suggests that Sir Toby and Maria are rather cruel in the way they take advantage of him.

Act 1 Scene 4

Lines 1–8 Valentine notices that after only three days' service, Viola, now appearing as Cesario, has won Orsino's favour.

Lines 9–40 This is confirmed when Orsino enters, calling for Cesario, and sends Valentine away. He asks Cesario to carry his message of love to Olivia.

Lines 41–2 Viola admits that she has fallen in love with Orsino.

What happens

Each scene so far has involved different characters in a different location. This is the first scene to come back to a location – Orsino's court, last seen in Act 1 Scene 1 – and it brings together Orsino and Viola, except that Viola is now in the disguise she spoke of at the end of Act 1 Scene 2 and is known as Cesario. She remains as Cesario until the end of the play.

The action has moved forwards three days, but Cesario has already integrated himself successfully at Orsino's court. A close relationship has developed between Cesario and Orsino, who says that he has 'unclasp'd / To thee the book even of my secret soul' (lines 13–14). Having failed so far to persuade Olivia to hear his messages of love, he thinks that Cesario may have better success. Orsino thinks that Cesario's youth, which makes him seem more like a woman, will make him a more suitable messenger. Of course, in comparing Cesario to a woman, he is unconsciously seeing through the disguise and recognising Viola's femininity. Having reluctantly agreed to go to Olivia's house, Viola admits in a final **aside** that she has fallen in love with Orsino herself. However, dressed as a man, she is unable to express this to him.

The characters

Viola appears for the first time as Cesario. She has been successful in her disguise, obtaining employment in Orsino's court and gaining his personal confidence. It is clear she is passing as a young man, rather than a 'eunuch' (Act 1 Scene 2 line 56), as Orsino addresses her as 'good youth' (line 15) and 'Dear lad' (line 29). He also makes several remarks about Cesario's femininity (lines 31–4), suggesting that Cesario is seen as a teenager. The difficulty of Cesario's task as a messenger between Orsino and Olivia is revealed to the audience at the end of the scene, when Viola admits that she would like to be Orsino's 'wife' herself (line 42).

Orsino is still besotted with Olivia and is determined to overcome her reluctance to see him, asking Cesario to 'Be clamorous and leap all civil bounds' (line 21). He has also become close to Cesario, feeling that he is a kindred spirit with whom he can share his most private thoughts.

> ### Activity 14
> Think about Orsino's instructions to Cesario. Do you admire his persistence with Olivia, or do you think that his behaviour would be viewed as harassment today? What quotations would you use to support your opinion?

Dramatic techniques
Viola's male disguise enables the plot to progress, while creating elements of humour for the audience through **dramatic irony**. The audience is aware of Cesario's real identity, while other characters are not. The aside at the end of the scene supports the dramatic irony, as Viola takes the audience into her confidence and speaks to them directly. Costume cannot do all the work as disguise – in some way, Viola will have to behave as a man too, and her choices of mannerisms could provoke humour in the theatre. The comedy of this situation would be doubled in Shakespeare's theatre, as boys played all female roles: Cesario would have been a young man being played by a woman being played by a boy.

> ### Activity 15
> Discuss in small groups what typical elements of young male behaviour Viola could imitate to appear convincingly as Cesario. How might these be slightly exaggerated to create humour for the audience, developing the dramatic irony?

Dramatic irony is pushed further when Orsino comments on Cesario's feminine features – his 'smooth and rubious' lips (line 32) and high-pitched voice are all 'semblative a woman's part' (line 34). The aside at the end of the scene confirms the complicit relationship between the audience and Viola; only they know the secret of her true identity and recognise the complexities of her situation.

Language

The intimacy which has been quickly established between Orsino and Cesario is apparent in Orsino's **metaphor**: 'I have unclasp'd / To thee the book even of my secret soul' (lines 13–14). The secrecy of his private thoughts is emphasised by making them seem to be held in a chest with big clasps to keep it shut, but these clasps have been opened for Cesario. Orsino's excessive love for Olivia remains, though, reflected in his commands to Cesario: 'Be not denied' (line 16); 'Be clamorous and leap all civil bounds' (line 21); 'unfold the passion of my love' (line 24).

Act 1 Scene 5

Lines 1–28 Maria reprimands the Clown (Feste) for his absence from Olivia's house.

Lines 29–92 Feste gets himself out of trouble with Olivia by making witty jokes at her expense, which win her over. Malvolio, her steward, expresses his disapproval of Feste.

Lines 93–159 In turn, Maria, Sir Toby and Malvolio all announce the arrival of Cesario as a messenger from Orsino. His persistence persuades Olivia to see him.

Lines 160–277 Viola, as Cesario, presents Orsino's message and discusses love with Olivia.

Lines 278–300 Olivia reveals that she finds Cesario attractive. She pretends that he has left a ring with her from Orsino and sends Malvolio after Cesario to return it. In fact, it is a love token from herself.

What happens

This scene completes the initial exposition and the audience finally meets Olivia. Even this is delayed, though, as Maria first tells Feste that Olivia will 'hang thee for thy absence' (line 3). Withdrawing from society and sending Maria to remonstrate with both Sir Toby Belch and Feste, Olivia sounds quite a forbidding character. This seems to be confirmed when her first line on entering is to dismiss Feste: 'Take the fool away' (line 34). However, it doesn't take long for her to change, as she succumbs to Feste's jokes, even though she is their target – he 'proves' that she is the fool, rather than he, because she mourns for her brother when her brother, having lived a virtuous life, must be in heaven (lines 52–66). This not only changes Olivia's mood, but subtly points out the folly of her continued extreme response to her brother's death.

Malvolio, Olivia's steward, is also introduced, and continues the disapproval of Feste, expressing surprise that Olivia 'takes delight in such a barren rascal' (lines 77–8). This quickly establishes Malvolio's character as joyless and superior, lacking generosity towards others. Olivia seems to agree with this view of him.

> **Activity 16**
> Discuss your response to Malvolio. Write down two or three key quotations from his exchange with Olivia about Feste that seem to you to be particularly revealing.

The audience may remember that Orsino demanded that Cesario keep his 'fixed foot' (Act 1 Scene 4 line 17) at Olivia's gate; it becomes clear he is obeying orders when first Maria, then Sir Toby, report that 'a fair young man' (line 96) is at the gate. Malvolio is sent to dismiss him, but even he returns to report that the 'young fellow' (line 132) refuses to move. Olivia is intrigued enough to invite him in. She calls her women and disguises herself with a veil so that Cesario will not be certain which of the women is Olivia. The way Cesario approaches the task of wooing Olivia is unexpected and humorous, suggesting the strangeness of seeking the love of a woman for another person by pointing out that he has learned an excellently written speech. Just as Feste's jokes puncture the extremity of Olivia's mourning, Cesario's comments puncture the excess of Orsino's romantic language. It is this unusual quality in Cesario, as well as his refusal to leave, that fascinates Olivia, and eventually she agrees to listen to him alone, sending her women away.

The dialogue that follows shows an open relationship developing between Olivia and Cesario. Cesario praises Olivia's beauty and argues strongly in favour of Orsino; while Olivia says that she 'cannot love him' (line 246), Cesario cannot 'understand it' (line 256). The audience might see that Cesario's speech (lines 257–64) about how he would love Olivia is probably expressing Viola's own love for Orsino, and feel sympathy for her awkward position. Cesario gives riddling replies about his

ACT AND SCENE NOTES

parents to maintain the disguise. However, it is already clear that Olivia is attracted to him when she suggests that Cesario might 'come to me again' (line 270) to report on Orsino's response – when she is clearly not interested in Orsino. This is confirmed by her **soliloquy** (lines 278–87) when she dwells on Cesario's 'perfections' (line 285), making clear another stage in the comic confusions of the play. Her pretence about the ring that she sends after Cesario takes this further and prepares for a later scene. By the end of Act 1, Shakespeare's love triangle between Orsino, Olivia and Viola/Cesario is complete. The rest of the play will tease it out.

The characters

Feste appears in the script as **Clown** and is in fact only referred to once by his name in the play (Act 2 Scene 4 line 11). However, he is usually known as Feste, as this character has much more significance than the generic 'Clown' suggests. He is an 'allow'd fool' (line 88), someone whose job is to entertain by joking and singing. In this position, he can take liberties with those who employ him – as he does in this scene by making jokes about Olivia's mourning.

Malvolio, whose name suggests 'ill-wishing', is quickly revealed to be a sneering, pompous character in his attitude to Feste and Cesario. As Olivia says, he is 'sick of self-love' (line 84).

Olivia is portrayed as a thoughtful and generous woman. She forgives Feste, is patient with Malvolio and eventually relents and agrees to meet Cesario. Cesario notes that her face is 'beauty truly blent' (line 227) and the audience sees her gradually being won over by Cesario's charm and wit. She is firm in her refusal of Orsino, but feels herself becoming fascinated by Cesario – 'Not too fast! Soft, soft!' (line 282) she tells herself, but still sends him the ring.

> **Activity 17**
> Discuss with a partner what risks Olivia runs by sending her servant Malvolio with the ring to Cesario, who is Orsino's servant. At the time, it would be unusual for a woman to send unsolicited gifts to a man. Why do you think Shakespeare chooses a ring as the token?

Viola performs her duties as Cesario fully, consistently presenting Orsino's case even though she is in love with him herself. Her disguise causes even more unforeseen complications.

Dramatic techniques
Feste's role as the fool links him with several comic characters in Shakespeare's plays, such as Touchstone in *As You Like It* and the Fool in *King Lear*. They suggest that there is wisdom behind their fooling and they often know more than they admit, such as Feste's gentle criticism of Olivia's excessive mourning. Feste also provides a link between the households of Orsino and Olivia, moving freely between them.

The dramatic irony created by Viola's disguise develops further here. The audience will feel the poignancy of Cesario pleading for Olivia to accept Orsino while Viola is in love with him herself, but will also appreciate the humour of Olivia falling in love with Cesario, who is in fact a young woman. It is the Cesario disguise that allows the love triangle to take shape.

> **Activity 18**
> Consider who you think has shown the truest love so far – Orsino, Olivia or Viola. Note down your reasons, with some quotations from Act 1, and compare with a classmate.

Language
The idea that Orsino's romantic language is excessive is raised when Olivia says that 'poetical' words are more likely to be 'feigned' (lines 186–7). There is a deliberate humour in Shakespeare, a poet, writing these lines, and it is revealing that the dialogue between Cesario and Olivia, which begins in prose, moves into verse. Cesario begins on line 227, immediately disrupting the **iambic rhythm** at the beginning of lines 228 and 229 to emphasise 'Nature' and 'Lady', showing her admiration for Olivia and her beauty. Olivia follows, speaking verse from line 246. This is one of the means by which Shakespeare changes the tone of the scene as the dialogue becomes more intimate, and with the focus on love, Olivia begins to be attracted to Cesario. In her soliloquy, delivered with no other characters present so that she can speak her mind honestly, she uses the

ACT AND SCENE NOTES

metaphor of 'the plague' (line 284) for her feelings of love – love is like an infection that she has caught without realising.

> **Activity 19**
> As verse is usually used for the more important characters, or those of a higher social status, you might expect Shakespeare to show Malvolio's elevated view of himself by writing his speeches in verse. Consider the reasons why Malvolio's speeches are written in prose.

> **Task**
> Identify from Act 1 the different ways in which Shakespeare shows Orsino's infatuation with Olivia.
> - Consider the ways Orsino talks about love in Scene 1.
> - Look at the instructions he gives to Cesario in Scene 4.
> - What is your response to Shakespeare's portrayal of Orsino as a lover? How does this portrayal contrast with the romantic love developing in Viola and Olivia?

Act 2

Summary

Act 2 demonstrates Shakespeare's skill in plotting, as each scene picks up threads of the action from Act 1. This is clear when the first scene introduces Viola's twin, Sebastian, proving that the Captain's confidence in his survival in Act 1 Scene 2 was well placed. Now that the audience knows Sebastian is alive, well and in Illyria, they can expect that he and Viola will be reunited. However, in line with the conventions of comedy, they will have to wait for this until the last scene of the play.

In the same way, Scene 2 shows Malvolio bringing the ring to Cesario, as sent by Olivia in Act 1 Scene 5. In Scene 3, Maria, Sir Toby, Sir Andrew and Feste devise a plan against Malvolio, which comes to fruition in Scene 5, after an intervening scene where Orsino and Cesario discuss love. This dialogue is now coloured for the audience by the knowledge not only of Viola's love for Orsino, but also of Olivia's love for Cesario. The plotting is complicated, but by having a sequence of clear, focused scenes, Shakespeare ensures that the audience follows the action and can enjoy anticipating how events will play out.

Act 2 Scene 1

Lines 1–40 Sebastian reveals his true identity to Antonio and expresses his belief that his sister Viola is dead. He parts with Antonio to head to Orsino's court.
Lines 41–5 Antonio, who has enemies in Orsino's court, decides he will follow Sebastian anyway.

What happens

The conventions of comedy dictate that the problems and confusions of the play will be resolved at the end. So Sebastian's arrival in this scene reassures the audience that at some point he and Viola will be reunited, as he is the character who will bring the resolution – though of course there will be complications along the way. One of those complications is that he is convinced that his sister died in the shipwreck, while the audience knows that she is very much alive.

Sebastian's relationship with Antonio is interesting, as Sebastian reveals that he has been passing himself off as someone called Roderigo to disguise his identity. He has done so in order to create an easier relationship with Antonio, who is an ordinary sailor while Sebastian is the son of a well-known gentleman. It seems he has enjoyed a straightforward friendship with Antonio without the complications of class consciousness. Having revealed his identity, he feels that their friendship must end, but Antonio shows great loyalty, deciding to follow Sebastian even though he endangers himself by doing so. There are some parallels between this scene and the previous one, Act 1 Scene 5. An emotional connection develops between a character of high rank (Olivia and Sebastian) and another of lower status (Cesario and Antonio), but the expressions of devotion are reversed. In his soliloquy Antonio expresses his affection for Sebastian, but in her soliloquy the higher-class Olivia expresses her love for Cesario.

The characters

Sebastian shows a similar affection for Viola as she showed for him in Act 1 Scene 2. Although only appearing separately in the play so far, Shakespeare establishes a strong bond between them. Importantly, it is also made clear that they look similar – Sebastian says, 'it was said she much resembled me' (line 23). The comedy around them in the play can only work if they look very similar.

Antonio performs a similar role to Viola's Captain; it seems that he has been looking after Sebastian since his arrival in Illyria after the shipwreck. Sebastian speaks warmly of his friend's 'love' (line 7) and 'modesty' (line 11); he is an honest man who is devoted to Sebastian. Although he has 'many enemies in Orsino's court' (line 42), he will make 'sport' of 'danger' (line 45) and follow him.

> **Activity 20**
> Compare and contrast ways in which Antonio is similar to the Captain who rescues Viola. Make a list of the features and attitudes that they have in common and those that separate them.

Dramatic techniques
Although three scenes separate them, Shakespeare draws a clear parallel between Viola's arrival in Illyria and Sebastian's. They are both helped by a humble seaman and both fear the other is dead.

Biologically, the twins cannot be identical, but Shakespeare clearly intends them to resemble each other and the audience should be able to see the likeness between them immediately – Sebastian needs to look like Cesario. The two actors need to be of a similar height and build, and there should be an uncanny similarity between the costume of Viola's disguise as Cesario and Sebastian's clothing. While this is necessary for the play's mistaken identities, it should also provide a moment of humour when the audience first sees Sebastian. Ideally, there should be a double-take, checking that the character is not Cesario.

Language
Shakespeare uses imagery of water in this scene – Antonio has rescued Sebastian 'from the breach of the sea' which, he believes, 'drown'd' Viola (line 20). The sea, of course, is 'salt

water' (line 28) and Sebastian links that with his own tears of sorrow for her death.

The word 'love' is also used by both Sebastian and Antonio (lines 7 and 32) about their relationship, Antonio stating 'I do adore' Sebastian (line 44). While this may raise questions about the nature of their relationship, in Elizabethan times such language was commonly used about service and friendship. Antonio is both Sebastian's servant and his friend.

> **Activity 21**
> Consider in what ways, apart from appearance, Sebastian is similar to Viola. Look at how they express themselves and what they say about each other. Why do you think that Shakespeare creates these similarities?

Act 2 Scene 2

Lines 1–14 Malvolio brings Olivia's ring to Cesario.
Lines 15–39 Viola, puzzled by the ring, realises that Olivia has fallen in love with her male identity, Cesario.

What happens

Olivia sent Malvolio to take the ring to Cesario at the end of Act 1. As he delivers it in this scene, he shows more of his unpleasant nature, throwing the ring to the ground for Cesario to pick up. Viola, knowing that she did not leave any ring with Olivia, soon realises that there is only one explanation: 'She loves me, sure' (line 20). Olivia's behaviour suggested that she was distracted and Viola realises the unexpected consequence of her disguise as Cesario, which creates complications. She herself recognises the love triangle: 'My master loves her dearly, / And I, poor monster, fond as much on him; / And she, mistaken, seems to dote on me' (lines 31–3). Viola notes despairingly that the situation is too difficult for her to sort out herself.

The characters

Malvolio is carrying out his duties as Olivia's servant, and he does so faithfully. His final speech and action, though, show his superior and sneering side, as he invents the idea that Cesario

ACT AND SCENE NOTES

'peevishly threw' the ring at Olivia (line 12). He himself now throws it on the ground.

Viola here shows a full understanding of the predicament she has got herself into through adopting a male disguise.

Dramatic techniques
After Malvolio has left, Viola delivers a soliloquy – a speech given by one character, usually alone on stage. This enables the playwright to give the audience a direct insight into the character's mind, revealing their thoughts, motives and intentions. Shakespeare uses the soliloquy here to share with the audience Viola's realisation of Olivia's love and the difficulty of her situation. This begins a sympathetic relationship between the character and the audience.

> **Activity 22**
> Make some notes on why you think this soliloquy is important, both in terms of the plot development and how an audience might respond to Viola at this point in the play. Discuss your ideas with others in the class.

Language
Viola's language in this scene highlights the idea that love can be dangerous because it cannot be controlled. She concludes that the assumed identity of Cesario has 'charm'd' Olivia (line 16). The connotations of this verb include spells and enchantment as well as attraction, an idea continued when she refers to 'the cunning of [Olivia's] passion' (line 20). This suggests that love is active and crafty. Viola also notes that Olivia spoke 'distractedly' (line 19), suggesting her lack of control.

Viola returns to that idea of control at the end of the soliloquy, concluding that the situation is too complicated to solve immediately, using the metaphor of a complex 'knot' that only 'Time' will be able to 'untangle' (lines 38–9).

Act 2 Scene 3
Lines 1–65 Sir Toby and Sir Andrew are in party mood and ask Feste to sing for them.

TWELFTH NIGHT

Lines 66–80 Maria comes to persuade them to stop making such a noise during the night. She is unsuccessful.

Lines 81–117 Malvolio arrives to reprimand them but they make fun of him.

Lines 118–79 After Malvolio has left, the other characters are angry about his behaviour and Maria comes up with a plan to trick and embarrass him.

What happens

This scene, which begins the play's subplot, takes place in the middle of the night at Olivia's house. Sir Toby is enjoying himself, encouraging Sir Andrew to stay up with him and drink. When Feste arrives, the party becomes livelier – it is clear that Sir Andrew has been taken in by Feste's nonsense the previous evening, adding to the audience's understanding of his foolishness. Feste sings a love song, in keeping with the central concern of the play. Appreciating the song, Sir Toby and Sir Andrew are about to join in and sing another, probably much louder, when Maria appears. She tells them off and warns of Malvolio's possible appearance, but it is clear that they are not bothered. Sir Toby, rather drunk, dismisses her concerns and launches into song.

When Maria reprimands Sir Toby, it is obvious that this is more of a warning; his response shows that they are on very good terms. It is a great contrast when Malvolio appears and tells them off in stern, disparaging terms. While Malvolio is no more successful than Maria, the reactions of Sir Toby and Feste show they have a very different relationship with him. Their direct insults and continued singing, this time about Malvolio, show their contempt for him. This mutual scorn is the basis for the plot against Malvolio, which begins in this scene and is all Maria's idea. While Sir Andrew wants, comically, to challenge Malvolio to a duel, Maria has a far subtler plan. Shakespeare does not reveal the full details straight away, but Maria suggests that she will imitate Olivia's handwriting and leave a letter for Malvolio to find. This will suggest that she is in love with him. As Malvolio is Olivia's servant, there is clearly a lot of potential for embarrassment in Maria's plan, and the other characters look forward to it.

Just before the end of the scene, there is a revealing moment of tension between Sir Toby and Sir Andrew. Sir Andrew suggests he has spent a lot of money staying in Illyria trying to win Olivia's favour and that he depends on marrying her, and her fortune, to recover his costs. Sir Toby tells him to send for more money. In this short exchange, the audience understands that Sir Toby is taking financial advantage of Sir Andrew, who has perhaps been paying for all the drinks Sir Toby has been enjoying.

> **Activity 23**
> This scene takes place in Olivia's house, but Olivia herself does not appear. Instead we see gentlemen (Sir Toby and Sir Andrew) and servants of different kinds (Feste, Maria and Malvolio). Look carefully at the interactions between characters and find evidence to show who holds power at different points in the scene, and how they achieve it. Link your findings to the comic traditions of misrule.

The characters
Sir Toby shows his lively, carefree nature in this scene, intent on enjoying himself. However, it is possible that the audience begins to see a different side to his character too – he is careless about his behaviour in Olivia's house and is very rude to Malvolio, although he is provoked. The idea that he may be taking financial advantage of Sir Andrew suggests that he is also a manipulative character.

Sir Andrew's foolishness is again made apparent. The exchange with Feste shows that he has accepted incomprehensible names and ideas as actual learning, revealing his gullibility. For the rest of the scene he is mainly an onlooker until Malvolio has left, whereupon he suggests challenging him to a duel. His 'joke' is that he then would not turn up, suggesting that this would 'make a fool' of Malvolio (line 121). He doesn't realise that he would look the bigger fool, as well as a coward. An audience, though, might feel some sympathy for his financial situation and also from his melancholy remark that he 'was ador'd once' (line 171).

Feste continues his role as paid entertainer, singing for Sir Toby and Sir Andrew, but the way he joins in with the mockery of Malvolio suggests it is also personal for him. Remember that Malvolio dismissed him as 'a barren rascal' in Act 1 Scene 5 (lines 77–8).

Maria, although anxious on Olivia's behalf when she enters the scene, shows that she is more at home with the easier-going members of her lady's household, joking with Sir Toby and devising the plan against Malvolio.

Malvolio confirms his growing reputation as a sneering killjoy. He is, on the one hand, doing his job by ensuring that Olivia is not disturbed, but he acts high-handedly, insulting Sir Toby, Sir Andrew and Feste. Sir Toby and Sir Andrew are his social superiors, and Sir Toby is his employer's uncle.

> **Activity 24**
> Think carefully about your responses to the characters in this scene. Make a list of all the points that demonstrate Malvolio's strict moral puritan values, and another list of all the points that demonstrate how Sir Toby embraces the spirit of carnival. How do they balance? Is it possible to argue that either one of them is in the right?

Dramatic techniques
Music is mentioned in the first line of the play and Feste's songs are a key part of it. Singing is part of his professional role and Shakespeare uses the songs to reinforce the play's themes. Feste's companions in this scene demand a love song, but his song is full of melancholy. The first verse depicts the joining of the lovers, but the second points out that youth 'will not endure' (line 49) and the future is uncertain.

Language
While Malvolio acknowledges that he is speaking to his 'masters' (line 81), he shows no politeness to them, despite the fact that he is a servant. He says that they 'gabble like tinkers' (lines 82–3), reducing their status as gentlemen to that of itinerant manual workers. He dismisses their singing as 'squeak[ing] out your cozier's catches' (lines 84–5), another insult about the noise they

are making while comparing them to ordinary working people. Malvolio's language here is revealing: he shows disregard for his social superiors, but his comparisons also demonstrate that he has no respect for working people. While a servant himself, he is clearly a snob and perhaps resents his own lowly position.

Act 2 Scene 4

Lines 1–13 Orsino calls for music to fit his mood.
Lines 14–40 Orsino and Cesario discuss love.
Lines 41–77 Feste arrives and sings at Orsino's request. On this occasion, he refuses payment.
Lines 78–124 Orsino asks Cesario to visit Olivia again, leading to a further discussion of love and a disguised reference to Viola's feelings for Orsino.

What happens

The play returns to Orsino's palace, where the Duke is again wallowing in his melancholy mood and asking for music, as he was in the first scene of the play. He is impressed with the way Cesario speaks about love, which leads to a discussion layered with concealed meaning, as Cesario admits he is attracted to someone of Orsino's age and looks. Of course it is Orsino himself. Orsino remains blind to this as he assumes that Cesario is talking about a woman. This leads to a discussion of men's and women's love. Orsino expresses the view that men's loves 'are more giddy and unfirm' (line 32) than women's, but also notes, using the simile of roses, that women's beauty is short-lived, which echoes Feste's song in Scene 3. Cesario's agreement signals Viola's awareness that, while trapped in her disguise, she is missing her chances with Orsino.

These sad feelings are reflected in Feste's song, which is about death caused by unrequited love. It was a common idea in the traditions of romantic courtly love that the lover would die if their feelings were not reciprocated. Shakespeare uses the song to reinforce the tone and content of the dialogue between Orsino and Cesario. Interestingly, although he is keen to earn money elsewhere in the play, Feste refuses to be paid here.

After Feste's departure, the discussion of men's and women's love continues. Orsino claims that no woman can love as much as he does – 'no woman's heart / So big to hold so much' (lines 95–9). He is unaware that he is addressing these remarks to a woman, but as Cesario, Viola is able to challenge him, arguing that women 'are as true of heart as' men (line 106). The story of Cesario's father's daughter of course refers to Viola herself, and the speech expresses the sorrow of her necessary 'concealment' (line 111). Her last speech in the scene implies that Cesario's 'sister' died from her unrequited love, like the lover in Feste's song. While the audience knows that this is not true, it brings a melancholy mood to the end of the scene.

> **Activity 25**
> Look at the dialogue between lines 89 and 121. Discuss ways in which Viola's responses to Orsino challenge his view of love, identifying three key quotations to support your ideas.

The characters
Viola was in a tricky position with Olivia, but the conversation in this scene is even more complicated for her, and the tone here is much more serious. Trapped in her male disguise, she has to defend the female position on love. She does so by telling her own story as if discussing her sister.

Orsino persists in his pursuit of Olivia. His moodiness and refusal to accept Olivia's decision begin to look more and more self-centred. His conviction that no woman's love can match his own adds to this impression.

Feste's refusal of payment for his song suggests that the song is personal to him.

Dramatic techniques
Dramatic irony is at its most poignant here; there is little of the comedy we witnessed in the scene with Olivia. Orsino's repeated use of the word 'boy' (lines 14, 23, 31, 119) when addressing Cesario reminds the audience of his error over her identity. This dramatic irony has a twofold effect: it highlights Orsino's self-absorption as well as Viola's challenging position. Her speech (lines 110–18) is a moving account of her hidden suffering, 'Smiling at grief' (line 115).

Language

Throughout this scene, Orsino uses the language of a traditional courtly lover. He describes Olivia as 'sovereign cruelty' (line 80) and describes his 'passion' (line 94) with the hyperbolic or exaggerated simile 'as hungry as the sea' (line 100). The excess of his language emphasises that he is only concerned with his own feelings, while dismissing those of women. This suggests that Shakespeare is satirising such attitudes. A **satire** makes fun of something in order to criticise it. The contrast between Orsino's and Viola's speeches is marked; whereas his is excessive and showy, hers is about 'concealment', 'Patience' and 'grief' (lines 111, 114, 115). She subtly says that men 'say more, swear more' (line 116), which Orsino demonstrates himself. As well as humour, there is **pathos** in this scene; it appeals to the audience's emotions, encouraging pity for Viola's position.

> ### Activity 26
> Compare the ways in which different characters speak about men's and women's love. Do they suggest that men and women have different aims and express love in different ways? Do you think that these views are still relevant today?

Act 2 Scene 5

Lines 1–20 Fabian, Sir Toby, Sir Andrew and Maria wait in the garden for Malvolio. Maria leaves her forged letter for Malvolio to find.
Lines 21–75 Malvolio, talking to himself, imagines a love affair with Olivia and having authority over Sir Toby. The other characters, all hiding, overhear every word.
Lines 76–167 Malvolio finds the letter and falls for the trick quickly. He is thrilled to discover that Olivia is apparently in love with him, and decides to follow the letter's instructions.
Lines 168–94 Fabian, Sir Toby, Sir Andrew and Maria celebrate the success of the plan and await its next stage.

What happens

This is the big set-piece comic scene of the play, eagerly anticipated by Fabian, Sir Toby, Sir Andrew and Maria, who hopes that the plan will make 'a contemplative idiot' of

Malvolio (line 17). If the audience has any doubt whether he deserves mockery, Shakespeare shows Malvolio's arrogant behaviour before he even sees Maria's letter. Not knowing that the other characters are hiding behind trees, bushes and hedges in the garden, he speaks unguardedly and reveals that he has already half convinced himself that his employer, Olivia, has fallen in love with him. He gleefully imagines the social advancement that such a match would create, imagining himself as 'Count Malvolio' (line 32). The other characters are infuriated, particularly Sir Toby, who repeatedly needs to be restrained to avoid revealing his presence. This reaches its peak when Malvolio imagines having authority over Sir Toby.

> **Activity 27**
> Discuss in pairs why a relationship between people from different social levels might be challenging. Consider whether this kind of consideration is still relevant in modern society. Share your thoughts with the rest of the class.

When Malvolio finds the letter, he reads what appears to be a set of riddles, but he rapidly interprets that the message comes to him from Olivia. It gives him a number of ridiculous instructions, including to dress in 'yellow stockings' (line 142) and to 'smile' constantly (line 165). He goes off determined to carry these out. The audience already knows that smiling does not come naturally to Malvolio and Maria says that Olivia 'abhors' the colour yellow (line 187). Shakespeare makes both the audience and these characters wait in anticipation until the end of Act 3 for Malvolio's reappearance.

The characters
Fabian is introduced as another servant in Olivia's household and a friend of Maria and Sir Toby.

Sir Toby, while enjoying the plot against Malvolio, is so infuriated by Malvolio's attitude towards him that he nearly spoils the whole plan.

Sir Andrew has quite a passive role in the scene, though he adds comedy when he immediately recognises himself in Malvolio's reference to a 'foolish knight' (line 72).

Maria shows that she is skilful, not only in imitating Olivia's handwriting, but also in constructing a letter which, although ludicrous to the audience, still deceives Malvolio.

Malvolio reveals his character clearly in this scene. Note that his exploration of the possibility of a relationship between him and Olivia and of his authority over Sir Toby occurs before he is tricked by the letter and when he believes he is alone. In this way Shakespeare both questions his character and makes his belief in the letter plausible.

Dramatic techniques

Shakespeare clearly enjoyed writing this kind of farcical scene, where there is visual and physical comedy and characters overhear each other. There are similar scenes in *Love's Labours Lost* and *Much Ado About Nothing*. Such a scene depends for its effectiveness on the creation of visual comedy – the audience must see the hidden characters while believing that Malvolio does not see them. For example, positioning, movement and timing are crucial when Sir Toby emerges from the shrubbery in fury, ready to punch Malvolio, and is pulled back by Fabian just in time before Malvolio turns round. While the comedy in much of the play comes from situations or language, this scene's physical comedy creates a lot of potential with which the director and actors can experiment.

Activity 28
In groups, rehearse a section of this scene. Substitute chairs and tables for bushes and see how the comedy depends on physical positioning and timing. Try to make the hidden characters' interventions as obvious as you can while remaining unseen by Malvolio. Perform your different versions for the class and discuss their effectiveness.

Language

As well as the visual and physical humour of this scene, there is comedy in the language too, as Malvolio convinces himself that Olivia is the author of the letter. The way he persuades himself that the initials 'M.O.A.I.' mean Malvolio (line 112) is an example; he has to reorder the letters to make his interpretation work. The language Shakespeare uses in Maria's letter is chosen carefully to appeal to Malvolio – even referring to 'Fortune' (line 146), the word on his lips when he enters the scene (line 21). Maria appeals to his interest in status, with four references to 'great' and 'greatness' (lines 133–5) and a reminder that he is currently a 'steward' (line 145). Maria also highlights aspects of Malvolio's personality – he needs little encouragement to be 'opposite with a kinsman, surly with servants' (lines 138–9). The image created by the idea of 'yellow stockings' which are 'cross-garter'd' (lines 142–3) is vivid, even before the audience sees the actual costume.

> **Task**
> From Act 2, find evidence for the different methods that Shakespeare uses to present Malvolio.
> - Look at the language of his speeches to Cesario in Scene 1.
> - Consider Malvolio's speeches in Scene 5 as well as the effects of the stage business with the letter and the other characters watching him.
> - What judgements of Malvolio might an audience make at the end of this act?

Act 3

Summary

In this central part of the play, Shakespeare develops key plot elements. Olivia confirms that she has fallen for Cesario and the audience is reminded of Sebastian's presence in Illyria. These plot strands come together in final scene of Act 3, along with the much-awaited appearance of Malvolio in his yellow stockings.

Act 3 Scene 1

Lines 1–58 Viola (as Cesario) and Feste exchange witty remarks at Olivia's gate.
Lines 59–67 Left alone, Viola admires Feste's wisdom as well as his wit.
Lines 68–82 Sir Toby and Sir Andrew greet Cesario.

ACT AND SCENE NOTES

Lines 83–162 Cesario continues wooing Olivia for Orsino. Olivia refuses to listen and makes clear her growing affection for Cesario.

What happens

Returning to Olivia's house as Cesario, Viola encounters Feste and they exchange verbal jokes, showing that Viola is as witty as a professional entertainer. It is Feste, though, who demands payment for his jokes and drops a hint that he may be aware that Cesario isn't quite what he seems to be: 'who you are and what you would are out of my welkin' he says (lines 56–7). In her short soliloquy, Viola acknowledges there is more to Feste than meets the eye, too.

Sir Toby invites Cesario in to meet Olivia. His role here is twofold. By bringing Sir Toby to the gate rather than Malvolio, Shakespeare maintains the suspense waiting for Malvolio's appearance in yellow stockings. Secondly, because Sir Andrew accompanies Sir Toby, he has the opportunity to see and hear Cesario and become jealous of his success with Olivia. This gives Sir Toby the opportunity for further scheming in the next scene.

When Olivia and Cesario are alone, Olivia dismisses thoughts of Orsino and apologises for her trick in sending the ring. It would have been unusual for a woman to make such a bold move and Olivia is aware that by doing this she has made herself vulnerable; she tells Cesario 'Under your hard construction must I sit' (line 113). Olivia is torn; on the one hand, she wants to send Cesario away, but on the other she cannot deny her feelings for him. Eventually she has to declare her love: 'I love thee so' (line 149). Cesario tells her candidly that 'no woman' shall have his heart (line 157) because, of course, Cesario is really Viola. Olivia ends the scene sadly, begging Cesario to 'come again' (line 161).

The characters

Viola begins the scene enjoying jokes with Feste, but it ends in difficulty after Olivia has openly declared her love for Cesario.

Feste shows light-hearted verbal wit, with some suggestion that his careful observations have made him doubtful about Cesario.

Sir Andrew admires Cesario's social ease and courtly vocabulary, which contrast so much with his own social awkwardness.

Olivia battles with herself. She knows she has broken social conventions by sending the ring and feels she should not fall for Orsino's servant. But she does, and openly admits it at the end of the scene.

Dramatic techniques

On one level, this is quite a social scene. Cesario has discussions with Feste, then Sir Toby and Sir Andrew, before Olivia and Maria enter. It is a sequence of public conversations, made clear when Sir Andrew comments on what Cesario says to Olivia. Notice how that changes when Olivia asks the other characters to 'leave me' (line 90) and the stage direction is '*Exeunt all but* OLIVIA *and* VIOLA' (line 91). The stage now becomes the focus of private conversation, emphasised by Olivia's command that 'the garden door be shut' (line 90). This sets the mood for a highly personal exchange between Olivia and Cesario, preparing for Olivia's declaration of love.

The dialogue between the two characters again illustrates the importance of dramatic irony. Viola's roundabout way of answering Olivia's question in line 94 allows her to maintain her disguise and avoid lying about her real name, while the audience is aware throughout of that balance between her disguise and the truth. It occurs again in Viola's words 'I am not what I am' (line 139). When Olivia declares her love so stridently in line 149, the audience can recognise the problem in her mistake, but will probably also find it funny – when Olivia abandons her self-imposed mourning and separation from men, she falls for someone who isn't actually a man. This is accentuated by Cesario's embarrassed and hasty departure.

> **Activity 29**
> With a partner, improvise a dialogue where you ask each other questions. Your responses should conceal the truth, but avoid telling direct lies. This should give you a good understanding of Viola's quick-witted mind and care for the truth.

Language

The Elizabethans prized quick verbal wit very highly. This was often based on puns, which play on different meanings of the same or similar words. The opening of this scene offers a good example, showing that the word in question can be seemingly unimportant, as Feste makes a joke out of the different meanings of the word 'by'. Viola's question (line 2) uses 'by' to mean 'by means of', whereas Feste pretends to understand 'by' to mean 'close to', thus creating a deliberate misunderstanding. Feste makes a further pun by linking names to identity (lines 18–20) – someone playing with his sister's name (the word) could be understood as taking liberties with his sister (the person). We need words to communicate, but words can be slippery; as Feste says, 'How quickly the wrong side may be turn'd outward!' (lines 12–13).

> **Activity 30**
> Puns are often used by headline writers in popular newspapers and by advertisers, because they are catchy and memorable. See if you can find some examples, and make some up yourself. You could start with the different meanings of 'play', 'fool' and 'scene/seen'. Try to keep track of the puns that Shakespeare includes in the dialogue as you read the rest of the play.

It is also worth noting Shakespeare's variations in the iambic pentameter of the verse. In line 109, for example, the suddenness of Olivia's interruption is emphasised by the initial stress on '**Give** me leave' and the way she concludes highlights the strength of her feelings: 'a cypress, not a bosom, / **Hides** my heart.' (lines 119–20).

Act 3 Scene 2

Lines 1–59 Sir Andrew, feeling that he cannot compete with Cesario in winning Olivia's favour, decides to leave. Sir Toby persuades him to stay and to challenge Cesario to a duel to impress Olivia with his valour.

Lines 60–77 Maria brings news that her plan has worked and that Malvolio has carried out the instructions of the letter. The characters are keen to see the results.

What happens

This short scene begins suddenly, with Sir Andrew announcing his decision to leave. After his comments on Cesario's courtly language in the previous scene, he now feels that Olivia prefers Cesario, despite his lowly status as 'the Count's serving man' (lines 4–5). Fabian and Sir Toby join forces to convince Sir Andrew that he has misunderstood the situation, arguing that Olivia has been deliberately provoking him, hoping that he will react and demonstrate some bravery. Although Sir Andrew is initially suspicious, asking whether they are trying to 'make an ass' of him (line 10), which of course they are, he falls into their trap and asks them to 'bear me a challenge' to Cesario (line 36). He means to show knightly valour in a duel with Cesario and he goes off to write his challenge. Sir Toby and Fabian look forward to the duel. Though they do not know Cesario's real identity, they recognise that he is as ill-suited to fighting as Sir Andrew is. Toby also admits to Fabian that Sir Andrew has spent 'two thousand' ducats funding their drinking and entertainment, a reminder of their dialogue at the end of Act 2 Scene 3.

> ### Activity 31
> Sir Toby's revelation about how much money he has cost Sir Andrew is important. What is your judgement of these characters now? Look through the play so far for evidence of Sir Toby's exploitation of Sir Andrew.

By sending Sir Andrew off to write his challenge, Shakespeare sets in motion another part of the plot. When Maria enters, she lets Sir Toby, Fabian and the audience know how an earlier plan is progressing. She delightedly reports that Malvolio is dressed in 'cross-garter'd' 'yellow stockings' and 'does smile' (lines 65–7, 71), exactly matching the instructions in her forged letter from Act 2 Scene 5.

The characters

Sir Andrew starts with a moment of self-knowledge, recognising that he cannot marry Olivia, but then comically falls for another of Sir Toby's schemes. We saw in Act 2 Scene 5 how little he understands the practice of duelling. While there is comedy in his resolve to write a challenge, the audience might also feel some pity for him, particularly when Sir Toby admits he has spent so much of Sir Andrew's money.

Fabian and **Sir Toby** develop the plan for the duel, seeing opportunities for great amusement. Fabian has the main persuasive speech (lines 15–26), but never expects the plan to be carried out. Sir Toby is determined to see it through. His statement that he has cost Sir Andrew 'two thousand strong' (line 49–50) confirms how he is using him, rather than being a friend.

Maria is full of laughter at the success of her plan and is sure the others will soon 'laugh yourselves into stitches' (lines 61–2). Having already seen Malvolio, she previews his bizarre costume for the audience.

Dramatic techniques
This scene begins **in media res**, which means in the middle of the action. Sir Andrew's 'No, faith, I'll not stay a jot longer' (line 1) shows that he has announced his departure before he enters and that Sir Toby and Fabian have already been trying to change his mind. This is more naturalistic than beginning each scene with an opening speech and is also used by dramatists to suggest that characters have a life beyond what the audience sees of them on stage. This argument seems to have been going on for some time and Sir Andrew is clearly exasperated with his situation. The others are desperate for an explanation, clear from Sir Toby's 'Thy reason' (line 2), so that they can argue against it.

For a moment here the Malvolio plot (set up by the letter in Act 2 Scene 5) seems to be reaching its conclusion when Maria comes in full of her success. But Shakespeare makes the audience wait a little longer, building up the suspense for Malvolio's eventual appearance.

Language
Fabian uses metaphors to persuade Sir Andrew to challenge Cesario. He refers to his 'dormouse valour' (line 16), which mocks him because the dormouse is a tiny, very sleepy animal. He also balances the language of heat and the language of cold. In suggesting action, he uses the metaphors of 'fire', 'brimstone' and 'fire-new' (lines 17, 19), each of which is associated with

heat, passion and anger. In contrast Fabian, using a simile, associates Sir Andrew with 'an icicle' – not only icy, but static. He also suggests that the young knight is in 'the north of my lady's opinion' (line 23) because northern lands are associated with cold. Not only is Sir Andrew cold and inactive, but his lack of bravery makes Olivia cold and unfriendly towards him, implies Fabian.

Sir Toby's imagery also belittles Sir Andrew. Elizabethans believed that the liver was the source of blood; in fact, it filters and purifies blood. Blood is also associated with courage, so when Sir Toby says that all the blood in Sir Andrew's liver will hardly be enough to 'clog the foot of a flea' (lines 56–7), he is joking that Sir Andrew possesses only the tiniest amount of courage.

Act 3 Scene 3

Lines 1–49 Antonio has caught up with Sebastian and they are reunited. Antonio gives Sebastian advice on where to stay in Illyria, and lends him some money.

What happens

At the end of Act 2 Scene 1, Antonio decides to follow Sebastian despite the risk to himself. In this scene the two meet again and Sebastian, far from being cross, is overwhelmed at Antonio's good nature: 'thanks, / And thanks, and ever thanks' he says (lines 14–15). However, Antonio is unwilling to spend time showing Sebastian the sights. He was involved previously in a naval battle against Orsino's forces, and fears he might be recognised and arrested. This raises questions about Antonio's history, but Shakespeare is careful to retain audience sympathy for him – Antonio reassures Sebastian that his offence against Orsino is not of 'bloody nature' (line 30). As a further sign of his generosity, he recommends a suitable inn and offers to go there to order food. He also lends Sebastian his purse of money. It may seem odd for a man in the position of a servant to lend money to a gentleman, but Sebastian has lost all his goods in the shipwreck and Antonio recognises that, as a young gentleman, Sebastian might well see 'some toy' (line 44) he wants to buy, and would be unused to having no money.

ACT AND SCENE NOTES

> **Activity 32**
> From the limited details Shakespeare provides, what role do you think Antonio played in the 'sea-fight' (line 26)? Does it make a difference to the way you judge his character?

The characters
Antonio, despite the colourful past he reveals to Sebastian, again demonstrates that he is a thoughtful and generous friend, putting himself in danger for Sebastian as well as providing for him.

Sebastian not only accepts the renewal of Antonio's company, but also recognises the spirit of generosity that lies behind it and is delighted to see him again. He takes Antonio's advice and accepts his loan with good grace.

Dramatic techniques
In a play that depends so much on disguise, this is a scene where the lack of disguise is important. Antonio seems honest, and is honest. More than that, he knows he might be recognised in Illyria from his role in the sea battle – 'Only myself stood out' he tells Sebastian (line 35). Shakespeare uses Antonio as a point of contrast with the various characters in the play who disguise themselves, either through costume or behaviour.

The character of Antonio is also useful in setting up another part of Shakespeare's complex plotting. That purse of money will become important in later scenes.

Language
As in their first scene, Antonio uses the language of love and service to Sebastian that relates to male friendship bonds. He has followed him because of his 'desire' (line 4) and, as well as being motivated by 'love' (lines 6, 11), he has been worried about how Sebastian will cope in a place where he is 'Unguided and unfriended' (line 10).

> **Activity 33**
> Look at ways in which Antonio expresses his devotion to Sebastian and compare his language with that used by Orsino about Olivia, Olivia about Cesario, and Viola about Orsino. What similarities do you find?

Act 3 Scene 4

Lines 1–15 Olivia is expecting Cesario, but is told that Malvolio has gone mad.

Lines 15–80 Malvolio enters in his new costume, following the instructions of Maria's letter, which leads Olivia to agree that he is not in his right mind. Malvolio convinces himself that Olivia's reaction shows that he has interpreted the letter correctly.

Lines 80–137 Sir Toby, Fabian and Maria enter and provoke Malvolio further.

Lines 137–92 Sir Andrew enters with his challenge to Cesario, which is ludicrously inappropriate. Sir Toby decides he will deliver the challenge orally to make it more convincing.

Lines 193–209 Cesario continues to plead Orsino's case to Olivia, who continues to express her devotion to Cesario.

Lines 210–99 Sir Toby and Fabian engineer a duel between Cesario and Sir Andrew. Both are terrified and reluctant, but agree to cross swords for form's sake.

Lines 300–60 Antonio, mistaking Cesario for Sebastian and thinking the duel is serious, intervenes on his behalf. The commotion attracts attention and Antonio is recognised and arrested. He asks for the return of his money from Cesario, who of course does not have it.

Lines 361–72 Viola recalls that Antonio mentioned Sebastian and realises that, as she has been mistaken for him, he must be alive.

Lines 373–82 Sir Toby and Fabian have noticed what they understand as Cesario's dishonesty towards Antonio, and urge Sir Andrew to attack him again.

Activity 34
You will see there are nine distinct stages to the action in this scene. In groups, create tableaux to represent these sections of the scene, conveying characters, action and mood. Each character can have one line to describe their feelings.

What happens

This is one of the most complex, and comic, scenes in the play, as several strands of the plot come together. The first of these is, finally, the appearance of Malvolio in his cross-gartered yellow stockings, constantly smiling. His strange behaviour and puzzling speeches, where he quotes from Maria's letter, persuade Olivia that he has lost his mind – none of it makes sense to her. Shakespeare pushes the comedy further through Malvolio's misinterpretation of Olivia's reaction, convincing himself that he will gain 'the full prospect of my hopes' with Olivia (lines 78–9).

> **Activity 35**
> Research images of Malvolio in his yellow stockings from different film and theatrical productions. Consider how his costume in this scene contrasts with his character and costume earlier in the play. Choose the three images that you think are the most successful, and explain why.

Maria, Sir Toby and Fabian are delighted with the success of their plot and provoke Malvolio further by suggesting to him that they believe he has gone mad and is possessed by the devil. Malvolio, believing he has Olivia's special favour, scorns them harshly, calling them 'idle shallow things' (line 119) and promising that they will discover more later. This amuses them further, but events take a more sinister turn when Sir Toby suggests that they should lock Malvolio 'in a dark room' (line 131).

Shakespeare then swiftly moves from the Malvolio plot to that of Sir Andrew's duel, as he enters with his written challenge. Every sentence of it is contradictory and makes little sense, but Fabian and Sir Toby pretend it is excellent. Sir Toby, realising that Cesario would recognise the folly of Sir Andrew's letter, decides it will be funnier to deliver the challenge 'by word of mouth' (line 182). He looks forward to the amusement of seeing both Sir Andrew and Cesario, terrified of each other, fight a duel.

The audience will have this in mind when Viola and Olivia replace Sir Toby, Fabian and Maria on stage. It is a brief interlude, but Viola, as Cesario, continues to try to persuade Olivia to accept Orsino's attentions, while Olivia presses on

Cesario a small cameo – a tiny portrait of herself in a jewel case, which might be hung on a necklace.

As soon as Olivia leaves, the next stage of the duel plot begins, as Sir Toby delivers Sir Andrew's challenge orally, persuading Cesario that, as Sir Andrew is a skilled fighter, he is in considerable danger.

> **Activity 36**
> Make a list of all the words and phrases used by Sir Toby and Fabian to enhance Sir Andrew's reputation as a fighter. Opposite this, list words and phrases used by Sir Andrew that reveal how inexperienced and afraid he is.
> Repeat this with Cesario – the duelling skills that Sir Tony claims for him and how Viola tries to avoid the fight.
> Consider how Shakespeare balances these differences to create the comedy of the scene.

Sir Toby's plan works to perfection and the audience's amusement is complete when Sir Andrew and Cesario, both quaking in fear, are brought to face each other with swords drawn. At this point, the unexpected happens. Antonio enters, thinks he sees Sebastian in danger, and draws his sword on his behalf. However, Antonio's earlier fear of being recognised and arrested proves well founded; Orsino's officers have clearly been following him, and they move in to make their arrest. The mock duel has suddenly turned into something much more serious.

Matters are complicated further when Antonio asks for the return of his money. He thinks he is addressing Sebastian, but Viola has no idea who he is or what money he refers to. Although she is happy to lend him some of the small amount she has, this act seems ill-mannered and ungenerous to Antonio after his kindnesses towards Sebastian. Both are bewildered by the situation. However, Antonio's final speeches promise a plot resolution. He tells the story of Sebastian's rescue and although he does so despairingly, he names Sebastian in front of Viola before he is hauled away to prison. Viola seizes upon her brother's name. She realises Antonio's mistake and concludes that her brother must be alive and close by.

The episode with Antonio, however, has convinced Sir Toby, Fabian and Sir Andrew that Cesario is a 'very dishonest paltry boy' (line 373), which renews Sir Andrew's courage as he intends to follow and 'beat' Cesario (line 378).

The characters

Malvolio is finally seen again after his discovery of the letter in the garden. His appearance and behaviour are both absurd.

Sir Toby and **Fabian** often collaborate in this scene, developing the plots against firstly Malvolio and then Sir Andrew and Cesario. They understand each other's train of thought quickly and take delight in their scheming, right to the end of the scene. It is Sir Toby's idea, though, to have Malvolio put 'in a dark room and bound' (line 131), which reveals a cruel side to his character.

Sir Andrew is again the butt of the jokes, but his own ignorance and foolishness makes a big contribution to this. As Sir Toby says, his letter of challenge to Cesario is clearly written by 'a clodpole' (line 181).

Viola is aware of the difficulties caused by her disguise, and in this scene those difficulties take an unexpected and comic turn: she is challenged to a duel by Sir Andrew. However hard she tries, she cannot avoid it. The end of the scene marks a key turning point; although she is baffled by Antonio's sudden action on her behalf, the mention of her brother's name creates hope.

Antonio's role as a faithful friend reaches its peak as he draws his sword to protect Sebastian (in fact, Cesario). It is a cruel moment for him when he is refused the money he has loaned, as his friendship and service seem forgotten and rejected.

Dramatic techniques

This is a scene of big emotional shifts, from high comedy to heart-rending sadness. Much of the visual comedy revolves around Malvolio and depends on costume. His yellow stockings have been mentioned five times in the play before this scene (Act 2 Scene 5 lines 142, 154, 158–9, 187; Act 3 Scene 2 lines 65–6) to build suspense in the audience. As Malvolio parades his vibrant cross-gartered legwear, this suspense is released. Compared with a servant's normal plain, dark-coloured clothes, especially suitable for the sober Malvolio of previous scenes, his appearance here should shock Olivia and prove highly amusing to the audience.

While there is verbal humour in the unsuitability of Sir Andrew's letter, visual humour is once again important, as he and Cesario are persuaded to draw swords against each other while neither can bear the thought of fighting. We can imagine that they do not hold their swords very firmly, and Sir Toby and Fabian probably have to push them towards each other.

> **Activity 37**
> This is such a key moment in the play's humour, it is worth trying it out. In groups, rehearse the scene – using pens as 'swords' – and see how hard Sir Toby and Fabian have to work to get Cesario and Sir Andrew to enter the duel. Experiment with different ways of staging it, and consider any reactions or comments from your audience.

Antonio's disillusionment when he is refused the return of his purse produces quite a different response in the audience. Though we know the mistake he has made, it is sad to see him rejected in this way. However, Shakespeare has also sown a seed of hope for reconciliation, as we understand that Antonio will at some point discover the truth.

Language
While Malvolio's appearance provides the visual humour, his dialogue makes a key contribution too. Initially there is his misunderstanding of Olivia's concerned 'Wilt thou go to bed, Malvolio?' (line 29), which he thinks is an invitation. He then recites a number of quotations from Maria's letter, which the audience will recognise. The dramatic irony is accentuated by Olivia's nonplussed interruptions: 'What mean'st thou by that, Malvolio?' 'Ha?' 'What say'st thou?' (lines 38, 40, 42). The audience will enjoy her bewilderment as much as Malvolio's behaviour. There is something less attractive in his metaphor 'I have lim'd her' (line 71): he sees himself as a hunter and Olivia as a small bird that he has caught by trickery. The audience knows, however, that if anyone has been trapped, it is Malvolio himself.

Maria and Sir Toby make several references to 'devil', 'fiend' and 'Satan' (lines 82, 88, 94, 97, 107, 113). In Elizabethan times, madness was often understood to be possession by the devil, and they are building a pretence of Malvolio's madness.

> **Task**
> Consider ways in which Antonio and Sebastian are presented in Act 3.
> - Find examples of Antonio's use of the language of affection and care in Scene 3.
> - Consider Antonio's generosity in Scene 3, and Sebastian's response.
> - How does your reading of Scene 3 affect your response to Antonio's intervention in the duel in Scene 4 and his belief that Sebastian has refused to help him?

Act 4

Summary
The confusions of the play reach a peak in Act 4, but the beginning of the **resolution** occurs before the end, as plot problems begin to be settled. The act starts with confusion, with Feste, Sir Andrew, Sir Toby and then Olivia all mistaking Sebastian for Cesario. While this causes Sebastian bewilderment and anger in the first three cases, Olivia's appearance causes puzzlement of a very different nature, when this beautiful unknown woman approaches him in such a friendly way. Elsewhere in Olivia's house, the plot against Malvolio takes a darker turn before the focus returns to Sebastian and Olivia, who agree to marry.

Act 4 Scene 1
Lines 1–22 Feste confuses Sebastian for Cesario and tries to take him to Olivia.
Lines 23–42 Sir Andrew and Sir Toby also mistake Sebastian for Cesario and attack him.
Lines 43–63 Finally, Olivia mistakes Sebastian for Cesario, stops the fight and invites Sebastian into her home.

What happens

The audience has already seen Antonio mistake Cesario for Sebastian; in this scene the confusion is reversed and multiplied as a sequence of characters assume that Sebastian is Cesario. First, Feste has a rather bad-tempered exchange with Sebastian, who cannot understand why Feste claims to have been sent to fetch him for his 'lady' (line 5). As Sebastian is threatening Feste, Sir Andrew enters and hits him, following encouragement from Sir Toby at the end of Act 3 Scene 4. Since Sebastian was getting hot under the collar at Feste's verbal insistence, the audience is not surprised that he loses his temper when struck unexpectedly by a stranger. Sir Andrew, however, who is convinced that he has struck a cowardly Cesario, is shocked to be fiercely attacked in return – Sebastian hits him at least three times: 'Why there's for thee, and there, and there' (line 25). This prompts Sir Toby to draw his sword and there is the prospect of a duel between him and Sebastian. It is Olivia's arrival that prevents the clash, and she becomes the fourth person to mistake Sebastian for Cesario. She addresses him as 'dear Cesario' (line 48) and 'gentle friend' (line 49), inviting him in 'to my house' (line 52). After such a bewildering sequence of interactions, it is no wonder that Sebastian is confused.

The characters

Sebastian shows that he is quite hot-headed, responding impatiently to Feste and aggressively to Sir Andrew. However, his reactions are understandable and provide more comedy for the audience. He is equally confused by Olivia, but decides to follow her, as he is intrigued by what seems to be a 'dream' (line 61).

Activity 38

You have previously noted similarities between Sebastian and Viola. This scene shows that Shakespeare is careful to give them their own distinctive characteristics, even though they look alike. Compare how they react to other characters in Illyria, considering that Viola needs disguise in Illyria, whereas Sebastian can be himself. How far does the odd situation in this scene excuse Sebastian's aggression? Why do you think Shakespeare creates these differences?

Feste grows impatient – as far as he is concerned, Cesario is being bafflingly uncooperative.

Sir Andrew and **Sir Toby** finally get caught out in this scene. They assume they can take advantage of Cesario, but have to make a rapid readjustment when the reaction is not what they expected, creating a farcical outcome for the audience.

Olivia shows her feelings in her dismissal of Sir Toby as well as her welcome of Cesario. As the shocked Sebastian struggles to work out what is happening, she takes control, believing that Cesario is finally compliant when he agrees to take her lead after she asks 'Would thou'dst be ruled by me!' (line 62).

Dramatic techniques

The audience witnessed the misidentification of Sebastian at the end of Act 3, but in this scene the mistake is repeated for dramatic and comic effect. Shakespeare explored the comic potential of twins in his earlier play *The Comedy of Errors*, where there are two sets of twins, though he shows greater subtlety in his handling of the idea in *Twelfth Night*. Sebastian is absent for much of the play, but the importance of his brief appearance at the beginning of Act 2, making him known to the audience, becomes clear once he enters the plot fully. By including three misidentifications in this scene, Shakespeare builds up the level of humour. The comedy is also dependent on Sebastian's changes of mood, from irritated to violently angry to amazed.

> **Activity 39**
> Look carefully at Sebastian's reactions in the three encounters he has in this scene:
> - with Feste
> - with Sir Andrew and Sir Toby
> - with Olivia.
>
> For each, write down two or three quotations from Sebastian's speeches that demonstrate his different moods.

The humour throughout depends on the dramatic irony of the audience's correct identification of Sebastian. The audience will also recognise that Olivia's meeting with him presents a resolution of the problem that she has fallen in love with a woman in disguise – Sebastian really is a man.

Language

Perhaps emboldened by the sight of Cesario in possible danger, Olivia uses language that clearly reveals her impassioned state. She insults Sir Toby using **lexis** including 'Ungracious wretch', 'barbarous' and 'Rudesby' (lines 45, 46, 49) and then refers to him as 'uncivil' and 'ruffian' to the person she believes is Cesario (lines 51, 54). Her word choices in addressing Cesario are markedly different, calling him 'gentle friend' and referring to his 'fair wisdom' (lines 49–50). She then takes the initiative, using the **imperative** three times to Cesario: 'Go with me', 'Thou shalt not choose' and 'Do not deny' (lines 52, 55–6).

Sebastian shows his lack of understanding in his short speech. He uses the metaphor of a 'stream' (line 58) to imply that he is borne along without control and as he cannot explain the situation he begins to consider that he is either 'mad' or that it is 'a dream' (line 59). The word 'dream', used in both lines 59 and 61, also has connotations of fantasy, suggesting that he is already falling for Olivia's charm and beauty.

Act 4 Scene 2

Lines 1–69 Feste, encouraged by Maria and Sir Toby, talks to the imprisoned Malvolio in the disguise of Sir Topas.
Lines 61–128 Using his own voice and that of Sir Topas, Feste agrees to bring pen and paper to Malvolio so that he can write to Olivia. Feste departs with a song.

What happens

At this point the play takes a darker turn, with Malvolio imprisoned, as Sir Toby had suggested in Act 3 Scene 4. Nowadays this would seem cruel for a person suffering a real psychiatric disorder, but as part of a practical joke it might be seen as particularly nasty. The joke is pushed further, though, with Maria and Toby persuading Feste to put on the costume and voice of a priest, Sir Topas, to talk to Malvolio.

Feste's dialogue with Malvolio continues the pretence that he is mad, calling him 'Malvolio the lunatic', 'hyperbolical fiend' and 'dishonest Satan!' (lines 21–2, 24, 30). Malvolio insists that he is 'not mad' (line 39) and, quite unlike his behaviour earlier in the play, is rational and dignified, although in great distress. Perhaps Sir Toby recognises that distress and it persuades him to change his mind about the plot, which he now calls 'knavery' (line 66). Feste, however, in his own voice, sings lines from a song about a woman who 'loves another' (line 77), a reference to Malvolio's vanished hopes for Olivia, and continues to joke with Malvolio about being 'mad' and having 'no better…wits than a fool' (lines 86–7). Eventually Feste agrees to bring 'some ink, paper, and light' to Malvolio (lines 106–7), who intends to write to Olivia, an ironic parallel to the letter he believes was from her. Even as he departs, however, Feste sings about the devil – another reminder of the pretence that Malvolio is possessed.

> **Activity 40**
> Write your own version of Malvolio's letter to Olivia. What does he have to tell her about what has happened? What tone will he take in the letter? Consider everything that has happened to Malvolio since he found the letter in the garden. You will be able to compare your letter with Malvolio's later in the play.

The characters
Maria and **Sir Toby** continue to be the chief architects of the plan against Malvolio, but Sir Toby eventually feels it has gone far enough, wishing to be 'rid of this knavery' (line 65), which now endangers his position in his niece's house.

Feste performs the role required of him, at first seeming to enter into the spirit of the Sir Topas disguise, though his line 'Nay, I am for all waters' (line 61) may indicate a degree of frustration. However, the fact that he continues to make jokes at Malvolio's expense once Sir Toby has left, and uses his songs to irritate him, suggests that he still holds a personal grudge towards Malvolio.

Malvolio is very different in this scene, a striking contrast with his presentation earlier in the play. He is more controlled, insisting on his rationality but in considerable distress after being imprisoned in the dark.

Dramatic techniques

This is another scene that uses disguise, but its tone is quite different from previous scenes. Right at the start, Maria asks Feste to put on 'this gown and this beard', the disguise for 'Sir Topas the curate' (lines 1–2). She is continuing the pretence that Malvolio is possessed by the devil by calling in a clergyman to talk to him. This may continue the thread of disguise running through the play, but it is a strange decision. After all, Malvolio, locked away in the dark, is unable to see Feste, making his costume unnecessary. Maria herself admits: 'Thou mightst have done this without thy beard and gown: he sees thee not' (lines 62–3).

> **Activity 41**
> Since the disguise of Sir Topas is unnecessary to deceive Malvolio, why do you think Shakespeare included it? Think about what it contributes to the dramatic effects of the scene and how it develops the audience's understanding of the characters.

Malvolio's behaviour and speech make this disguise scene different from previous ones. Depending on how it is produced, there could be very little humour here at all apart from the one-person dialogue between Feste and Sir Topas, perhaps (lines 96–8).

Language

The change is tone is mainly caused by Malvolio's language. Gone is the sneering pomposity of earlier in the play. He speaks clearly about his predicament, in straightforward language that is a contrast with Feste's mock complexities in his role as Sir Topas. While Feste talks elaborately of 'windows transparent as barricadoes' and 'clerestories [...] as lustrous as ebony' (lines 35–7), Malvolio explains that 'never was man thus wronged' and that 'they have laid me here in hideous darkness' (lines 27–9). Feste tests his patience with irrelevant questions about 'Pythagoras', but Malvolio's answers are patient and clear (lines 48–54). Importantly, when Feste drops his disguised voice, Malvolio addresses him four times as 'good fool' (lines 78, 82,

102, 106) – remember that 'fool' is Feste's title and role, not an insult, and compare this with how Malvolio addressed him at the beginning of the play. When Malvolio says that he is 'as well in my wits as any man in Illyria' (lines 103–4) it is simply phrased and undeniably true.

> **Activity 42**
> Discuss in pairs in what ways this scene affects your judgement of Malvolio. How far do you agree that he has been 'notoriously abus'd' (line 84), or has he appropriately been humbled?

Act 4 Scene 3

Lines 1–21 Sebastian expresses his puzzlement about events since his arrival in Illyria, including the disappearance of Antonio and the behaviour of Olivia.

Lines 22–35 Olivia brings a priest; Sebastian agrees to go with her and be married, ending Act 4.

What happens

This short scene is a crucial one for the plot: at the end of it, Olivia exits to get married. She thinks she is marrying Cesario, but it is in fact Sebastian who accompanies her and the priest. It begins with a soliloquy by Sebastian, who is in such a confused state that he has to check the reality of his surroundings. He longs for Antonio's advice, but has not been able to find him at the Elephant, the inn where they agreed to meet. The source of his confusion is Olivia, whose attentions to him he cannot understand, though she seems sane and stable. On cue, Olivia arrives, accompanied by a priest, and suggests immediate marriage. Perhaps surprisingly, Sebastian readily agrees to go with her and marry.

The characters

Sebastian shares his confusion directly with the audience, thinking that either he or Olivia must be mad. However, he is quite sure of his own sanity and has observed that Olivia runs her household carefully and effectively. Although none of this quite makes sense to him, he agrees to marry her.

Olivia, on the other hand, is delighted by the new level of compliance in the man she believes to be Cesario. Note that in the scene, she never addresses him by name, which would have revealed the misidentification. Perhaps the young man's ready agreement is the reason why she is in such a hurry to get married – she may fear Cesario will change his mind.

> **Activity 43**
> Write a short soliloquy (6–8 lines would be enough, or one prose paragraph) for Olivia, which gives her reactions to Cesario's apparent new attitude towards her and explains her decision to go and fetch a priest. Look carefully at her speech in lines 22–31 for ideas.

Dramatic techniques
There have been many times in *Twelfth Night* when the audience has had to suspend disbelief. Viola has decided on a male disguise and nobody has been able to see through it. Olivia has fallen in love with that disguise virtually at first sight, and still cannot tell the difference between Cesario and Sebastian. In this scene, the audience has to accept that Sebastian is willing to marry a woman he has only just met, despite the fact that her behaviour towards him makes little sense. Comedy depends on such **suspension of disbelief** – the plot would not work without it, and Shakespeare's audiences would be accustomed to watching plays that required them to accept these conventions. The play's subtitle is *What You Will*, which could allude to this, suggesting audience members can make of it what they please. The closer a playwright pushes the plot to the very edge of plausibility, the funnier it can be.

Language
The idea of madness runs through Sebastian's soliloquy, with variations of the word occurring four times (lines 4, 10, 15, 16). There is no suggestion of being possessed by the devil here, as there was with Malvolio, but Sebastian feels he cannot trust his rational understanding. He checks off items at the beginning, reassuring himself that they are tangible and his senses are working. Even so, he feels that he might 'distrust mine eyes / And wrangle with

my reason' (lines 13–14) because of Olivia's behaviour. 'Reason' is the opposite of 'madness' and he suggests that he has to fight it to persuade his mind of the reality of events. The structure of his own speech suggests a rational mind carefully working through problems and balancing evidence. It is very different from a conventional love speech, like Orsino's at the beginning of the play. The words he uses to describe Olivia's actions all contradict the disorder of madness: 'command', 'smooth, discreet and stable' (lines 17, 19), which assure him all is well.

> **Activity 44**
> Look carefully at Sebastian's opening speech in this scene. Pick out all the concrete nouns – words that refer to actual, tangible objects – and the abstract nouns – those that refer to ideas, thoughts or feelings. Think about how they are balanced in the speech to show the things that Sebastian understands and those that still puzzle him. How does his expression of his own confusion help the audience to suspend disbelief?

> **Task**
> From Act 4, consider ways in which Shakespeare presents Feste's varied role as the play's clown.
> - Find examples of Feste's wordplay in his dialogue with Sebastian at the beginning of Scene 1.
> - List particular examples of his role-play as Sir Topas, including costume and language.
> - What is your judgement of the way Feste treats Malvolio in this act?

Act 5

Summary

Taking the form of one long scene, Act 5 is the big finale, resolving at last all the confusions of the play. The mistaken identities are corrected and, as is traditional with Shakespeare's comedies, marriage rounds off the action. Not everyone, however, is included in the festivities.

Act 5 Scene 1

Lines 1–45 Orsino, with Cesario, arrives at Olivia's house and enjoys some word-play with Feste.

Lines 46–96 Orsino's officers appear with Antonio, who again mistakes Cesario for Sebastian.

Lines 97–167 Olivia's appearance brings confusions to a head, as she dismisses Orsino's love and reveals her marriage to, as she believes, Cesario. Orsino is understandably furious.

Lines 168–97 Sir Andrew and Sir Toby enter, both bearing wounds from a further attack. They believe Cesario is the culprit, whereas the audience realises it must have been Sebastian.

Lines 198–271 As Sir Andrew and Sir Toby depart, Sebastian arrives. Finally he and Cesario are on stage together and the mistakes can be reconciled. Sebastian and Viola are reunited.

Lines 272–401 Feste brings Malvolio's letter, which Fabian reads aloud. Malvolio, released from his imprisonment, complains about his ill-treatment, prompting Fabian to admit the plot against him. Malvolio exits, the couples are united and Feste sings to end the play.

What happens

The scene begins with anticipation – Feste has Malvolio's letter and Fabian begs to see it. Their discussion, however, is interrupted by the arrival of Orsino and Cesario. This is the first time that Orsino has visited Olivia's house himself, which gives his entry greater significance. Since Cesario is with him, the audience will keenly anticipate a meeting with Olivia, following the marriage to Sebastian at the end of the previous scene. Shakespeare creates suspense by delaying the meeting as Feste engages Orsino in wordplay for 40 lines to gain more money from him. Antonio's arrival then delays Olivia further. Orsino immediately recognises him from the sea battle, but Cesario defends him, in gratitude for his intervention in the duel with Sir Andrew, which he still cannot understand. Antonio, thinking that he is facing Sebastian again, addresses Orsino in a passionate speech about Sebastian's ingratitude. He now believes his former devotion to Sebastian must have been the result of 'witchcraft' (line 72) or 'false cunning' (line 82). However, Orsino dismisses his story without much consideration, since Antonio claims to have spent 'three months' (line 90) with the 'ingrateful boy' (line 73), the same time that Cesario has spent with him.

> **Activity 45**
> Antonio is very clear about what he thinks at this moment in the scene, as Shakespeare gives Antonio a 21-line speech in which he clearly expresses his shock and disappointment in his friend. However, the audience has fewer clues about what Viola and Orsino think about the situation. Write a short speech, no more than five lines, for each of them to express what they privately think of Antonio's speech.

Only then does Shakespeare bring Olivia into the scene. She addresses herself to Cesario, with no time for Orsino, dismissing his attention to her as 'howling' (line 106). The destructiveness of Orsino's jealousy is made clear when he threatens to kill Cesario, whom he believes has stolen Olivia's love and 'sits crowned in his master's spite' (line 124). This section reaches a climax when Cesario declares devotion to Orsino. Olivia reacts with shock, then declares that he is her husband. Naturally, Orsino is taken aback – as is Cesario. While the priest confirms the wedding and Orsino responds with fury, poor Viola is trapped in her disguise knowing that such a marriage is impossible.

Since Cesario has just arrived with Orsino, it is also impossible for him to be responsible for the attack on Sir Andrew and Sir Toby, who accuse him as they stagger on, wounded. Sir Toby is particularly angry and finally rudely rejects Sir Andrew with a stream of insults which leave him speechless. Only at that point, after over 200 lines of dialogue in the scene, with confusions that have caused anger and hurt, does Shakespeare bring Sebastian into the action. He enters with an apology for hurting Sir Toby, not seeing Cesario. It is Orsino who first acknowledges the similarity between the two, followed by Antonio, who is confused about which of the two figures is in fact Sebastian. Olivia follows, finding the prospect of two Cesarios 'wonderful!' (line 219). Only then does Sebastian lay eyes on Cesario, puzzled by seeing an apparent brother instead of a sister who he believed drowned. In a moving dialogue, he and Viola exchange details of their shared parentage to be sure of each other's identity before Viola reveals her 'masculine usurp'd attire' (line 244) in which she has served Orsino. Sebastian reassures Olivia that she has married a man, and Orsino, remembering some of Cesario's speeches about love, accepts and returns Viola's love. The mistakes are over and all seems set for a happy ending.

However, the final moments of the play return to Malvolio. Fabian reads his letter, which outlines his cruel treatment, and when Malvolio appears he accuses Olivia of doing him 'Notorious wrong' (line 322). Still believing the letter he found came from Olivia, he outlines its contents, only for Olivia to recognise the handwriting as Maria's. Fabian admits the other details of the plot. He tries to balance 'injuries […] on both sides' (lines 361–2), but Feste continues to tease Malvolio. Malvolio exits, spoiling the party mood, swearing revenge on 'the whole pack' of his tormentors (line 371). On that sour note, the other characters turn back to their unions and Feste sings his final song, closing the play with verses about life and ageing.

> **Activity 46**
> As *Twelfth Night* is a comedy, how surprising do you find it that Shakespeare ends it with a melancholy song? Discuss with a partner how appropriate to the play you find Feste's song.

The characters

Viola and **Sebastian** are reunited, bringing the misidentifications to an end. Viola is able to drop her disguise and both look forward to joining their loving partners.

Olivia and **Orsino** are reconciled, but only because they choose different partners and only after considerable discord. All ends happily for the play's four main characters.

Feste maintains his criticism of Malvolio, but ends the play in a traditional manner, with a song.

Sir Andrew and **Sir Toby**'s relationship comes to an end after Sebastian's attack on them, which was caused by Sir Toby's search for entertainment and funds at Sir Andrew's expense.

Malvolio ends the play as a sorrowful figure, broken by his experience and swearing revenge.

Antonio, although overjoyed to discover the real Sebastian again, is then left in limbo, his fate unresolved. He seems excluded from the final festivities.

ACT AND SCENE NOTES

Dramatic techniques

As one of the conventions of comedy is to restore order after chaos, the problems and puzzles are always resolved at the end. It is the same in Shakespeare's other comedies, such as *Much Ado About Nothing* and *The Comedy of Errors*, and even a play like *The Tempest* shares many of the same structural features. An audience might be expecting this resolution as Cesario arrives with Orsino at Olivia's house, but Shakespeare increases the suspense by delaying Olivia's entry. Then he pushes the confusions one final stage further when Olivia names Cesario as her husband. It is not until Sebastian's arrival that the errors can be uncovered; the first line of dialogue acknowledging the similarity between the twins occurs in line 210. Viola first decided on her disguise in Act 1 Scene 2 line 54; since then, there have been 2165 lines of dialogue over 15 scenes, which demonstrates how well Shakespeare maintains the comic momentum of the drama.

> **Activity 47**
> Make a list of every scene in the play, horizontally across the middle of a piece of landscape A4 paper. Choose a different-coloured pen for each of the following elements of the plot:
> 1 Cesario's visits to Olivia
> 2 Cesario's scenes with Orsino
> 3 The plot against Malvolio
> 4 Sir Toby's and Sir Andrew's challenge to Cesario and its aftermath
> 5 Sebastian's arrival and scenes
>
> For each plot element, draw a box around each relevant scene in its chosen colour. Then draw lines to join up the boxes of the same colour, similar to the sample below. When you have finished, you will have a colourful diagram that will give you a visual image of the complexity of Shakespeare's plotting across the play. Some lines will arc across a number of scenes, showing how Shakespeare prepares for later events, and finally the lines will join together.
>
>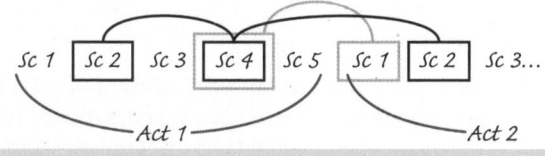

TWELFTH NIGHT

While the play ends in union and marriage, *Twelfth Night* is consistent with Shakespeare's other comedies in that the ending is not entirely happy. The joyful resolution of *A Midsummer Night's Dream* depends on the love potion remaining in one lover's eyes; at the end of *Much Ado About Nothing*, Hero marries the man who previously humiliated her at the altar; the marriages at the end of *Love's Labours Lost* are delayed by the news of death. In *Twelfth Night*, the happiness of the reunited twins and the joy of their marriages are undercut by Malvolio's angry, vengeful exit.

> **Activity 48**
> What effect does Malvolio's 'I'll be reveng'd on the whole pack of you' (line 371) have as he leaves? Do you think that this alters an audience's view of the play's happy ending? Consider too that Antonio has not been spoken to since line 215 and, as far as the script indicates, is still under arrest. Discuss the effects of these aspects in pairs, then share your conclusions.

Language

The climax of the play is the twins, Viola and Sebastian, finally coming face to face after so many characters have accepted Cesario as a young man and failed to spot any difference between him and Sebastian. It is not surprising, then, that Shakespeare emphasises the characters' shock, and the twins' likeness, in the dialogue. Orsino first comments on the uncanny similarity between the two, his words balancing the **paradox** of 'one' and 'two': 'One face, one voice, one habit, and two persons!' (line 210). Antonio, meeting the real Sebastian again after the earlier confusion, is still not certain, having to check: 'Sebastian are you?' (line 215), while Olivia finds the likeness between the two 'Most wonderful!' (line 219). When Sebastian catches sight of Viola, even he is confused, asking 'Do I stand there?' (line 220). The key reference to their visual similarity comes from Antonio, who uses the metaphor of an apple sliced in half: 'An apple cleft in two is not more twin' (line 217). In this final scene of the play, Viola can return to her true identity; when

ACT AND SCENE NOTES

Sebastian says, 'Thrice welcome, drowned Viola!' (line 235), it is the first time her name is mentioned in the play.

> **Activity 49**
> Though Viola remains in her male clothes, she refers to her 'maiden weeds' – her female clothes (line 249) – and her 'maid's garments' (line 269). In this way her true sex is made clear to Orsino. Look at the lines addressed to Viola by Olivia and Orsino between lines 308 and 318 and pick out all the words that refer to gender. How is Shakespeare using this lexis to solve the confusion between these three characters, and bring Orsino and Viola together as partners?

> **Task**
> Consider ways in which Shakespeare brings the play to its resolution in Act 5.
> - Find three ways in which Shakespeare creates more tension and confusion before Sebastian's entrance.
> - List different reasons why Shakespeare writes extended dialogue (32 lines) between Viola and Sebastian when they meet.
> - Which characters do you think have the most favourable resolution at the end of the play, and which characters the worst? What is the effect of this variation?

A GUIDE TO THE PLAY'S THEMES

Love

Romantic love

> **Key scenes:** Act 1 Scenes 1 and 5; Act 2 Scenes 2, 4 and 5; Act 3 Scene 1; Act 4 Scenes 1 and 3; Act 5

Twelfth Night is a romantic comedy, exploring the difficulties and ultimately the joys of love in different ways. The characters' success in finding a suitable love match seems impossible until the very end of the drama and, through their challenges, Shakespeare examines the nature of love itself. He begins the play with Orsino's showy demonstration of his own feelings, moody and changeable because of the 'spirit of love' (Act 1 Scene 1 line 9). Shakespeare characterises Orsino as a typical Petrarchan lover, bearing the hallmarks of the literary style of love made popular 200 years earlier by the Italian Renaissance poet Petrarch (1304–74). Such a lover idolises the woman and sees himself as a victim of love, helpless until she accepts him. This type of love is very much a literary convention rather than a reality, and Shakespeare seems to be making fun of it in Orsino's character.

Viola's love for Orsino is presented in a contrasting way; she cannot express her love as she is restricted by her disguise, but she speaks of being 'like Patience on a monument, / Smiling at grief' (Act 2 Scene 4 lines 114–15). While Orsino is interested in the story of Cesario's 'sister' (line 119), he is still convinced that a woman's love is inferior to a man's, being unable to bear 'the beating of so strong a passion' as his own (Act 2 Scene 4 line 94). This view is actively challenged by Viola in Cesario's answer to him and by her behaviour throughout the play. Orsino's idealised version of love finally amounts to nothing, as he realises the true value of companionship, mutual respect and affection at the end.

> **Activity 50**
> Research the lyrics of pop songs about love and relationships. Try to find a range of songs from different times since the mid-twentieth century. Discuss how they reflect changing

A GUIDE TO THE PLAY'S THEMES

attitudes and see if you can recognise any connection with Petrarchan ideas of male/female relationships.

Twelfth Night also includes characters who fall in love at first sight. Shakespeare's comedy depends on the improbability of this for part of its humour. That is emphasised, of course, when Olivia falls for Cesario, whom the audience knows is another woman. Olivia herself comments on the speed of her attraction to Cesario, stating 'this youth's perfections' have led her into love as 'quickly' as catching 'the plague' (Act 1 Scene 5 lines 284–5). Viola recognises the impossibility of the match, remarking that 'she were better love a dream' (Act 2 Scene 2 line 24). Later, Olivia's own speed of falling in love is matched by Sebastian's acceptance of her love in Act 4.

Sir Andrew Aguecheek and Malvolio also seek the love of Olivia, and they create further comparisons. Sir Andrew, despite being a knight, lacks any kind of social awareness, while Malvolio's feelings for Olivia are complicated by class. Although he claims that 'the Lady of the Strachy married the yeoman of the wardrobe' (Act 2 Scene 5 lines 36–7), his position as Olivia's servant makes any relationship between them highly unlikely. None of Olivia's suitors is a good match for her, including Cesario, until Sebastian's arrival.

Sibling love

Key scenes: Act 1 Scene 2; Act 2 Scene 1; Act 5

The audience is introduced to the separated twins, a brother and sister, early in Acts 1 and 2. Their affection for each other is clear; Viola asks about her brother's welfare as soon as she lands in Illyria (Act 1 Scene 2), desperate to hear that he may have survived the shipwreck. While she is reassured by the Captain, her brother Sebastian is convinced that Viola has 'drown'd' (Act 2 Scene 1 line 21). He pays tribute to her 'mind that envy could not but call fair' (line 27) and weeps for her loss. This idea of sibling love is reinforced when they meet at the end of the play, gently questioning each other about shared memories of their father to reassure themselves of the reality of their reunion (Act 5 Scene 1 lines 226–42).

Viola's and Sebastian's love for each other is contrasted by Olivia's mourning for the death of her brother. The excess of her sorrow, separating herself not just from Orsino but from the world 'like a cloistress' for seven years (Act 1 Scene 1 line 29) is questioned by Feste's jokes, proving her a fool for her exaggerated mourning (Act 1 Scene 5 lines 52–66). The speed at which she falls in love with Cesario also leads the audience to question the sincerity of excessive emotional response.

Friendship

> **Key scenes:** Act 2 Scene 1; Act 3 Scenes 3 and 4

Sebastian enters the play with Antonio, who has helped him since the shipwreck that brought him to Illyria. Although Sebastian is determined to approach Orsino's court alone, Antonio, who is a wanted man in Illyria, follows, dismissing 'danger' as 'sport' because he 'adore[s]' Sebastian (Act 2 Scene 1 lines 44–5). This affection is clear when he catches up with him in Act 3 Scene 3, referring to his 'willing love' (line 11) and lending Sebastian money. Shakespeare gives Antonio the language of service and friendship. While Antonio acts as a servant towards the socially superior Sebastian, there is also a shared bond between them. Such language of love is often used between true friends in Shakespeare's plays.

No such language is used in the dialogue between Sir Toby and Sir Andrew, and it becomes clear this friendship is of a very different nature. Sir Toby amuses himself at Sir Andrew's expense. He encourages him in his impossible quest to gain Olivia's love and arranges the mock duel between Sir Andrew and Cesario, creating false reputations for both of them as skilled swordsmen so that he and Fabian can enjoy the spectacle of two terrified people duelling. In a direct contrast with Antonio, apart from amusement, Sir Toby's prime motivation is spending Sir Andrew's money. He knows he has 'three thousand ducats a year' (Act 1 Scene 3 line 20) and has already cost him 'some two thousand strong' (Act 3 Scene 2 lines 49–50). The falseness of this friendship is confirmed when Sir Toby finally dismisses Sir Andrew as 'an ass-head and a coxcomb and a knave, a thin fac'd knave, a gull' (Act 5 Scene 1 lines 200–1).

Disguise

Costume and cross-dressing

> **Key scenes:** Act 1 Scenes 2, 4 and 5; Act 2 Scenes 2 and 4; Act 3 Scenes 1 and 4; Act 4 Scene 2; Act 5

Disguise plays an important role in a number of Shakespeare's plays, with the use of costume and accompanying performance relating it directly to the theatre. All actors are disguised within their roles and costumes, and in the Elizabethan theatre the female roles were played by boys. This means that Cesario was the role of a young man being performed by a young woman being performed by a boy, creating extra layers of humour and irony. The idea of disguise is established quickly in the play's second scene, when Viola asks the Captain to 'Conceal me what I am' so that she can seek employment at Orsino's court (Act 1 Scene 2 line 53).

After one intervening scene and three days' passage of time, we meet Viola as Cesario, who has already established 'himself' in a position of trust with Orsino. From that point on, Viola maintains the male identity of Cesario until the end of the play. This disguise gives her opportunities to seek employment and converse frankly with both women and men in a way she would be unable to do as a woman. However, it also traps her so that she is unable to show her feelings for Orsino and unintentionally becomes the object of Olivia's love. The audience is always aware of Cesario's real identity, and Shakespeare exploits this in Orsino's observations about his new servant's feminine qualities, commenting on his 'smooth and rubious' lips (Act 1 Scene 4 line 32).

Viola's appearance in Cesario's costume creates both humour and poignancy, whereas Malvolio's costume following the instructions in Maria's letter is designed for comedy. With bright yellow stockings, emphasised by contrasting strapping, Shakespeare is aiming for maximum visual impact when Malvolio finally appears. The plotters and the audience find it funny and even Olivia's bewilderment is probably accompanied by laughter at her servant's ludicrous appearance as she asks, 'Why, how dost thou, man? What is the matter with thee?' (Act 3 Scene 4 lines 24–5).

Malvolio's costume and accompanying behaviour are used by Maria to persuade Olivia that he is suffering from 'midsummer madness' (Act 3 Scene 2 line 52), which gives the Malvolio plot a sinister turn as he is 'bound' in 'a dark room' (line 131). Shakespeare gives the role of disguise another strange twist with Feste's performance as Sir Topas the curate, who supposedly comes to investigate Malvolio's 'madness'. Feste produces some baffling dialogue in his role, but Maria also provides him with a costume, including a 'gown' and 'beard' (Act 4 Scene 2 line 1), to play the part. This creates a strong visual image for the audience, but it is unnecessary to deceive Malvolio, who cannot see Sir Topas anyway.

> **Activity 51**
> Look back through the play and make a list of all the occasions where disguise and pretence are used. Think about how language is used to disguise and pretend as much as costume.

Deception and honesty

> **Key scenes:** Act 1 Scene 2; Act 2 Scenes 1 and 5; Act 3 Scene 4; Act 4 Scene 2

The initial deception of Malvolio is one of the high points of *Twelfth Night*'s comedy. Maria's plot plays on traits of Malvolio's own character – his pride, his scorn for others and his conviction of his place in Olivia's favour – all of which delight the audiences both on stage and in the theatre. Once he has persuaded himself that the letter he finds in the garden comes from Olivia, he is caught and convinced that 'greatness' is being 'thrust upon' him (Act 2 Scene 5 line 135). This leads to his yellow stockings and his smiling, both of which go against his natural characteristics.

Shakespeare is also careful to include examples of honesty, in characters who lack deceit and who can be trusted. He uses both the Captain and Antonio, the two humble characters who help Viola and Sebastian, to contrast with the deception in the play. Viola tells the Captain that appearances can be deceptive, that 'nature with a beauteous wall / Doth oft close in pollution,' (Act 1 Scene 2 lines 48–9), but the Captain himself shows 'a fair behaviour' (line 47) and she is convinced that he has 'a mind that suits / With this thy fair and outward character' (lines 50–1). Although Sebastian has deceived Antonio by passing himself off as Roderigo, Antonio remains devoted to him and fears for his friend, 'Unguided and unfriended' in Illyria (Act 3 Scene 3 line 10). He endangers himself by following him.

> **Activity 52**
> Although the Captain and Antonio are ordinary sailors, Shakespeare writes their speeches almost as formally as Viola's and Sebastian's. Rewrite some of their speeches in Creole or dialect, and perform the scenes with the original speeches for Viola and Sebastian. What difference does this make to your understanding of the characters and the scenes?

Illusion and reality

> **Key scenes:** Act 1 Scenes 4 and 5; Act 2 Scenes 4 and 5; Act 3 Scene 1

Viola's disguise in the play results in a number of awkward relationships, as she creates the illusion of a thoughtful young man, Cesario, when she is in fact a rather lost young woman. Orsino is quickly drawn to his new companion, showing him 'favours' after 'three days' (Act 1 Scene 4 lines 1–3). Shakespeare reminds the audience of the fine line between illusion and reality when Orsino almost sees through the disguise, commenting on Cesario's feminine characteristics: 'thy small pipe / Is as the maiden's organ, shrill and sound, / And all is semblative a woman's part' (lines 32–4). There are difficulties of a different kind with Olivia, who is immediately struck by Cesario's forthright character, declaring, 'I love thee so that, maugre all thy pride, / Nor wit nor reason can my passion hide' (Act 3 Scene 1 lines 149–50). She has fallen in love with an illusion.

Malvolio is self-deluding and his own illusions about his relationship with Olivia are exploited by Maria's forged letter. Act 2 Scene 5 is a staging masterpiece of illusion, where the audience enjoys the contrast between what Malvolio believes and the reality. He is convinced he is alone, that the letter is from Olivia, and that she loves him. The audience can see the other characters watching, knows the letter has been written by Maria and realises that Olivia has no romantic feelings for him at all.

At the centre of the plot, the pair of twins are frequently mistaken for one another: Cesario is taken for Sebastian and Sebastian is mistaken for Cesario by different characters at different points of the action. While Antonio's illusion that he is rejected by Sebastian in Act 3 is poignant, all the other mistaken identities contribute to the comic pattern of the play.

Strangeness

Malvolio's 'madness'

> **Key scenes:** Act 3 Scene 4; Act 4 Scene 2; Act 5

Malvolio is, of course, of sound mind, but it suits the trickery of Maria and Sir Toby to claim he is otherwise. It is Maria who first makes the suggestion to Olivia that Malvolio is 'possess'd' and 'tainted in's wits' (Act 3 Scene 4 lines 9, 13) and his strange behaviour seems to confirm this. The audience might feel that Malvolio is indeed delusional in imagining that he could have a relationship with Olivia, but in this scene his tormentors make that idea literal, suggesting that he is controlled by 'the fiend' (line 88) and 'bewitch'd' (line 98).

Malvolio's scornful dismissal of Maria, Sir Toby and Fabian as 'idle shallow things' (line 119) encourages the audience to enjoy the comedy at his expense. However, in Act 4 Scene 2 Shakespeare begins to influence the audience's response when Malvolio is discovered imprisoned. Feste's lines continue the idea of possession by the devil, with references to 'hyperbolical fiend' (line 24), 'dishonest Satan' (line 30) and 'dark as hell' (line 45). The contrast with Malvolio's own lines is striking. Rejecting the description of 'Malvolio the lunatic' (lines 21–2), he claims that 'never was man thus wronged' (line 27) and argues clearly that 'I am not mad' (line 39). The pretence of 'madness' through the humiliation of Malvolio's ridiculous costume at first provided the audience with much amusement, but in this scene the tone has changed and the audience may well agree with Malvolio that 'there was never man so notoriously abus'd' (line 84).

Activity 53
Imagine that Malvolio's revenge involves taking Sir Toby, Sir Andrew, Maria, Feste and Fabian to court for the abuse he has suffered. Appoint different students to present Malvolio's case against each of them and other students to present their defence. Look carefully at the dialogue and try to incorporate some of the characters' lines. Vote as a class on a verdict.

The strangeness of Illyria

> **Key scenes:** Act 4 Scenes 1 and 3

Shakespeare sets a number of his plays in locations outside the normal confines of society, where strange, even magical things can happen. In Illyria he creates the impression of a far-distant place where nobody should be surprised by incomprehensible events. Both Viola and Sebastian are strangers there, and Sebastian, in particular, finds his experiences very puzzling. It is a place where different people insist they know him, despite his being a newcomer, and where he is attacked without provocation. Most puzzling of all, it is a place where he is immediately welcomed by a beautiful woman. Unsurprisingly, he wonders whether 'I am mad, or else this is a dream' (Act 4 Scene 1 line 59) and is still confused two scenes later when he says he is 'ready to distrust mine eyes / And wrangle with my reason' (Act 4 Scene 3 lines 13–14). It is in that bewildered state that he agrees to marry Olivia.

Activity 54
Compare and contrast Shakespeare's presentation of the 'madness' of Malvolio and Sebastian. Make note of the language and imagery used by and about these characters, considering how they indicate different types of 'madness'.

Dreams and sleep

> **Key scenes:** Act 2 Scenes 2 and 5; Act 4 Scenes 1 and 3

Sebastian's sense of bewilderment at the strangeness of his experiences in Illyria makes him wonder if he might be dreaming. Shakespeare uses the language and imagery of dreams to suggest that Illyria is unreal, and perhaps a fantasy. In fact, it is such an attractive dream for Sebastian that he wants it to continue, saying 'Let fancy still my sense in Lethe sleep' (Act 4 Scene 1 line 60) – he wants 'sense', rationality, to be put to sleep and forgotten. A dream, though, is insubstantial and unreal, and that is the sense in which Viola uses the image when she realises that Olivia has fallen in love with her Cesario persona. She comments that 'she were better love a dream' (Act 2 Scene 2 line 24).

Malvolio's fantasy is a relationship with Olivia, and Maria's clever letter seems to have given him a sense of its reality. However, as Sir Toby says, Malvolio has been persuaded of a 'dream' (Act 2 Scene 5 line 181), one which for him will finally become a nightmare.

Money and society

Money and marriage

> **Key scenes:** Act 2 Scenes 1 and 3; Act 5

The marriages at the end of the play match couples within the higher levels of society. Orsino is a duke, the highest rank in the play, while Olivia is a countess, another character of rank and title. Viola and Sebastian have no title, but Sebastian assumes Antonio will have heard of 'Sebastian of Messaline', his father (Act 2 Scene 1 line 15), which indicates the family's importance, and Orsino reassures Olivia that Sebastian's 'blood' is 'right noble' (Act 5 Scene 1 line 258). These are characters in a comfortable position in society, with few worries about money. Through their marriage choices, they keep the wealth within their own social circle.

The difference in social status makes a relationship between Malvolio and Olivia highly unlikely. When he imagines being married to her, he significantly pictures playing with 'some rich jewel' (Act 2 Scene 5 line 57). In many productions this is emphasised by Malvolio fondling his steward's chain at this point. While Sir Andrew's pursuit of Olivia is equally unlikely, he is a knight. However, though he has an income of 'three thousand ducats a year' (Act 1 Scene 3 line 20), it also becomes clear that money is at least part of Olivia's attractiveness to him, as he tells Sir Toby that 'If I cannot recover your niece, I am a foul way out' (Act 2 Scene 3 line 174).

Earning and spending money

> **Key scenes:** Act 2 Scenes 1, 2 and 3; Act 3 Scene 1; Act 5

Unlike the wealthy, some characters in the play clearly need to earn a living. While Feste is Sir Toby's and Sir Andrew's companion, joining them in the plot against Malvolio, he still earns money from them, getting 'sixpence' from Sir Toby and 'a testril' from Sir Andrew as payment for his song (Act 2 Scene 3 lines 30–2). It is unusual that in Orsino's court he refuses money for a song, saying that he takes 'pleasure in singing' (Act 2 Scene 4 line 67), whereas later in the play he uses a sequence of jokes to gain more coins from both Cesario and Orsino. In Act 3 Scene 1, he suggests to Cesario, who has just given him one coin, 'Would not a pair of these have bred, sir?' (line 49) and in Act 5 Scene 1, he persuades Orsino to be a 'double-dealer' with his money and pay him twice (line 31).

Sir Toby likes spending money on having a good time. However, it seems to be Sir Andrew's money that he squanders; he tells him that he 'hadst need send for more money' (Act 2 Scene 3 lines 172–3) and admits he has already spent 'some two thousand' of Sir Andrew's ducats (Act 3 Scene 2 line 49).

> **Activity 55**
> Orsino and Olivia are a duke and a countess, characters of wealth and position. Before their shipwreck, Viola and Sebastian seem to have been from an affluent family. Money for them, therefore, is not a key concern. Make a note of references in the play which show that money is important to some characters.

Fools and foolery

Feste

> **Key scenes:** Act 1 Scene 5; Act 2 Scene 3; Act 3 Scene 1; Act 4 Scenes 1 and 2; Act 5

Feste appears in the list of characters as 'Clown'. He is the licensed fool of the play, an entertainer or jester. The fact that his character is usually known and discussed as Feste, rather than

Clown, is indicative of his impact on *Twelfth Night*. Shakespeare creates similar characters elsewhere in his plays, the Fool in *King Lear* and Touchstone in *As You Like It* being the closest examples. In each case, the character creates humour but also shows a sharp intelligence and insight. Feste's role as entertainer explains the frequency of his songs, which are a key feature of the play. While he sings for the entertainment of other characters, Shakespeare uses the content of the songs to reflect the concerns of the play. He sings melancholy love songs, and even undercuts the celebratory end of the play with a cynical portrayal of the limited span of human life. These songs imply that he has a deeper level of understanding than his jester role might initially suggest. The audience can see that he is stung by Malvolio's disparaging remarks in Act 1 Scene 5 and perhaps he has his own knowledge of unhappy love. Sir Andrew refers to Feste's 'leman', his sweetheart (Act 2 Scene 3 line 24), which gives a hint. Feste's wisdom, though, is demonstrated by his well-aimed challenge to Olivia's depth of mourning for her brother in Act 1 Scene 5. In Act 2 Scene 1 there are slight indications that he may, alone of all the characters, have seen through Viola's Cesario disguise, with his suggestion that Cesario needs a 'beard' (line 45) and the enigmatic comment that 'who you are and what you would are out of my welkin' (lines 56–7).

Unconscious fools

> **Key scenes:** Act 1 Scene 3; Act 2 Scenes 3 and 5; Act 3 Scene 2; Act 5

Despite his title of Clown, Feste is in many ways far from foolish. Other characters deserve that description rather more, particularly Sir Andrew Aguecheek and Malvolio. Both these characters have their own foolishness exploited by other characters, for their amusement or gain. There is a big difference in the audience's reaction to them, however, as Malvolio's early arrogance and snobbery makes him a very unattractive figure. Sir Andrew is a much gentler character and Shakespeare gives him moments of comic self-knowledge, such as when he recognises himself in Malvolio's reference to a 'foolish knight' (Act 2 Scene 5 line 72).

However, it is also possible to view Orsino and Olivia as examples of foolishness. Initially at least, they both wallow in extreme versions of love – Orsino for Olivia, Olivia for her brother – which the action of the play questions. In this way Shakespeare widens the range of 'fools' on stage.

> **Activity 56**
> Both Feste and Malvolio are employed in Olivia's household, and both provide a great deal of comedy in the play. Starting with the idea that Feste is a licensed fool and that Malvolio is an unconscious one, draw up a list of bullet points that compares and contrasts their roles in the play.

Fate and time

> **Key scenes:** Act 1 Scene 2; Act 2 Scene 2

An unforeseen accident wrecks the ship on which Viola and Sebastian are travelling and they both arrive unexpectedly on Illyria's coast. Sebastian sees this as evidence that Fate is working against him, bringing him bad luck. He says to Antonio that 'My stars shine darkly over me' and refers to 'the malignancy of my fate' (Act 2 Scene 1 lines 3–4). The inability to be in control of the action is exaggerated for Viola when she takes on the disguise of Cesario and loses her true identity. Shakespeare exploits the coincidences, mistakes and problems faced by his characters to create both the humour and the poignant moments of the play. Viola herself recognises her powerlessness, saying that 'Time' will have to resolve the problems as 'It is too hard a knot for me t' untie!' (Act 2 Scene 2 lines 38–9).

Fate and time are almost used as **synonyms** in the play and water is a similar recurring **motif** in the language that delivers these themes. Viola and Sebastian are brought to Illyria by a fateful storm; they are both rescued 'From the rude sea's enrag'd and foamy mouth' (Act 5 Scene 1 line 74). When Sebastian is puzzled by events in Illyria, he asks, 'What relish is in this? How runs the stream?' (Act 4 Scene 1 line 58), linking his fate to the unpredictable, meandering motion of water.

It is not only the twins who feel they are powerless, however. Maria's forged letter for Malvolio states that 'some have greatness thrust upon 'em' by the 'Fates' (Act 2 Scene 5 lines 134–5) and even Olivia feels that 'Fate' is in control, rather than she, and that 'What is decreed must be' (Act 1 Scene 5 lines 299–300).

> **Activity 57**
> Individually, decide which character you think feels the greatest satisfaction with their fate at the end of *Twelfth Night*. Consider how Viola, Sebastian, Orsino and Olivia might reflect on the events, their behaviour and what they have learned about other characters. Explain your choice to the rest of the class.

> **Task**
> Shakespeare makes disguise central to the plot and comedy of Twelfth Night. Consider ways he uses disguise in the play.
> - Choose an example where disguise creates humour, and another example where the use of disguise is not comic.
> - Give two examples where disguise is an advantage to Viola, and two examples where it creates problems for her.
> - What connections can you make between the use of disguise and Shakespeare's exploration of love in the play?

EXAM PRACTICE FOR CSEC® ENGLISH B

Exam-style question 1

'*Twelfth Night* is a play that explores different kinds of loving relationships.'
Write an essay in which you describe TWO loving relationships in the play. In this essay, you must also discuss how the MAIN character is affected in ONE of the relationships, and examine ONE dramatic technique Shakespeare uses to present these loving relationships in the play as a whole.
(35 marks)

Mid-level sample response
Read the following mid-level annotated response to the question above and the overall comment at the end.

'Twelfth Night' is a romantic play which focuses on love, and in particular the loving relationships of Viola, [1] who is the play's central character. When she arrives in Illyria after the shipwreck, she has already heard of Duke Orsino and plans to find a job in his household. However, she cannot serve him as a woman, so she must pretend to be a young man and asks the Captain to help her make a disguise. [2]

Shakespeare uses disguise in the play to show how Viola gets close to Orsino, by pretending to be Cesario, but that also means that she cannot tell him how she feels about him. This would be an unusual thing for a woman to do anyway in Shakespeare's time, [3] but she is trapped by her disguise. It soon becomes clear that Orsino gets on well with Cesario. Valentine comments on the 'favours' Orsino has shown towards him in only 'three days' and Orsino himself says that he has 'unclasp'd / To thee the book even of my secret soul.' [4] The dramatic irony of the disguise creates humour here. [5] This comedy is made even funnier when Orsino seems almost to see through the disguise and comments on

Cesario's features, which he thinks are like a woman's. He talks about Cesario's 'smooth and rubious' lips and his 'shrill' voice, [6] suggesting it is high-pitched, rather than low like a man's. Orsino sends Cesario straight away to try to woo Olivia for him, which is hard for her, because Viola admits to the audience in an aside [7] that she wishes that she 'would be his wife'. This makes the audience feel sympathy for Viola, because she will faithfully try to do something that would make her unhappy if she succeeded.

The problems for Viola are developed later in the play when she, as Cesario, discusses love with Orsino. Orsino thinks he is talking to another man, so he is open in his thoughts about women's and men's love. He thinks women cannot bear 'so strong a passion' as men. Viola does not agree because she feels a powerful love for Orsino but cannot speak about it openly because of her disguise. So Cesario claims that women 'are as true of heart as' men and speaks of her concealed love, pretending that Viola is Cesario's sister. Cesario talks about his sister's suffering as she 'sat like Patience.' The audience will find this moving, as they know that Viola is really talking about herself and Shakespeare is again using dramatic irony. [8] She does not reveal the disguise until the end of the play, and only then does Orsino recognise and accept her love and says, 'Give me thine hand'.

However, Shakespeare creates more complications for Viola before the happy ending with Orsino, and it is disguise again which causes the problems. On arrival at Olivia's house, Malvolio also notes that Cesario has a high voice, but thinks he is 'between boy and man'. Despite Cesario's youth, and the fact that he is trying to win Olivia for Orsino, Olivia finds that she is attracted to him [9] as she is fascinated by his clever speeches. She notices his 'perfections' and says, 'Even so quickly may one catch the plague?' This metaphor shows that she didn't mean to fall in love and finds that it is a problem. [10] However, she sends Malvolio with a ring for Cesario, which makes it clear that she has fallen for him. Again, Shakespeare uses the dramatic irony for comedy as the audience knows that Cesario is a woman. As Viola herself says, 'she were better love a dream'. There cannot be a relationship between Olivia and Cesario, because Cesario is in fact a woman who loves Orsino. This dramatic irony caused by the disguise is both moving and comic [11] when Olivia declares her love to Cesario, saying 'I love thee so'. The disguise makes things difficult for Viola, who answers in riddles, saying that she has 'one heart' which 'no woman has' a claim to. The audience might feel sorry for Olivia, but also for Viola, [12] who is in two impossible relationships – Olivia loves her as Cesario, but she cannot return this love as she is a woman, and she loves Orsino, but she cannot express that love because she is disguised as a man.

Shakespeare therefore creates comedy from the disguise, but he also encourages the audience to think carefully about why people fall into loving relationships. [13] It is only at the end of the play, when Sebastian is revealed as Viola's twin, that Cesario's real identity can be revealed and the marriages that traditionally end Shakespeare's comedies can take place. [14]

[1] Acknowledges the question's focus and identifies Viola as the key character for the essay
[2] Introduces disguise as the dramatic technique to be discussed
[3] Shows some awareness of the historical context
[4] Useful quotation, but no specific analysis of Shakespeare's choice of metaphor
[5] Identifies another technique, arising from the disguise, and one of its effects
[6] Relevant quotations to illustrate the limits to Viola's disguise
[7] Shows awareness of asides to communicate private thoughts to the audience
[8] Good suggestion of how an audience might respond to the scene, simply stated
[9] Focus moves to the second loving relationship for the essay
[10] Attempts to analyse the metaphor, a little clumsily
[11] Shows awareness that dramatic irony can have different effects on an audience
[12] Recognises an audience's possible different responses

TWELFTH NIGHT

[13] Straightforward conclusion that shows its relevance by using the terms of the question
[14] Acknowledges the conventions of comedy

Comment on response

This response covers appropriate areas of the play relevant to the question clearly, though without much development. The expression of ideas and the sentence structure is unsophisticated, which is another indicator of a mid-level response. There is some appreciation of the dramatic techniques of disguise and dramatic irony, though the analysis of Shakespeare's language is rather limited. The difficulties of Viola's relationship are clearly recognised, though the response would have been improved by a more subtle exploration of the ironies of her situation.

High-level sample response
Read the following high-level annotated response to the same question and the overall comment at the end.

Loving relationships are central to 'Twelfth Night', a romantic comedy. They include the love between siblings and between friends, but Shakespeare's prime focus in this comedy is the development of romantic relationships between men and women. [1] As an audience would expect with a Shakespearean comedy, those loving relationships develop through a number of complications and confusions before their resolution [2] and by these means, Shakespeare examines the nature of love itself.

Viola is Shakespeare's central character, on stage for most of the scenes of the play, and it is mainly through her relationships that he explores love. That exploration is never straightforward, however, as it is complicated by disguise. [3] Shakespeare establishes this theatrical technique early in the play, when Viola is shipwrecked in Illyria and asks the Captain to 'Conceal me what I am' so that she can serve Duke Orsino. From this point onward in the play, Viola appears in the costume of Cesario and acts as a young man, but the audience is always aware of her real identity.

Being disguised as Cesario allows Viola some freedom, which she would not be able to enjoy as a woman at the time the play was written. [4] She can talk to Orsino openly and freely, but Shakespeare exploits the ironies of that position. She can enjoy close discussion with Orsino who himself says that he has 'unclasp'd / To thee the book even of my secret soul' to Cesario, but Viola's own 'secret soul' remains hidden to other characters. The audience, however, fully aware that Cesario is Viola in disguise, feels both the comic and the poignant effects of the dramatic irony. [5] This is heightened when Orsino's lines indicate that he is more perceptive than he realises as he comments on Cesario's feminine qualities, his 'smooth and rubious' lips and 'shrill' voice, suggesting its high pitch. [6] Shakespeare plays with the idea that Viola's disguise might be discovered: there is comedy in how close Orsino comes to the truth and this comically emphasises the audience's suspension of disbelief. However, Viola's aside to the audience, admitting that she 'would be his wife' is moving – this has to be an aside, because it is impossible for her to express her feelings openly. [7] The disguise has given her the freedom of access to Orsino's court, but her male role has also become a trap. [8] Shakespeare further exploits the dramatic irony of Viola's position when Orsino sends Cesario as his messenger to convey his love to Olivia. In effect she agrees to attempt something that will cause her great pain if she succeeds, and the audience is aware of the poignancy of her carrying out her duties faithfully.

In Act 2 Scene 4, Shakespeare develops Orsino's and Viola's different loving relationships in a private dialogue about love between Orsino and Cesario. Orsino, believing that he is talking with another man, is quite open about his views on gender differences between men's and women's attitudes to love. While the audience's understanding of Cesario's real identity encourages sympathy for Viola's predicament, it perhaps also provokes criticism of Orsino, who regards himself as an example of the courtly lover in his devotion to Olivia. However, he is made to seem foolish by his declaration that women cannot bear 'so strong a passion' as men. [9] The dialogue maintains the comparison between the biased and opinionated Orsino and the careful responses of Cesario, who argues Viola's view that women 'are as true of heart as' men without revealing her disguise. Cesario speaks movingly about his sister, whom the audience recognises as a reference to Viola herself, whose love was not reciprocated. He tells Orsino that 'She pin'd in thought' and 'sat like Patience on a monument, / Smiling at grief.' Unable to speak openly to Orsino about her love, which convention would prohibit her from doing even if she were not disguised, Viola finds an alternative way to challenge Orsino's views. Shakespeare is also exploring the lack of freedom women at his time had in the expression of their feelings compared with men. The audience will see the irony in that Viola can speak about the true feelings of women only when disguised as a man. [10]

Cesario's role as 'Orsino's embassy' to Olivia causes further complications, which are difficult for Viola, but comic for the audience. [11] Similar to Orsino recognising Cesario's feminine qualities, Malvolio is also unable to define Cesario, describing him as 'between boy and man' and commenting that 'he speaks very shrewishly'. Shakespeare creates the comedy of the scene when Malvolio stumbles near the truth of the disguise, but Olivia falls in love with it. She is fascinated by Cesario's manner and witty speeches, despite her position as a wealthy countess and his role as Orsino's servant. She quickly notices the 'youth's perfections' and expresses how quickly and unexpectedly love has affected her by comparing it to catching 'the plague', a metaphor that also suggests that love is an unwanted infection. [12] Although Shakespeare creates a situation that is challenging for both Olivia and Viola, the audience enjoys the humour of the mistaken identity and the impossibility of a relationship between them. As Viola says, it would be better for Olivia to 'love a dream' than Cesario. She perhaps also recognises that Olivia's unrequited love mirrors her own, referring to her sympathetically as 'Poor lady'. [13] Shakespeare uses the disguise in the play to create both moving moments and comedy, but Viola's choice has created enormous complications for her; she admits 'Disguise, I see thou art a wickedness' because she cannot control its effects.

The dual effects of the dramatic irony are brought to a head when Olivia cannot 'her passion hide' and declares 'I love thee so' to Cesario. Still disguised, Viola answers in riddles, rejecting Olivia by saying that she has 'one heart' which 'no woman has' a claim to. Shakespeare's impossible love triangle is complete and can only reach its comic resolution by the appearance of Sebastian and Viola's abandonment of her disguise. [14]

Viola's disguise, primarily using costume but also depending on the actor's performance, [15] is therefore central to the comedy of 'Twelfth Night'. However, by using the technique to complicate Viola's relationships and elsewhere in the play, Shakespeare also explores the nature of human relationships and what we understand of love. While the play might be seen as light and funny, it also examines one of the most important aspects of human life. [16]

[1] Acknowledges the range of relationships before choosing a focus
[2] Shows awareness of the conventions of comedy
[3] Focuses on the central character and chosen theatrical technique
[4] Gives useful reference to historical context
[5] Considers dramatic irony, a further theatrical technique, as one of the effects of the disguise
[6] Well-integrated quotations and comment
[7] Appreciation of asides as another dramatic technique
[8] Develops a nuanced argument about the effects of disguise
[9] Widens the argument to consider the audience's judgement of Orsino, with reference to the context of courtly love
[10] Develops a wider argument about the play, making appropriate use of contexts
[11] Moves to the essay's second example with awareness of the complexity of response
[12] Comments carefully on Shakespeare's use of imagery
[13] Links the two relationships discussed in the essay
[14] Offers an overview of the play, making reference to the conventions of comedy, including the appearance of Sebastian
[15] Links a dramatic technique to theatrical performance
[16] Clear conclusion, with quick acknowledgement that Viola's is not the only disguise

Comment on response

This response considers some of the broader issues raised by the play. In exploring the use of Viola's disguise, it considers the different responses of characters and audience and the combination of comedy and poignancy. It makes helpful references to contexts, such as gender expectations and the conventions of comedy. References are clear and quotations are well integrated, though there could be more analysis of Shakespeare's language and imagery. The reference to performance towards the end is good and could have been better developed if it was introduced earlier. However, the essay is clearly organised, placing the chosen relationships within the context of the whole play and developing its ideas in fluently linked and structured paragraphs.

Essay plan – high-level response

It is worth considering the structure of this high-level response, to note how the student has formed a coherent argument. The question asks the candidate to consider loving relationships, with a focus on a key character and an important theatrical technique. The plan breaks down like this:

Introduction: clear focus on the question, the range of relationships and the comic genre

Paragraph 2: introduction of the key character for the question (Viola) and the theatrical technique (disguise)

Paragraph 3: discussion of Viola's relationship with Orsino, exploring ways in which the disguise makes the relationship complicated through Viola's hidden feelings

Paragraph 4: further development of Viola's relationship with Orsino, with discussion of the characters' contrasting views of men's and women's love

Paragraph 5: disguise used as the link between the first relationship discussed and the second, between Viola/Cesario and Olivia

Paragraph 6: further evidenced development of this second relationship, with reference to the comedy's resolution

Conclusion: pulls together the two strands of the question, loving relationship and disguise, to comment the nature of the play's comedy

Exam-style question 2

Now write your own response to the following exam-style question.

> 'Though *Twelfth Night* is a comedy, the play does not end happily for all characters. 'Write an essay in which you describe TWO characters' experiences at the end of the play. In this essay, you must also discuss how the MAIN character is affected in ONE of the experiences, and examine ONE dramatic technique Shakespeare uses to portray characters' responses at the end of the play. (35 marks)

TWELFTH NIGHT

THE ALEXANDER SHAKESPEARE
Twelfth Night

TWELFTH NIGHT

ACT 1 SCENE 1

Notice how quickly and effectively Shakespeare introduces two of his main characters, the Duke in person, and Olivia by report. It is never his practice to leave us guessing just for the fun of it. The delicate, almost sugary atmosphere of the scene, with the richly clad nobles elegantly relaxed around the Duke, the music, and the lyrical declarations of love-sickness, all tell us a great deal – perhaps all there is to know – about Orsino. There is a touch of unreality about his distress, as if he is unconsciously enjoying the situation, and being the Duke, with no shortage of courtiers to echo his mood, he can indulge his emotions in comfort. The cause of his desperation, Olivia's coolness, and her reasons for it, are made plain. And so, furnished with this essential piece of the main plot, and with a fairly strong impression of Orsino already forming in our minds, we can move on to learn the other piece of the pattern, in the next scene.

1–3. What Orsino is saying here is that he wants the musicians, with their evocative music, to help him to 'use up', as it were, all the love-sick thoughts that are torturing him, and so be rid of them. (But does he really want this? Is he not unconsciously enjoying every minute of it? Look at lines 41–2.)

2. *surfeiting* having more than it can contain.

4. *fall* cadence or concluding phrase (a musical term).

5–7. A subtle comparison between sound and scent which is spoiled if we try to render it in prose.

9. *spirit*. This is pronounced as one syllable, 'sprite', or more probably 'spreet'. 'Sprite' and 'spirit' were virtually the same word. *quick* lively.

10. We should probably insert the words 'the fact that' after **notwithstanding**.

12. *validity* value. *pitch* height (probably a hawking term).

13. *abatement and low price* These two are synonymous here, meaning 'worthless condition'. Orsino's description of the working of love is somewhat involved. He seems to be saying that it matters not who they are who fall in love, or how passionately, the effect on them is the same. They are alike reduced to the same condition of helplessness.

14–15. Again, the meaning is obscure. Orsino seems to be saying that a love-sick person's thoughts (*fancy*) are so occupied imagining fond things (*shapes*), that they end up in an utterly unreal world (*high fantastical*).

16. *go hunt* go hunting.

ACT 1
SCENE 1

The Duke's palace

[Enter ORSINO, *Duke of Illyria,* CURIO, *and other* LORDS; MUSICIANS *attending]*

Duke
    If music be the food of love, play on,
    Give me excess of it, that, surfeiting,
    The appetite may sicken and so die.
    That strain again! It had a dying fall;
    O, it came o'er my ear like the sweet sound   5
    That breathes upon a bank of violets,
    Stealing and giving odour! Enough, no more;
    'Tis not so sweet now as it was before.
    O spirit of love, how quick and fresh art thou!
    That, notwithstanding thy capacity   10
    Receiveth as the sea, nought enters there,
    Of what validity and pitch soe'er,
    But falls into abatement and low price
    Even in a minute. So full of shapes is fancy,
    That it alone is high fantastical.   15
Curio
    Will you go hunt, my lord?
Duke
                       What, Curio?
Curio
    The hart.

19–23. Orsino describes his love-at-first-sight. He is referring to an ancient Greek myth in which Actaeon, when out hunting, came upon the goddess Diana while she was bathing, which so displeased her that she turned him into a stag, to be savaged by his own hounds. Orsino is saying that, as soon as he saw Olivia, his passion, like Actaeon's hounds, began to torture him, and has gone on doing so ever since.

20. *purg'd the air of pestilence!* Elizabethans were still preoccupied with the physical manifestations of evil. Darkness, fog and bad weather generally were to them more than just unpleasant natural conditions. They saw them almost as the outward signs of the evil forces surrounding mankind. So when Orsino describes the effect of Olivia's beauty, it is not surprising that he will think first of this aspect of her beneficent influence.

22. *fell* fierce.

25–33. Valentine has been sent to woo the Countess Olivia (or at least take the first steps) on behalf of Orsino, who apparently feels that, as Duke, he can hardly go in person at this stage. (The kind of courtship practised by Orsino follows the medieval style, with its long and not dishonourable history, and we should not think of the Duke as behaving in an unconventional way in all this.)

25. *might not be admitted* was not allowed in.

27. *element* sky; ***seven years' heat*** seven summers (and so, seven years).

28. *at ample view* in public.

29. *cloistress* nun (who keeps to the cloisters, which are part of a monastery or nunnery, and is thus withdrawn from the outside world).

30–1. *water . . . brine* a poetic way of saying that she will weep every day. 'Brine' is salt-water, and tears are thought to be salt; ***'eye-offending'***, because weeping makes our eyes sore.

31. *season* We season food with salt, to bring out the full flavour and to keep it fresh. Olivia is trying to keep alive the memory of her dead brother by weeping over him. The use of this elaborate imagery perhaps leaves us today with a feeling of artificiality. Is Olivia really as heart-broken as she believes she is? Is she possibly getting a kind of satisfaction out of the strict conditions of mourning she has set herself, in just the way that Orsino appears to enjoy his love-sickness?

ACT 1 SCENE 1

Duke
    Why, so I do, the noblest that I have.
    O, when mine eyes did see Olivia first,
    Methought she purg'd the air of pestilence!   20
    That instant was I turn'd into a hart,
    And my desires, like fell and cruel hounds,
    E'er since pursue me.
                [Enter VALENTINE]
    How now! what news from her?
Valentine
    So please my lord, I might not be admitted,   25
    But from her handmaid do return this answer
    The element itself, till seven years' heat,
    Shall not behold her face at ample view;
    But like a cloistress she will veiled walk,
    And water once a day her chamber round   30
    With eye-offending brine; all this to season
    A brother's dead love, which she would keep fresh
    And lasting in her sad remembrance.

34–40. Ever hopeful, Orsino reasons that if Olivia can have had such affection for a brother, she will be even more whole-hearted when she falls in love – with himself, as he hopes!

36–8. How will she love . . . live in her Once she has fallen in love, affection for everyone and everything else will cease.

36. rich golden shaft Cupid, the love-god, shot golden-tipped arrows at people to make them fall in love.

38–9. liver, brain, and heart, These sovereign thrones The physical organs were still generally held to be the seat of emotion and thought. They are spoken of here as 'sovereign (all-powerful) thrones' because it was believed that whatever occupied them would then be in effective control of the whole person, like a king on his throne, ruling his subjects.

40. *one self king!* one and the same king. The 'sole ruler' Orsino hopes for in Olivia's case is 'love', and he is duly dazzled as he conjures up the prospect.

41–2. On which optimistic note, Orsino can now turn and enjoy his romantic mood again, this time in the garden!

Duke
    O, she that hath a heart of that fine frame
    To pay this debt of love but to a brother,   35
    How will she love when the rich golden shaft
    Hath kill'd the flock of all affections else
    That live in her; when liver, brain, and heart,
    These sovereign thrones, are all supplied and fill'd,
    Her sweet perfections, with one self king!   40
    Away before me to sweet beds of flow'rs:
    Love-thoughts lie rich when canopied with bow'rs.
        [Exeunt]

SCENE 2

This is an abrupt change from the security and leisureliness of Orsino's palace. Here we see bedraggled survivors from the sea, under much greater actual stress than Orsino and Olivia, for all their protestations of emotion. We get our first glimpse of Viola, an integrated, resourceful creature who impresses us at once with her 'no-nonsense' genuineness. Her arrival in Illyria spells the end of what promised to be a quite predictable pattern of courtly wooing. The whole of the main plot will turn upon the interaction of these three with their utterly distinct personalities. As well endowed with feelings as any, Viola is as yet in no position to show them. All she has time for is simply to ensure her survival.

Again, much sheer information is packed into this scene; and Viola's reason for taking this most crucial step – joining Orsino's service – is explained and justified quite acceptably.

2. *Illyria* probably the Adriatic coast; though we might feel that any country with a coast-line would do as well. The actual locality has little significance in this play.

4. *Elysium* the equivalent of Heaven in the religion of the Ancient Greeks.

5. A very natural touch: Viola suddenly clutches at a hope, and at once turns to the sailors for their support.

6. *perchance* only by chance.

7–8. The Captain comforts her by describing her brother's brave efforts to save himself from the wreck, which, as far as he can see, may well have been successful.

11. *driving* being driven by the wind.

12. *provident* taking appropriate action.

14. *liv'd* managed to keep afloat.

15. *Arion* a semi-mythical poet of the ancient Greeks, who managed to foil a murderous attempt to drown him, by charming a dolphin with one of his songs, to carry him to safety on its back.

16. *hold acquaintance with* keep on struggling against.

18–20. Viola rewards him for this cheering news, and reasons with herself that, as she herself has escaped, so there is every cause to hope that her brother, too, is safe – especially now that the Captain's story points the same way (***serves for authority***).

21. Only now does Viola turn to her own needs – her first thoughts have all been for her brother.

SCENE 2

The sea-coast

[*Enter* VIOLA, *a* CAPTAIN, *and* SAILORS]

Viola
  What country, friends, is this?
Captain
  This is Illyria, lady.
Viola
  And what should I do in Illyria?
  My brother he is in Elysium.
  Perchance he is not drown'd – what think you,
  sailors? 5
Captain
  It is perchance that you yourself were saved.
Viola
  O my poor brother! and so perchance may he be.
Captain
  True, madam, and, to comfort you with chance,
  Assure yourself, after our ship did split,
  When you, and those poor number saved with you, 10
  Hung on our driving boat, I saw your brother,
  Most provident in peril, bind himself—
  Courage and hope both teaching him the practice—
  To a strong mast that liv'd upon the sea;
  Where, like Arion on the dolphin's back, 15
  I saw him hold acquaintance with the waves
  So long as I could see.
Viola
  For saying so, there's gold.
  Mine own escape unfoldeth to my hope,
  Whereto thy speech serves for authority, 20
  The like of him. Know'st thou this country?
Captain
  Ay, madam, well; for I was bred and born
  Not three hours' travel from this very place.

30–41. A few more useful bits of background information.

32. *fresh in murmur* the latest piece of gossip.

35. *What's she?* 'Who's she?' (A frequent Shakespearean usage.)

40. *abjur'd* sworn to do without.
41–4. Viola sees a chance here for herself to find some sort of safe if temporary concealment. The construction is a little involved, but the meaning is plain – she wants to serve Orsino so that for the time being she can remain in obscurity (***not be delivered to the world***) till she has found a suitable opportunity (***made mine own occasion mellow***) to assume her proper rank and position.

44. *compass* achieve, bring about.

Viola
  Who governs here?
Captain
  A noble duke, in nature as in name.   25
Viola
  What is his name?
Captain
  Orsino.
Viola
  Orsino! I have heard my father name him.
  He was a bachelor then.
Captain
  And so is now, or was so very late;   30
  For but a month ago I went from hence,
  And then 'twas fresh in murmur – as, you know,
  What great ones do the less will prattle of—
  That he did seek the love of fair Olivia.
Viola
  What's she?   35
Captain
  A virtuous maid, the daughter of a count
  That died some twelvemonth since, then leaving her
  In the protection of his son, her brother,
  Who shortly also died; for whose dear love,
  They say, she hath abjur'd the company   40
  And sight of men.
Viola
                    O that I serv'd that lady,
  And might not be delivered to the world,
  Till I had made mine own occasion mellow,
  What my estate is!
Captain
                    That were hard to compass,
  Because she will admit no kind of suit—   45
  No, not the Duke's.

47–51. Viola is so well impressed by the Captain's manner that she confidently believes that he is good at heart; though she realises that an attractive exterior (***beauteous wall***) often only disguises a rotten character (***Doth oft close in pollution***).

53. *Conceal me what I am* Modern English would either say 'conceal me' or 'conceal what I am'. (Compare St Mark's Gospel, Chapter I, Verse 24 (A.V.), 'I know thee who thou art'), So 'keep my identity secret'.

54. *become* suit.

55. *The form of my intent* 'whatever role I decide to adopt'.

56. *eunuch* Eunuchs (castrated males) were, for obvious reasons, frequently found as intimate servants in wealthy households particularly in the Middle East. It would clearly seem a good idea for Viola to assume this rôle; it would tend to stop people asking too many questions about her un-masculine voice and appearance. It is odd, perhaps, that this is never referred to again. But it is not allowed to become what would only be a further complication in Viola's ensuing involvement with Orsino and Olivia.

59. 'That will guarantee that I can give worthwhile service' – a suitable qualification for the job, as we would say today. Viola's musical talent will be a good recommendation in her hoped-for employment with Orsino.

60. 'The future must be left to take care of itself.'

61. 'Treat my scheme with due secrecy.' (Literally, 'make your silence appropriate to my scheme'.); ***wit*** has many meanings. Here, it signifies the finished product of her wit or intelligence.

62. *Be you . . . I'll be* 'All right, you be his eunuch and I'll be your mute.' ***mute*** a dumb servant. (Like a eunuch, but for different reasons, a mute would have his uses in a household – secrets would always be safe with him!)

63. 'May I be struck blind if I betray your secret.' ***blabs*** betrays confidence.

Viola
   There is a fair behaviour in thee, Captain;
   And though that nature with a beauteous wall
   Doth oft close in pollution, yet of thee
   I will believe thou hast a mind that suits 50
   With this thy fair and outward character.
   I prithee, and I'll pay thee bounteously,
   Conceal me what I am, and be my aid
   For such disguise as haply shall become
   The form of my intent. I'll serve this duke: 55
   Thou shalt present me as an eunuch to him;
   It may be worth thy pains, for I can sing
   And speak to him in many sorts of music,
   That will allow me very worth his service.
   What else may hap to time I will commit; 60
   Only shape thou thy silence to my wit.
Captain
   Be you his eunuch and your mute I'll be;
   When my tongue blabs, then let mine eyes not see.
Viola
   I thank thee. Lead me on.
            [Exeunt]

SCENE 3

It is now time for some light relief; the action up to now has been at a high pitch. The blank verse and stately language, therefore, give place to informal, conversational prose. (This is a fairly regular practice of Shakespeare at this stage in his career, though his later plays make increasing use of prose for serious dialogue and soliloquy.)

But the break is only in mood. The very first line takes up the thread again – Olivia's excessive mourning is in question once more, this time to be condemned by the down-to-earth common-sense of her uncle, Sir Toby Belch.

Sir Toby's position in her household is worth noting. Things were still at the stage where a person of rank and possession would be only too pleased to provide permanent hospitality to dependants, who might not be relatives. These, if able-bodied men, would provide some kind of security for the Lord and Lady of the house, who, alone, would be hard put to it to defend a large residence. So we must not think of Sir Toby as just a parasite in his niece's house. Even he could be a quite comforting person to have about the place if danger threatened.

4. *cousin* In Shakespeare, this could denote any close relationship, not necessarily of blood.

5. *ill hours* bad hours (and so 'late hours').

6. *except before excepted* word-play on a Latin legal phrase 'exceptis excipiendis'. Sir Toby is suggesting that Olivia has already taken quite enough exception to his behaviour.

7. *confine* restrain.

9. *confine . . . finer*. Another pun, playing on the two meanings of 'fine'.

11. *an* if (a fairly regular Shakespearean usage).

11–12. *hang themselves in their own straps*. A more vivid way of saying 'Let them be hanged'. (Modern English still has the quite common phrase, 'I'll be hanged if . . .'.) There was an Elizabethan saying, 'To be hanged in one's own garter', which may have been in Sir Toby's mind.

16. The very idea of sponsoring Sir Andrew Aguecheek as a serious suitor for the Countess was almost ludicrous, as we may well agree when he makes his appearance. There was certainly a financial interest in it for Sir Toby, even if only indirectly, to the tune of 3000 ducats a year – a sizeable fortune by any reckoning (see Note, line 20). But Sir Toby is likely motivated as much by his irrepressible sense of fun, in much the way that he joins in Maria's later device to push Malvolio into the same impossible position with his niece.

ACT 1 SCENE 3

SCENE 3

Olivia's house

[Enter SIR TOBY BELCH *and* MARIA*]*

Sir Toby
What a plague means my niece to take the death of her brother thus? I am sure care's an enemy to life.

Maria
By my troth, Sir Toby, you must come in earlier o' nights; your cousin, my lady, takes great exceptions to your ill hours. 5

Sir Toby
Why, let her except before excepted.

Maria
Ay, but you must confine yourself within the modest limits of order.

Sir Toby
Confine! I'll confine myself no finer than I am. These clothes are good enough to drink in, and so be these 10 boots too; an they be not, let them hang themselves in their own straps.

Maria
That quaffing and drinking will undo you; I heard my lady talk of it yesterday, and of a foolish knight that you brought in one night here to be her wooer. 15

Sir Toby
Who? Sir Andrew Aguecheek?

Maria
Ay, he.

18. *tall* brave, or simply 'good' as in our modern phrase 'a good fellow'.
19. Somewhat cynically 'What's that got to do with it?'
20. *ducat* There were ducats in more than one European currency. The value in England in Shakespeare's day was equivalent to something like 33p.
21. ***he'll have but a year in all these ducats*** 'his whole fortune is likely to last him only a year.'
22. *prodigal* one who spends and gives away his wealth with no thought for the future.
23. *Fie* an expression of disapproval or disgust. Sir Toby pretends to be disgusted with Maria for saying such a thing.
23. *viol-de-gamboys* (for 'viola-da-gamba') bass viol, a stringed instrument like a 'cello, held between the legs.
27. *natural* Maria is here using 'natural' to mean 'half-witted', which it often meant at this period.
29–30. *gust . . . quarrelling* taste for quarrelling.
31. ***have the gift of a grave*** 'meet his death'. (The idea of 'gifts' of nature is thus carried further.)
32. *substractors* detractors (those who take away his good name). Sir Toby's indignant outburst is not seriously meant to take anyone in. He knows as well as Maria that Sir Andrew is a figure of fun.
36. Like Falstaff, Sir Toby is adept at turning an argument against his critics. He can always talk himself out of an unfavourable situation, yet without really trying to dodge the blame he knows he deserves. His excuse in this instance – drinking his niece's health – is one he doesn't expect Maria to take seriously. It would spoil his joke if she did.
38. *coystrill* worthless fellow.
40. *parish-top* a large spinning-top kept in a parish to provide the parishioners with wholesome exercise when bad weather prevented them from working on the land.
40. *What . . . !* simply an exclamation. ***Castiliano vulgo!*** This mysterious phrase suggests that Sir Toby is urging Maria to behave more seriously now that Sir Andrew is approaching, but no one knows the exact meaning.
41. *Agueface.* To get someone's name wrong on purpose, in this way, is a familiar trick of the comedian.

Sir Toby
He's as tall a man as any's in Illyria.
Maria
What's that to th' purpose?
Sir Toby
Why, he has three thousand ducats a year. 20
Maria
Ay, but he'll have but a year in all these ducats; he's
a very fool and a prodigal.
Sir Toby
Fie that you'll say so! He plays o' th' viol-de-gam-boys,
and speaks three or four languages word for word
without book, and hath all the good gifts of 25
nature.
Maria
He hath indeed, almost natural; for, besides that he's
a fool, he's a great quarreller; and but that he
hath the gift of a coward to allay the gust he hath in
quarrelling, 'tis thought among the prudent he would 30
quickly have the gift of a grave.
Sir Toby
By this hand, they are scoundrels and substractors that
say so of him. Who are they?
Maria
They that add, moreover, he's drunk nightly in your
company. 35
Sir Toby
With drinking healths to my niece; I'll drink to her as
long as there is a passage in my throat and drink in
Illyria. He's a coward and a coystrill that will not drink
to my niece till his brains turn o' th' toe like a
parish-top. What, wench! Castiliano vulgo! for here comes 40
Sir Andrew Agueface.

[Enter SIR ANDREW AGUECHEEK]

Sir Andrew
Sir Toby Belch! How now, Sir Toby Belch!

46. Accost. The confusion initiated by the introduction of this word has the desired effect of putting Sir Andrew off-balance from the start. (He is not over-endowed with poise, in any case.) Having thus drained him of self-confidence, Sir Toby now intentionally over-supplies him, with the result that he has Sir Andrew dancing to his tune, and literally so at the end of the scene. This is a delightful episode. Or is it a bit cruel, like a cat playing with a mouse? The word 'accost' is used quite properly ('Approach and start conversing'). But its abruptness here has Sir Andrew clearly bewildered.

47. What's that? This can equally mean 'Who's that?' in Shakespearean English (see Act 1, Scene 2, line 35). This latter meaning is the one Sir Toby chooses to take, and answers accordingly. But Sir Andrew's reaction shows that it was the word, not the person, he wanted explained. Sir Toby may well have been wilfully misunderstanding him – he certainly does nothing to clear up the confusion, not, that is, till he has had his fun out of it.

52–3. front her, board her, woo her, assail her This sudden string of indelicate synonyms has Sir Andrew believing that nothing less than instant love-making is now expected of him.

56. Fare you well, gentlemen Why does Maria suggest leaving just now? Is she embarrassed by all this, or simply pretending to be, to keep up the joke?

57. An if. The meaning of Sir Toby's observation here is almost – 'You're not the man I took you for, if you let her go just like that'.

59. Notice how meekly Sir Andrew echoes him, almost word for word. This emphasises neatly his pathetic dependence upon Sir Toby's judgment and experience. He is almost mesmerised by it.

60–1. do you think you have fools in hand? 'do you think you are having to deal with fools?'

62. I have not you by th' hand Maria has taken 'in hand' literally – intentionally, of course.

63. Marry by (the Virgin) Mary (a mild oath); **here's my hand** This, for Sir Andrew, is real progress in amorousness.

Sir Toby
   Sweet Sir Andrew!
Sir Andrew
   Bless you, fair shrew.
Maria
   And you too, sir.   45
Sir Toby
   Accost, Sir Andrew, accost.
Sir Andrew
   What's that?
Sir Toby
   My niece's chambermaid.
Sir Andrew
   Good Mistress Accost, I desire better acquaintance.
Maria
   My name is Mary, sir.   50
Sir Andrew
   Good Mistress Mary Accost—
Sir Toby
   You mistake, knight. 'Accost' is front her, board her,
   woo her, assail her.
Sir Andrew
   By my troth, I would not undertake her in this
   company. Is that the meaning of 'accost'?   55
Maria
   Fare you well, gentlemen.
Sir Toby
   An thou let part so, Sir Andrew, would thou mightst
   never draw sword again!
Sir Andrew
   An you part so, mistress, I would I might never draw
   sword again. Fair lady, do you think you have fools in   60
   hand?
Maria
   Sir, I have not you by th' hand.
Sir Andrew
   Marry, but you shall have; and here's my hand.

64. *thought is free* (proverbially) 'one may think what one likes.'

65. *butt'ry-bar* rather like our modern serving-hatch, where refreshment of both kinds was dispensed (the word originally meant a place where bottles were stored, from the French word ***Bouteille***, bottle).

66. *What's your metaphor?* 'What double meaning are you now implying? (Or, more simply, 'What are you hinting at now?') Sir Andrew tries hopefully to keep abreast of all this 'double-talk', but he never quite catches up. The ensuing dialogue is typical Elizabethan wordplay, if a little one-sided. By nimbly substituting now one meaning, now another, for her words, Maria has Sir Andrew helplessly trailing behind her.

68–9. *I can keep my hand dry* Sir Andrew's meaning here is probably quite literal – he is protesting that he won't spill his liquor. But Maria has in mind a popular belief that a 'dry hand' indicated an un-amorous disposition. But the word 'dry' in ***A dry jest*** has yet another meaning – stupid – and this is how Sir Andrew seems to take it.

72. When Maria says she has the 'dry jests' ***at her fingers' ends***, she is referring to Sir Andrew's hand which she is holding, and which amuses her because it is dry; and so, when she lets it go, her cause for amusement goes too. Sir Toby has been enjoying all this. He and Maria share the humour, which has gone over Sir Andrew's head.

74. *canary* a popular wine, from the Canary Islands.

77–8. *Methinks . . . an ordinary man.* Such crestfallen frankness might have elicited some sort of pity – but not from Sir Toby!

79–80. *eater of beef . . . wit.* A popular belief, that beef had this effect when eaten to excess.

82. *forswear* do without, give up.

85. *What is 'pourquoi' . . . ?* Sir Andrew is apologetic about the gaps in his education.

Maria
  Now, sir, thought is free. I pray you, bring your hand
  to th' butt'ry-bar and let it drink. 65
Sir Andrew
  Wherefore, sweetheart? What's your metaphor?
Maria
  It's dry, sir.
Sir Andrew
  Why, I think so; I am not such an ass but I can keep
  my hand dry. But what's your jest?
Maria
  A dry jest, sir. 70
Sir Andrew
  Are you full of them?
Maria
  Ay, sir, I have them at my fingers' ends; marry, now
  I let go your hand, I am barren.

  [Exit MARIA]

Sir Toby
  O knight, thou lack'st a cup of canary! When did I see
  thee so put down? 75
Sir Andrew
  Never in your life, I think; unless you see canary put
  me down. Methinks sometimes I have no more wit
  than a Christian or an ordinary man has; but I am a
  great eater of beef, and I believe that does harm to my
  wit. 80
Sir Toby
  No question.
Sir Andrew
  An I thought that, I'd forswear it. I'll ride home
  tomorrow, Sir Toby.
Sir Toby
  Pourquoi, my dear knight?
Sir Andrew
  What is 'pourquoi' – do or not do? I would I had 85
  bestowed that time in the tongues that I have in

89. The conversation now switches to Sir Andrew's lank, pale yellow hair, an obvious feature to make capital out of in such a scene.

91. ***thou seest it will not curl by nature***. Sir Toby is punning here on the word 'tongues'. When Sir Andrew regretted his neglect of the 'tongues' he meant 'foreign languages'. But Sir Toby takes it as 'tongs' (curling tongs) which might, of course, have done something to improve Sir Andrew's hair. (There may also be a reference to the antithesis between 'art' and 'nature'.)

93. ***flax on a distaff***. Flax is a plant used in the making of linen and other materials. The distaff was the spindle on to which it was spun, normally within the home, by the **huswife** (housewife). The pale yellow colour of flax gives us our word 'flaxen'.

96–9. Sir Andrew's present loss of confidence we can well understand. What does surprise us is that he ever allowed himself to be talked into this courtship.

102. ***there's life in't*** 'you still have a sporting chance.'

103–5. ***I am a fellow . . . sometimes altogether***. A small but telling sign here of Sir Andrew's vanity, a side of his character just as fundamental as his more obvious self-deprecation. There is one cause for both – he takes himself far too seriously – hence his blithe assumption here that other people will be as fascinated as he is by what goes on in his mind.

104. ***revels*** entertainments (like the very ones put on by the Inns of Court, with *Twelfth Night* as probably one of its items).

106. ***kickshawses*** trivial things that entertain or amuse. (The word seems to be a corruption of the French *quelquechose* in the sense of a trifle or small delicacy.)

107–9. How cautious can he get! He says he is as good as his equals! ***Compare with an old man***. This has been variously explained, but it is difficult to supply a meaning with any certainty. It may be that Sir Andrew has the phrase 'elders and betters' in mind; he has already spoken of his 'betters'.

110. ***galliard*** a quick, lively dance.

111. ***cut a caper*** One of the steps in the galliard was to beat the feet together in the air. The other meaning of 'caper' – a plant of which the buds are used for making sauce – is taken by Sir Toby (line 112) for an easy pun.

fencing, dancing, and bear-baiting. O, had I but
followed the arts!
Sir Toby
Then hadst thou had an excellent head of hair.
Sir Andrew
Why, would that have mended my hair? 90
Sir Toby
Past question; for thou seest it will not curl by nature.
Sir Andrew
But it becomes me well enough, does't not?
Sir Toby
Excellent; it hangs like flax on a distaff, and I hope to
see a huswife take thee between her legs and spin it
off. 95
Sir Andrew
Faith, I'll home to-morrow, Sir Toby. Your niece will
not be seen, or if she be, it's four to one she'll
none of me; the Count himself here hard by woos
her.
Sir Toby
She'll none o' th' Count; she'll not match above her 100
degree, neither in estate, years, nor wit; I have heard
her swear't, Tut, there's life in't, man.
Sir Andrew
I'll stay a month longer. I am a fellow o' th' strangest
mind i' th' world; I delight in masques and revels
sometimes altogether. 105
Sir Toby
Art thou good at these kickshawses, knight?
Sir Andrew
As any man in Illyria, whatsoever he be, under the
degree of my betters; and yet I will not compare with
an old man.
Sir Toby
What is thy excellence in a galliard, knight? 110
Sir Andrew
Faith, I can cut a caper.

113. *backtrick* a caper backwards.

115. *Wherefore are these things hid?* Almost the master-stroke in the process of flattery so successfully brought off by Sir Toby – 'If I could dance as well as you can, I'd be doing it all the time.'
116. *curtain* These were used to protect valuable pictures, and would be drawn aside only when the picture was to be viewed.
117. *Mistress Mall's picture*. 'Mall' is probably the same as 'Moll'. There is no clear indication whose portrait is referred to.
119. *coranto* another lively dance, similar to the galliard.
120. *make water . . . sink-a-pace* 'Sink-a-pace' is a corruption of *cinque pace*, a French dance. The picture here is crude, but it certainly drives the point home!
121. *Is it a world to hide virtues in?* Like Falstaff, Sir Toby now and then speaks as a true philosopher.
123. *form'd under the star of a galliard*. This is in astrological vein. It suits Sir Toby here to pretend that Galliard is a sign of the Zodiac, conferring dancing genius on those born under it.
124. Once more Sir Andrew's vanity is tickled into motion, though it doesn't venture beyond ***indifferent well*** (fairly well).
125. *stock* stocking.
126. *What should we do else?* 'What else is there to do?'
126. *Taurus* an authentic Zodiacal sign this time (the Bull), but it was not concerned with 'sides and heart' (each sign had a particular part or parts of the human anatomy assigned to it).
128. *legs and thighs*. Sir Toby gleefully points out Sir Andrew's error and takes the appropriate opportunity to make him dance ridiculously.

ACT 1 SCENE 3

Sir Toby
And I can cut the mutton to't.
Sir Andrew
And I think I have the backtrick simply as strong as any man in Illyria.
Sir Toby
Wherefore are these things hid? Wherefore have these gifts a curtain before 'em? Are they like to take dust, like Mistress Mall's picture? Why dost thou not go to church in a galliard and come home in a coranto? My very walk should be a jig; I would not so much as make water but in a sink-a-pace. What dost thou mean? Is it a world to hide virtues in? I did think, by the excellent constitution of thy leg, it was form'd under the star of a galliard.
Sir Andrew
Ay, 'tis strong, and it does indifferent well in a flame-colour'd stock. Shall we set about some revels?
Sir Toby
What shall we do else? Were we not born under Taurus?
Sir Andrew
Taurus? That's sides and heart.
Sir Toby
No, sir; it is legs and thighs. Let me see thee caper. Ha, higher! Ha, ha, excellent!

[Exeunt]

SCENE 4

A brief return to the fortunes of Viola. Her scheme has worked and she is duly installed in the Duke's service, as his latest and – as he optimistically believes – most promising go-between in his courtship of Olivia. How ill-placed his optimism is, we can judge from Viola's hint at the end.

This is an excellent example of Shakespeare's skill in linking scene with scene by a dexterous economy of word and material. There is a continuous moving forward, yet not so subtly expressed that we miss the connection, nor yet so laboured that we lose interest.

2. Cesario the masculine name Viola has adopted.
2. like likely.

5–7. 'You must have doubts about his reliability, or about the way I'm doing the job, if you are so uncertain whether he will go on being nice to me.'
5. humour natural tendency; **negligence** that is, in the carrying out of her job. It is beginning to mean a great deal to her that Orsino is being so kind, but she needs a lot of reassurance, and – typical of a young person in her first job and her first romance – has her fair share of diffidence.

9. Count Orsino is from now on thus addressed.

12. Stand you awhile aloof Spoken to all except Viola. Orsino seems to have decided already that he can confide more in Viola than in anyone else.
13. unclasp'd. Valuable books would, as sometimes even now, be secured by a clasp.
15. address thy gait 'make your way'.
16. Be not denied access 'Don't let them refuse to let you in.'
17–18. A very effective way for her to say that she won't move until they have let her in to speak to Olivia.

20. As it is spoke 'as it is reported' ('spoke' was a correct Elizabethan past participle).

ACT 1 SCENE 4

SCENE 4

The Duke's palace

[Enter VALENTINE, *and* VIOLA *in man's attire]*

Valentine
If the Duke continue these favours towards you,
Cesario, you are like to be much advanc'd; he hath
known you but three days, and already you are no
stranger.

Viola
You either fear his humour or my negligence, that you   5
call in question the continuance of his love. Is he
inconstant, sir, in his favours?

Valentine
No, believe me.

[Enter DUKE, CURIO, *and* ATTENDANTS*]*

Viola
I thank you. Here comes the Count.

Duke
Who saw Cesario, ho?   10

Viola
On your attendance, my lord, here.

Duke
Stand you awhile aloof. Cesario,
Thou know'st no less but all; I have unclasp'd
To thee the book even of my secret soul.
Therefore, good youth, address thy gait unto her;   15
Be not denied access, stand at her doors,
And tell them there thy fixed foot shall grow
Till thou have audience.

Viola
                    Sure, my noble lord,
If she be so abandon'd to her sorrow
As it is spoke, she never will admit me.   20

21. *Be clamorous* almost 'Make a great noise'; *leap all civil bounds* 'ignore (leap over) all the normal rules of polite behaviour.'
22. 'Don't come back empty-handed.'
23. Ever practical, Viola realises that she hasn't been told what to say if she does get invited in.

25. *dear faith* heartfelt fidelity.
26. 'You are well suited to convey my desperate feelings of love-sickness.'
28. *nuncio* messenger. Quite naturally, since he is not prepared to do it in person, Orsino would rather someone did it who was young enough to deliver the message with conviction.
29. Viola knows just how impossible this may be.
29–34. Emphasizing her youthful appearance, in order to convince her of her suitability, Orsino probably only embarrasses her, and makes her feel that her secret is less secure than ever.
29–31. 'Your carefree, youthful appearance (*happy years*) clearly proves wrong (*belie*) those who say you are grown up.'
32. *rubious* ruby-coloured; *pipe* windpipe. Conveniently for Viola, Orsino attributes her girlish voice to the fact that it has not yet broken.
34. *is semblative* resembles.
35. *constellation* Astrology teaches that a person's character is affected by the position of the stars at the time of birth. 'Constellation' here means 'character, as fixed by the stars'.
36. *attend* Here used as an imperative. Orsino is ordering them to go with Viola.
37–8. He prefers t o be alone in his present mood.

41. *barful* frustrating. (To bar the way to something is to hinder or frustrate whoever is trying to get to it.)
42. Some of the most significant lines in Shakespeare are conveyed in 'asides'.

ACT 1 SCENE 4

Duke
　Be clamorous and leap all civil bounds,
　Rather than make unprofited return.
Viola
　Say I do speak with her, my lord, what then?
Duke
　O, then unfold the passion of my love,
　Surprise her with discourse of my dear faith!　　　25
　It shall become thee well to act my woes:
　She will attend it better in thy youth
　Than in a nuncio's of more grave aspect.
Viola
　I think not so, my lord.
Duke
　　　　　　　　　　Dear lad, believe it,
　For they shall yet belie thy happy years　　　　　30
　That say thou art a man: Diana's lip
　Is not more smooth and rubious; thy small pipe
　Is as the maiden's organ, shrill and sound,
　And all is semblative a woman's part.
　I know thy constellation is right apt　　　　　　35
　For this affair. Some four or five attend him—
　All, if you will, for I myself am best
　When least in company. Prosper well in this,
　And thou shalt live as freely as thy lord
　To call his fortunes thine.
Viola
　　　　　　　　　　　I'll do my best　　　　　　40
　To woo your lady. *[Aside]* Yet, a barful strife!
　Whoe'er I woo, myself would be his wife.

TWELFTH NIGHT

SCENE 5

A busy scene, which gives us our first sight of the clown, Feste, in characteristic role; and Olivia, whose fortunes take a momentous step forward; and Malvolio, who manages, though in restrained fashion as yet, to present himself in his true colours. So, by the end of Act 1, we shall have made the acquaintance of all the main characters (except Sebastian and his loyal friend Antonio) intimately enough for us to size them up; and the main plot, at least, will be sufficiently under way for us to see where it is heading.

5. fear no colours The word 'colours' is used here in the military sense, meaning 'ensign' or 'standard'. The complete phrase, almost proverbial, means 'fear no foe', which in turn means 'fear no one (or nothing)'.
6. Make that good 'Explain that satisfactorily.'
7. A deliberate anticlimax – Feste's meaning suddenly becomes literal: 'Not only will a hanged man have no fears, he will have nothing else either!'
8. lenten answer a short answer, 'rationed', like food in Lent (a penitential season in the Christian calendar).

20. You are resolute then? 'You have made up your mind, then?'

21. points. A pun – 'points', or tagged laces, were used to keep up a man's gaskins or breeches.

SCENE 5

Olivia's house

[Enter MARIA *and* CLOWN*]*

Maria
Nay, either tell me where thou hast been, or I will not open my lips so wide as a bristle may enter in way of thy excuse; my lady will hang thee for thy absence.
Clown
Let her hang me. He that is well hang'd in this world needs to fear no colours. 5
Maria
Make that good.
Clown
He shall see none to fear.
Maria
A good lenten answer. I can tell thee where that saying was born, of 'I fear no colours'.
Clown
Where, good Mistress Mary? 10
Maria
In the wars; and that may you be bold to say in your foolery.
Clown
Well, God give them wisdom that have it; and those that are fools, let them use their talents.
Maria
Yet you will be hang'd for being so long absent; or to 15 be turn'd away – is not that as good as a hanging to you?
Clown
Many a good hanging prevents a bad marriage; and for turning away, let summer bear it out.
Maria
You are resolute then? 20
Clown
Not so, neither; but I am resolv'd on two points.

24–6. if Sir Toby . . . any in Illyria 'It makes about as much sense to call you the wittiest woman in Illyria, as to say that Sir Toby will give up drinking.'
26. Eve's flesh Eve was the first woman to be created, in the Genesis story in the Bible; hence all women are part of her 'flesh' – descended physically from her.

29. Wit . . . fooling! Feste calls on 'Wit', as on a god, to give him the gift of humour.
29–30. Those wits that think they have thee 'Those who are clever only in their own estimation.'
32. Quinapalus an authority of dubious authenticity, dragged in for the occasion!
32–3. 'Better a witty fool than a foolish wit.' Clearly a play on the two meanings of 'fool', which, in the first part means a 'professional clown', whereas 'foolish' later has its modern meaning. This theme is touched upon several times in *Twelfth Night*. Feste here seems particularly on the defensive, resenting the superficial assessment of his real intelligence made by those who, he feels, are his inferiors mentally.
36. dry dull, stupid.
38. Madonna 'my lady.'
39. Feste deliberately takes the literal meaning of 'dry'.
42. botcher one who patches things, usually unskilfully. (We use the word today figuratively – 'a botched-up job'.)
43–4. virtue that transgresses . . . patch'd with virtue. Nonsense – or does it come near the point of deep wisdom? The clown's role is not so different from that of the playwright, in observing and commenting on life and people, and being as often as not ignored or misunderstood. This is perhaps why Shakespeare seems to have a soft spot for his clowns, and to depict them so feelingly. Some of his shrewdest lines are entrusted to them.
45. syllogism a piece of systematic reasoning. (Feste is, of course, not entirely serious when he uses the word here.)

Maria
  That if one break, the other will hold; or if both break,
  your gaskins fall.
Clown
  Apt, in good faith, very apt! Well, go thy way; if Sir
  Toby would leave drinking, thou wert as witty a piece   25
  of Eve's flesh as any in Illyria.
Maria
  Peace, you rogue, no more o' that. Here comes my lady.
  Make your excuse wisely, you were best.
      [Exit. Enter OLIVIA *and* MALVOLIO*]*
Clown
  Wit, an't be thy will, put me into good fooling! Those
  wits that think they have thee do very oft prove fools;   30
  and I that am sure I lack thee may pass for a wise man.
  For what says Quinapalus? 'Better a witty fool than a
  foolish wit.' God bless thee, lady!
Olivia
  Take the fool away.
Clown
  Do you not hear, fellows? Take away the lady.   35
Olivia
  Go to, y'are a dry fool; I'll no more of you. Besides,
  you grow dishonest.
Clown
  Two faults, Madonna, that drink and good counsel will
  amend; for give the dry fool drink, then is the fool
  not dry. Bid the dishonest man mend himself: if he   40
  mend, he is no longer dishonest; if he cannot, let
  the botcher mend him. Anything that's mended is but
  patch'd; virtue that transgresses is but patch'd with
  sin, and sin that amends is but patch'd with virtue. If
  that this simple syllogism will serve, so; if it will not,   45

46. *cuckold*. The cuckoo's habit of laying its egg in another bird's nest – a sort of unfaithfulness – has given us this word, which denotes the husband of an unfaithful wife. His wife and her lover, by their adultery, are said to 'make him a cuckold'. But here he seems to be using the word in an active sense, to denote the one who commits the unfaithfulness, and thus refers to calamity's way of inflicting loss and humiliation. The main thing about this speech of Feste's is that he's rattling away so as to give Olivia no chance to rebuke him.

47. *so beauty's a flower*. Again, if sense is intended, this would be a comment on the transitoriness of beauty, which withers as a flower.

50–1. *Misprision* misunderstanding; **'*Cucullus non facit monachum*'** 'The hood (part of a monk's normal dress) does not make the monk.' (Contrast the proverb 'Fine feathers make fine birds'.)

52. *motley* apparel of various colours, which the professional clown normally wore. (Compare 'mottled' – speckled.) The word 'motley' has come to be used to denote professional foolery or humorous entertainment. Feste means that, though he is a fool by profession, that does not mean that his intelligence is in any way inferior.

55. *Dexteriously* A deliberate mispronunciation?

57. *catechize* to instruct orally, usually by question and answer (as in the Church Catechism).

57. *mouse*. Regularly used as a term of affection.

67. Malvolio is now for the first time brought into the picture. An innocent enough question is put, but his sour reply marks him out for what he is. He is especially bitter towards Feste, and the things he represents, gaiety and lightheartedness; and Feste never really forgives or forgets.

68. *mend* amend, improve, reform.

what remedy? As there is no true cuckold but calamity,
so beauty's a flower. The lady bade take away the fool;
therefore, I say again, take her away.
Olivia
Sir, I bade them take away you.
Clown
Misprision in the highest degree! Lady, 'Cucullus non   50
facit monachum'; that's as much to say as I wear not
motley in my brain. Good Madonna, give me leave to
prove you a fool.
Olivia
Can you do it?
Clown
Dexteriously, good Madonna.   55
Olivia
Make your proof.
Clown
I must catechize you for it, Madonna. Good my mouse
of virtue, answer me.
Olivia
Well, sir, for want of other idleness, I'll bide your
proof.   60
Clown
Good Madonna, why mourn'st thou?
Olivia
Good fool, for my brother's death.
Clown
I think his soul is in hell, Madonna.
Olivia
I know his soul is in heaven, fool.
Clown
The more fool, Madonna, to mourn for your brother's   65
soul being in heaven. Take away the fool, gentlemen.
Olivia
What think you of this fool, Malvolio? Doth he not
mend?

69. 'Shall' is used emphatically – it is Malvolio's desire and intention for the moment, that the rest of Feste's life *shall* be one long process of reformation.

70–1. *Infirmity ... fool* Infirmity (in this case, advancing age, with its increasing eccentricities) will add to the fool's equipment. This shows clearly what a poor opinion Malvolio has of Feste's brand of humour.

74. *fox* then, as now, thought of as the embodiment of cunning.

77–83. Malvolio's criticism here, of the professional jester (equivalent to our modern stage comedian) is not without justification. He despises their utter dependence on a suitable 'lead' from someone else, and their lack of spontaneity. Not that Malvolio is much interested in humour for its own sake – he simply resents the popularity enjoyed by such people, who, as he thinks, have far less intelligence than himself.

78. *put down* silenced, beaten in an argument.

80. *out of his guard* a fencing term, meaning 'off his guard' not ready to defend himself.

81. *minister* supply.

82. *crow* laugh in an empty, unintelligent way.

83. *set kind of fools* jesters who can be humorous only according to a set pattern. *zanies*. A clown was often accompanied by an assistant ('zany') who would clumsily imitate his antics.

84. *O, you are sick of self-love, Malvolio* A line to remember, in which Olivia puts her finger on the probable root-cause of Malvolio's unattractiveness.

85. *distemper'd* diseased, disordered.

86. *free disposition* more or less repeats the sense of *generous*. Those are the very virtues Malvolio lacks.

86. *bird-bolts* blunt-headed arrows for shooting birds.

88. *allow'd fool* recognised jester (that is, of course, the 'professional clown').

88. *rail* use abusive language.

88–90. *nor no railing ... reprove*. A not too gentle hint that Malvolio could have expressed his disapproval without growing abusive.

91. *Mercury* a Roman god, thought of not only as messenger but also as patron of thieves and cheating. *leasing* telling lies. So, mock seriously, Feste prays that Olivia may receive this reward – a skill in telling lies – to repay her for her kindness in speaking on his behalf. He is saying this against himself – implying that to speak well of fools is dishonesty anyway, and so Mercury will readily reward one of his own disciples!

93–4. Maria's announcement focuses all Olivia's attention now on the arrival of Viola with the Duke's latest message for herself. (In modern English we should put the word 'who' between *gentleman* and *much*.)

Malvolio
  Yes, and shall do, till the pangs of death shake him.
  Infirmity, that decays the wise, doth ever make the   70
  better fool.
Clown
  God send you, sir, a speedy infirmity, for the better
  increasing your folly! Sir Toby will be sworn that I am
  no fox; but he will not pass his word for twopence
  that you are no fool.   75
Olivia
  How say you to that, Malvolio?
Malvolio
  I marvel your ladyship takes delight in such a barren
  rascal; I saw him put down the other day with an
  ordinary fool that has no more brain than a stone.
  Look you now, he's out of his guard already; unless   80
  you laugh and minister occasion to him, he is gagg'd.
  I protest I take these wise men that crow so at these
  set kind of fools no better than the fools' zanies.
Olivia
  O, you are sick of self-love, Malvolio, and taste with a
  distemper'd appetite. To be generous, guiltless, and of   85
  free disposition, is to take those things for bird-bolts
  that you deem cannon bullets. There is no slander in
  an allow'd fool, though he do nothing but rail; nor
  no railing in a known discreet man, though he do
  nothing but reprove.   90
Clown
  Now Mercury endue thee with leasing, for thou speak'st
  well of fools!

              [Re-enter MARIA]

Maria
  Madam, there is at the gate a young gentleman much
  desires to speak with you.

100–1. *speaks nothing but madman* speaks entirely like a madman.

103. *what you will to dismiss it* 'make any excuse you like to get rid of him.'

106–9. There is a certain measure of affection in the relationship between Olivia and Feste. A clown needed to feel secure in his employer's affections, when so much of his time had to be spent saying things that people could find highly offensive, if they so chose.

107–8. *Jove cram with brains* '*may* Jove cram with brains.' Wishes are often thus expressed, by the simple verb without the auxiliary. (Compare 'God *save* the Queen'.)

109. *pia mater* brain (strictly a medical term for a membrane enclosing the brain).

110. Sir Toby in one of his less impressive moments. When sober, he manages some measure of deference towards Olivia; but at the moment his behaviour leaves much to be desired. There is probably as much resignation as indignation in Olivia's comments – but in any case she has more interesting things to occupy her, just now.

117–18. 'How have you managed to get so drowsy at this early hour?' (She knows the real reason, of course.) **lethargy** drowsiness.

Olivia
　From the Count Orsino, is it?　　　　　　　　　　　95
Maria
　I know not, madam; 'tis a fair young man, and well
　attended.
Olivia
　Who of my people hold him in delay?
Maria
　Sir Toby, madam, your kinsman.
Olivia
　Fetch him off, I pray you; he speaks nothing but　　100
　madman. Fie on him! *[Exit* MARIA*]* Go you, Malvolio:
　if it be a suit from the Count, I am sick, or not at home
　– what you will to dismiss it. *[Exit* MALVOLIO*]* Now you
　see, sir, how your fooling grows old, and people dislike
　it.　　　　　　　　　　　　　　　　　　　　　　　　　　　　　105
Clown
　Thou hast spoke for us, Madonna, as if thy eldest son
　should be a fool; whose skull Jove cram with brains!
　For – here he comes – one of thy kin has a most weak
　pia mater.

　　　　　　　[Enter SIR TOBY*]*

Olivia
　By mine honour, half drunk! What is he at the gate,　110
　cousin?
Sir Toby
　A gentleman.
Olivia
　A gentleman! What gentleman?
Sir Toby
　'Tis a gentleman here. *[Hiccups]* A plague o' these
　pickle-herring! How now, sot!　　　　　　　　　　　115
Clown
　Good Sir Toby!
Olivia
　Cousin, cousin, how have you come so early by this
　lethargy?

119. Sir Toby is so befuddled that he does not hear her properly. Or is he pretending to be stupid or deaf, so as to take the edge off her sarcasm?
120. **what is he?** We would probably say 'who is it?' (see line 110).

123–9. Olivia is genuinely distressed by her uncle's condition, and is becoming agitated at the prospect of a fresh messenger from Orsino. It is largely to settle her own thoughts, and play for time, that she turns to Feste. (We can see how valuable a function the clown could fulfil, in being at hand to provide artificial and irresponsible conversation which could tide people over an embarrassing or painful situation.)
125. **above heat** above his normal body temperature.
127. **crowner** coroner. The word means 'of the Crown' and a coroner was originally a King's special representative in legal administration. Olivia is using the word here in its modern sense (the official who investigates possibly suspicious deaths), for Sir Toby is **drown'd** in drink.

132–7. We can well picture such a scene as Malvolio recounts—
'I'm afraid the Countess isn't well.'
'Yes, I know all about that – I'm coming to see her.'
'No, actually she's still asleep.'
'I've heard that before, too – let me in.'

141. **sheriff's post** probably a post fixed at the Sheriff's door, for the display of public notices, **supporter to a bench** another necessary piece of wood, not to be lightly shifted!

Sir Toby
  Lechery! I defy lechery. There's one at the gate.
Olivia
  Ay, marry; what is he?   120
Sir Toby
  Let him be the devil an he will, I care not; give me
  faith, say I. Well, it's all one.
                              [Exit]
Olivia
  What's a drunken man like, fool?
Clown
  Like a drown'd man, a fool, and a madman: one
  draught above heat makes him a fool; the second mads   125
  him; and a third drowns him.
Olivia
  Go thou and seek the crowner, and let him sit o' my
  coz; for he's in the third degree of drink, he's drown'd;
  go look after him.
Clown
  He is but mad yet, Madonna, and the fool shall look   130
  to the madman.
                    [Exit. Re-enter MALVOLIO*]*
Malvolio
  Madam, yond young fellow swears he will speak with
  you. I told him you were sick; he takes on him to
  understand so much, and therefore comes to speak
  with you. I told him you were asleep; he seems to have 135
  a foreknowledge of that too, and therefore comes to
  speak with you. What is to be said to him, lady? He's
  fortified against any denial.
Olivia
  Tell him he shall not speak with me.
Malvolio
  Has been told so; and he says he'll stand at your door 140
  like a sheriff's post, and be the supporter to a bench,
  but he'll speak with you.

144. *of mankind* 'just a human being.'

146–7. *will you or no* 'whether you want him to, or not.'

150. *squash* unripe pea pod.
151. *codling* unripe apple.
152. *standing water* the turn of the tide, when the water level is stationary.
153. *well-favour'd* good-looking; ***shrewishly*** sharply, impatiently.
154–5. *mother's milk . . . out of him* only just weaned (an obvious exaggeration of Viola's youthfulness).

Viola's first encounter with Olivia is highly entertaining. The contrast between the two is excellently brought out. An apparent disparity in age or dignity makes Viola seem ingenuous and impetuous, for she has yet to learn Olivia's sophisticated wiles. (Though these will count for less and less with Olivia as she abandons herself to her new-found romance.) In sheer resolution and astuteness, Viola is more than her match. With none of her people to embarrass her by their presence, Olivia probably gets a perverse satisfaction out of Viola's unceremonious treatment of her. And before she is dismissed, Olivia has begun to fall in love.

Viola knows how to be courteous; her attitude to the Duke earlier was full of deference. What then is the reason for her awkwardness? Is it through loyalty to her master that she resents Olivia's indifference to him – or is it plain jealousy? Olivia could be a formidable rival, whose rare beauty had to be conceded, however grudgingly. Probably both motives are present – nothing has as yet taken final shape in Viola's mind and emotions.

161. *Speak to me . . . Your will?* Olivia deliberately dodges the question.

Olivia
  What kind o' man is he?
Malvolio
  Why, of mankind.
Olivia
  What manner of man? 145
Malvolio
  Of very ill manner; he'll speak with you, will you or no.
Olivia
  Of what personage and years is he?
Malvolio
  Not yet old enough for a man, nor young enough for a boy; as a squash is before 'tis a peascod, or a 150 codling when 'tis almost an apple; 'tis with him in standing water, between boy and man. He is very well-favour'd, and he speaks very shrewishly; one would think his mother's milk were scarce out of him. 155
Olivia
  Let him approach. Call in my gentlewoman.
Malvolio
  Gentlewoman, my lady calls.

  [Exit. Re-enter MARIA*]*

Olivia
  Give me my veil; come, throw it o'er my face; We'll once more hear Orsino's embassy.

  [Enter VIOLA*]*

Viola
  The honourable lady of the house, which is she? 160
Olivia
  Speak to me; I shall answer for her. Your will?

162. Viola starts to reel off the piece she has learned by heart, and then breaks off, still not sure which one is Olivia, and not wanting to feel that all her memorizing has been wasted (see also lines 170–1 and 181–3). This amuses Olivia greatly. Viola herself is not entirely serious either, probably.
165. *penn'd* written.
166. *con* learn by heart.
167. *comptible* susceptible.
168. *least sinister usage* 'the slightest unkindness.'

170–1. *I can say little more . . . out of my part.* Is there a slight dig here at certain actors who were incapable of improvization?

176. *I am not that I play.* The audience knows what Viola means by this cryptic statement, which, however, only adds to the mystery surrounding Viola, in the mind of Olivia.

181. *from my commission* 'not included in what I have been sent to convey.'

184–5. *I forgive you the praise* 'I will let you leave out that part of your message that simply flatters me.'

Viola
Most radiant, exquisite, and unmatchable beauty – I
pray you tell me if this be the lady of the house, for
I never saw her. I would be loath to cast away my
speech; for, besides that it is excellently well penn'd, 165
I have taken great pains to con it. Good beauties, let
me sustain no scorn; I am very comptible, even to the
least sinister usage.
Olivia
Whence came you, sir?
Viola
I can say little more than I have studied, and that 170
question's out of my part. Good gentle one, give me
modest assurance if you be the lady of the house, that
I may proceed in my speech.
Olivia
Are you a comedian?
Viola
No, my profound heart; and yet, by the very fangs of 175
malice I swear, I am not that I play. Are you the lady
of the house?
Olivia
If I do not usurp myself, I am.
Viola
Most certain, if you are she, you do usurp yourself; for
what is yours to bestow is not yours to reserve. But 180
this is from my commission. I will on with my speech
in your praise, and then show you the heart of my
message.
Olivia
Come to what is important in't. I forgive you the
praise. 185
Viola
Alas, I took great pains to study it, and 'tis poetical.
Olivia
It is the more like to be feigned; I pray you keep it in.
I heard you were saucy at my gates, and allow'd your
approach rather to wonder at you than to hear you.

191–2. *to make one in so skipping a dialogue* 'to take part in such a flippant conversation.'

194. *swabber* one who scrubs the ship's deck. (A fit reply to Maria, and in the same metaphor.); ***hull*** drift to and fro with no sails hoisted.
195. *Some mollification for your giant* 'Something to pacify this great protector of yours.' Maria is clearly presented as a very small person. (See Act 2, Scene 5, line 11, and Act 3, Scene 2, line 62.) The sight of her, then, adopting this rough, bullying tone, strikes Viola as very funny – hence her comment. We have the amusing spectacle of these two very slight persons trying to outface each other.
199. *Speak your office* 'Say what you have been instructed to say.'

201. *taxation of homage* demand for homage. ***olive*** olive branch (traditional symbol of peace).

203. *What are you?* See lines 110 and 120.
206. *from my entertainment* 'from the way I have been treated since I arrived at your house' – implying that Olivia and her people have 'got what they asked for'.
207. *maidenhead* virginity.
207–8. *to your ears . . . profanation* 'it is of such a highly personal (almost sacred) nature that it would be quite out of place for someone else to hear it.' (***Profanation*** is the abuse of something sacred.)
209. *Give us the place alone*. Olivia sends everyone else out. ***We will hear this divinity***. A touch of gentle irony.
There follows a fairly light dialogue, with typical Elizabethan verbal dexterity. Yet beneath their self-possession we see more than a little of their true emotions. Olivia is very concerned about how Viola will react when she sees her face; and Viola is momentarily taken aback when she sees for herself how beautiful Olivia is. The entire confrontation, with all that it means to both of them, is most delicately handled. At no time is their outward poise effectively disturbed; but the audience, knowing the true situation, is keenly aware of what lies behind each ambiguity.

If you be not mad, be gone; if you have reason, be   190
brief; 'tis not that time of moon with me to make one
in so skipping a dialogue.
Maria
  Will you hoist sail, sir? Here lies your way.
Viola
  No, good swabber, I am to hull here a little longer.
  Some mollification for your giant, sweet lady.   195
Olivia
  Tell me your mind.
Viola
  I am a messenger.
Olivia
  Sure, you have some hideous matter to deliver, when the
  courtesy of it is so fearful. Speak your office.
Viola
  It alone concerns your ear. I bring no overture of war,   200
  no taxation of homage: I hold the olive in my hand;
  my words are as full of peace as matter.
Olivia
  Yet you began rudely. What are you? What would
  you?
Viola
  The rudeness that hath appear'd in me have I learn'd   205
  from my entertainment. What I am and what I would
  are as secret as maidenhead – to your ears, divinity; to
  any other's, profanation.
Olivia
  Give us the place alone; we will hear this divinity.
          [Exeunt MARIA *and* ATTENDANTS*]*

210–18. Olivia purposely plays down the rather pompous setting of Orsino's love message. She finds his attentions increasingly tedious; and she is probably looking for some way to topple the confidence of this persistent 'young man' whom she cannot quite make out. By the use of the word 'divinity' in Viola's piece, Orsino's passion has been invested with a kind of sanctity. Irritated by this, Olivia seeks to deflate his pretentiousness by sustaining the metaphor up to a point, but in fact reducing his hopeful eloquence to the dreary level of a sermon. Hence her use of **text, chapter** and **heresy**.

216. To answer by the method 'to answer in the same kind of metaphor as you are using'.

221. out of your text 'saying something that has nothing to do with your text.' In other words, Olivia suggests – probably by now hopes – that Viola's request to see her face is entirely her own idea.
222. draw the curtain. Compare with Act 1, Scene 3, line 116.
225. if God did all 'if it is the way God made you' (i.e., with no artificial aid).

226. 'Tis in grain. 'Dyed in grain' meant 'indelible'. We have the word 'ingrained' meaning much the same.
227. blent blended.
228. cunning skilled. (The word then usually had no sense of underhandedness.)

230–1. 'If you will remain unmarried, and so childless, so that there is no one to inherit your good looks.'
232–4. Though delighted, no doubt, with the praise, Olivia pretends to misunderstand Viola's meaning, and answers flippantly enough: 'I will make sure that all my good looks are carefully listed and published.'
234. particle small part. **utensil** any article serving a useful purpose. (The modern usage is more limited.)

Now, sir, what is your text? 210
Viola
  Most sweet lady—
Olivia
  A comfortable doctrine, and much may be said of it.
  Where lies your text?
Viola
  In Orsino's bosom.
Olivia
  In his bosom! In what chapter of his bosom? 215
Viola
  To answer by the method: in the first of his heart.
Olivia
  O, I have read it; it is heresy. Have you no more to say?
Viola
  Good madam, let me see your face.
Olivia
  Have you any commission from your lord to negotiate 220
  with my face? You are now out of your text; but we
  will draw the curtain and show you the picture.
  [Unveiling] Look you, sir, such a one I was this present.
  Is't not well done?
Viola
  Excellently done, if God did all. 225
Olivia
  'Tis in grain, sir; 'twill endure wind and weather.
Viola
  'Tis beauty truly blent, whose red and white
  Nature's own sweet and cunning hand laid on.
  Lady, you are the cruell'st she alive,
  If you will lead these graces to the grave, 230
  And leave the world no copy.
Olivia
  O, sir, I will not be so hard-hearted; I will give out
  divers schedules of my beauty. It shall be inventoried,
  and every particle and utensil labell'd to my will:

235. *'item'* literally 'likewise'. We use the word 'itemise' today, meaning 'to set out in detail,' or 'make a detailed list'. In Shakespeare, the word 'item' is often used to preface each item in a list – in much the way we would say 'number one', 'number two' and so on.

239. Viola has just blamed Olivia for her hardheartedness; but goes on, 'But however bad you may be, no one can deny that you are beautiful.'

241. *but* only.

242. *nonpareil* one who has no equal. Loyal to her master, Viola claims that only if Olivia were the most beautiful lady in the world, could she deserve such love as Orsino has for her.

245. A paradoxical way of describing Orsino's pent-up passion. His 'groaning' is but a faint echo of the 'thunder' of his emotions, and the 'fire' of his passion can only be reflected by mere 'sighs'.

246. *I cannot love him*. Olivia simply means that love is not something that can be forced into existence. It takes possession when it chooses to do so. (A little later Olivia will have become thus possessed – perhaps she is already aware of this.) She is quite willing to admit that Orsino has many excellent qualities (lines 247–51), but these elicit her approval only, not her love. How ironical (but how true to life so often) that she cannot fall for the 'obvious' man, with so much to recommend their union; but instead becomes involved in what is likely to be a comparatively uncertain relationship – even granting that Viola were of the right sex!

249. *In voices well divulg'd* of good reputation.

250. *shape of nature* outward appearance.

253. *in my master's flame* 'with the same burning passion as my master feels.'

254. *such a deadly life* 'a life so full of love-sickness as to be more like death'. (Compare 'a living death'.)

256. *Why, what would you?* 'Why, what would you do?'

as – item, two lips indifferent red; item, two grey eyes 235
with lids to them; item, one neck, one chin, and so
forth. Were you sent hither to praise me?
Viola
   I see you what you are: you are too proud;
   But, if you were the devil, you are fair.
   My lord and master loves you – O, such love 240
   Could be but recompens'd though you were crown'd
   The nonpareil of beauty!
Olivia
   How does he love me?
Viola
   With adorations, fertile tears,
   With groans that thunder love, with sighs of fire. 245
Olivia
   Your lord does know my mind; I cannot love him.
   Yet I suppose him virtuous, know him noble,
   Of great estate, of fresh and stainless youth;
   In voices well divulg'd, free, learn'd, and valiant,
   And in dimension and the shape of nature 250
   A gracious person; but yet I cannot love him.
   He might have took his answer long ago.
Viola
   If I did love you in my master's flame,
   With such a suff'ring, such a deadly life,
   In your denial I would find no sense; 255
   I would not understand it.
Olivia
                    Why, what would you?

257. *cabin* hut. The willow tree was traditionally associated with unhappy love.
258. Viola simply means that she would call upon Olivia. Lovers have often referred to the object of their affection as their 'heart' or 'soul'. (Compare perhaps 'losing one's heart' to someone.)
259. *cantons* poems or sections of poems ('canto' is the more usual form). ***contemned*** despised.
261. *reverberate* reverberant, echoing.
262–3. The very air would echo the sound of Olivia's name. We have to admire the sheer poetry of these lines, whatever our view may be of the sincerity of the emotion behind them. Notice that here Viola is voicing her own ideas, and no longer simply repeating her memorised lines.
265. *But you should pity me* unless (or until) you took pity on me. ***You might do much***. Is this spoken as an 'aside'? Olivia is probably 'thinking aloud', as we say, as she has to admit, perhaps in spite of herself, that Viola's pleading, though on Orsino's behalf, is beginning to have an alarmingly potent influence on her.
267–8. It pleases Olivia, no doubt, to have this assurance, however disguised, that Viola comes from a 'good background', and is at least not ineligible on this score.
269–71. A lovely touch here – Olivia is about to say 'Don't come back with any more messages from Orsino', but then realises that, if so, she will be depriving herself of what she is coming to need desperately – Viola's company. Her reason for Viola's next visit, ***to tell me how he takes it***, is feeble in the extreme. But how life-like! She is so infatuated now that she acts less and less rationally.
273. *fee'd post* paid messenger.
273–7. Viola's indignation is entirely genuine. Loyal devotion to the Duke still comes first. It is the only relationship possible for her anyway – or so she thinks; and so it never occurs to her that Olivia's rejection of Orsino, which she has just been attacking so vehemently, may in the long run be her own gain.

Viola
    Make me a willow cabin at your gate,
    And call upon my soul within the house;
    Write loyal cantons of contemned love
    And sing them loud even in the dead of night;   260
    Halloo your name to the reverberate hills,
    And make the babbling gossip of the air
    Cry out 'Olivia!' O, you should not rest
    Between the elements of air and earth
    But you should pity me!
Olivia
                    You might do much.   265
    What is your parentage?
Viola
    Above my fortunes, yet my state is well:
    I am a gentleman.
Olivia
                    Get you to your lord.
    I cannot love him; let him send no more—
    Unless perchance you come to me again   270
    To tell me how he takes it. Fare you well.
    I thank you for your pains; spend this for me.
Viola
    I am no fee'd post, lady; keep your purse;
    My master, not myself, lacks recompense.
    Love make his heart of flint that you shall love;   275
    And let your fervour, like my master's, be
    Plac'd in contempt! Farewell, fair cruelty.
                    [Exit]

285–7. A description of love-at-first-sight that would be hard to improve upon. 287. **Well, let it be** Resignation, but of what kind – despairing, or contented?

289. *peevish messenger*. A familiar subterfuge in the first stages of romance is to show no sign of affection. Olivia must in any case maintain some appearance of propriety, to cover up her next undignified little scheme.
290. *County's man* Count's man. (It is probably a rendering of *Countes man* a legitimate possessive form in earlier English.)
290–1. She is, of course, going to 'plant' the ring on Viola. It is a foolish thing to do, because Viola will certainly see through it. Or does Olivia half hope that she will, and will then begin to 'put two and two together' and realise what is going on in Olivia's mind?
293–4. Notice the abrupt change. *I am not for him* is immediately followed by *If that the youth will come*. Olivia has to get this second part of her message in at once, before Malvolio goes out, taking with him only the general tone of rejection she started with.
297–8. 'I don't know what I'm doing; and I'm afraid I may have let this young man's looks go to my head.'
299. *owe* own.
300. Olivia's resignation probably has as much in it of pleasurable anticipation as of fear.

ACT 1 SCENE 5

Olivia
  'What is your parentage?'
  'Above my fortunes, yet my state is well:
  I am a gentleman.' I'll be sworn thou art;   280
  Thy tongue, thy face, thy limbs, actions, and spirit,
  Do give thee five-fold blazon. Not too fast! Soft, soft!
  Unless the master were the man. How now!
  Even so quickly may one catch the plague?
  Methinks I feel this youth's perfections   285
  With an invisible and subtle stealth
  To creep in at mine eyes. Well, let it be.
  What ho, Malvolio!
            [Re-enter MALVOLIO]

Malvolio
            Here, madam, at your service.

Olivia
  Run after that same peevish messenger,
  The County's man. He left this ring behind him,   290
  Would I or not. Tell him I'll none of it.
  Desire him not to flatter with his lord,
  Nor hold him up with hopes; I am not for him.
  If that the youth will come this way to-morrow,
  I'll give him reasons for't. Hie thee, Malvolio.   295
Malvolio
  Madam, I will.
            [Exit}

Olivia
  I do I know not what, and fear to find
  Mine eye too great a flatterer for my mind.
  Fate, show thy force: ourselves we do not owe;
  What is decreed must be; and be this so!   300
            [Exit]

ACT 2 SCENE 1

A short but necessary scene introducing Sebastian, Viola's twin brother, and Antonio. Vital to the main plot is Sebastian's present assumption that Viola is dead. Equally vital is the strong physical likeness between brother and sister, which Sebastian humorously points out. Though not vital, yet helping the play forward convincingly, and contributing much to its excitement and pathos, is the loyal attachment Antonio shows for Sebastian.

Most of this scene uses a dignified prose, not very different in its effect from the verse that ends the scene. The changed form marks the changed atmosphere when Antonio is alone, and 'thinking aloud'. Solitary thoughts are usually better conveyed in verse than in prose.

1–2. *nor will you not that I go with you?* (a double negative) 'Don't you want me to go with you either?'

3. *stars shine darkly* Refers to the effect, for good or ill, that the stars were thought to have upon people's lives.

4. *malignancy* bad influence. *distemper* disturb, blight. Sebastian and Antonio exhibit generous concern for each other's well-being. We are reminded of the earlier coast-scene when Viola's plight is greatly cheered by the loyalty of the Captain.

9. *determinate* intended.

10. *extravagancy* wandering. 'All I have in mind is simply to wander idly from place to place.' ('Vagrant' is still the legal word for a 'tramp', someone of 'no fixed abode'.)

12. *it charges me in manners* 'out of politeness, I ought . . .' Antonio has been considerate enough not to press Sebastian for information, and so Sebastian feels that the polite thing to do, in reply, is to tell Antonio about himself.

15. *Roderigo*. Sebastian has adopted a false name, almost automatically, as a security measure. (His predicament, and the remedy he has chosen, remind us of Viola's almost identical situation.)

17–18. *if the heavens had been pleas'd, would we had so ended!* 'I wish we had both drowned together (that is, within the same hour), if that had been God's will.' We may recall Viola's similar grief when she thinks Sebastian has been drowned.

18–19. *But you, sir, alter'd that.* Antonio has clearly saved Sebastian from drowning, and this, as they both imagine, prevented him from sharing his sister's fate.

ACT 2
SCENE 1

The sea-coast

[Enter ANTONIO and SEBASTIAN]

Antonio
Will you stay no longer; nor will you not that I go with you?

Sebastian
By your patience, no. My stars shine darkly over me; the malignancy of my fate might perhaps distemper yours; therefore I shall crave of you your leave that I may bear my evils alone. It were a bad recompense for your love to lay any of them on you. 5

Antonio
Let me yet know of you whither you are bound.

Sebastian
No, sooth, sir; my determinate voyage is mere extravagancy. But I perceive in you so excellent a touch of 10
modesty that you will not extort from me what I am willing to keep in; therefore it charges me in manners the rather to express myself. You must know of me then, Antonio, my name is Sebastian, which I call'd Roderigo; my father was that Sebastian of Messaline 15
whom I know you have heard of. He left behind him myself and a sister, both born in an hour; if the heavens had been pleas'd, would we had so ended! But you, sir, alter'd that; for some hour before you took me from the breach of the sea was my sister 20
drown'd.

Antonio
Alas the day!

23. *though it was said she much resembled me*. Is it modesty that prompts Sebastian to express surprise at Viola's reputation for beauty, since it will follow that he must share it, being so like her in appearance? Whatever his reason, there is a gentle humour in his comment.

24–6. *though I could not with such estimable wonder overfar believe that* 'though I couldn't go as far as to share their excessive admiration' (***estimable*** means 'esteeming highly'.)

26–7. *she bore a mind that envy could not but call fair*. Sebastian cannot, for reasons of modesty, enlarge upon her outward beauty; but he has no qualms about confirming her inner goodness. Even those who envy her have to admit that.

28–29. *drown her remembrance again with more*. Sebastian speaks of the tears he could easily shed as he calls her to mind.

30. 'I'm sorry I haven't been able to look after you better.' (For this use of 'entertainment', see Act 1, Scene 5, line 206.)

31. *forgive me your trouble* 'forgive me the trouble you have been put to (on my behalf).'

32. *If you will not* . . . 'Unless you wish to . . .' What Antonio means here is that it will be as bad as dying if he is not allowed to stay with Sebastian as his loyal servant.

35. *kill him whom you have recover'd*. Sebastian seems to be exaggerating the effect that Antonio will have if he stays there any longer; he goes on to explain exactly what this effect will be. He is so overwrought that he is likely to break down and weep if Antonio speaks so openly of his affection.

37. *yet so near the manners of my mother* 'still possessing so many unmanly feelings' – i.e. 'I feel like crying.' There is the further implication that he has not been long enough out in the world to become hardened.

38–9. *mine eyes will tell tales of me* 'by weeping I shall reveal that I am still not much more than a child.'

39. *I am bound* 'I am on my way.'

Antonio's affection for Sebastian (which plays a not insignificant part in the play) develops with lightning speed – to judge by the brevity of this conversation and the implied encounter that has preceded it. This 'compression' is sometimes forced upon a playwright. In this instance, it is clearly better to make secondary things happen over-rapidly, than to allow the proper lapse of time, which would then be taking up a disproportionate place in the play.

ACT 2 SCENE 1

Sebastian
    A lady, sir, though it was said she much resembled me,
    was yet of many accounted beautiful; but though I
    could not with such estimable wonder overfar believe   25
    that, yet thus far I will boldly publish her: she bore a
    mind that envy could not but call fair. She is drown'd
    already, sir, with salt water, though I seem to drown
    her remembrance again with more.
Antonio
    Pardon me, sir, your bad entertainment.   30
Sebastian
    O good Antonio, forgive me your trouble.
Antonio
    If you will not murder me for my love, let me be your
    servant.
Sebastian
    If you will not undo what you have done – that is,
    kill him whom you have recover'd – desire it not.   35
    Fare ye well at once; my bosom is full of kindness,
    and I am yet so near the manners of my mother that,
    upon the least occasion more, mine eyes will tell tales
    of me. I am bound to the Count Orsino's court.
    Farewell.   40
                          [Exit]

Antonio
    The gentleness of all the gods go with thee!
    I have many enemies in Orsino's court,
    Else would I very shortly see thee there.
    But come what may, I do adore thee so
    That danger shall seem sport, and I will go.   45
                          [Exit]

SCENE 2

Simply the sequel to Olivia's dismissal of Viola at the end of Act 1. But it becomes an occasion – a most effective one – for Viola to impart, in soliloquy, her growing realization that the worst has happened, and Olivia has, all unwittingly, fallen in love with her.

1. Malvolio's peremptory enquiry (entirely in character) has little effect on Viola, whose reply is completely unruffled.

2. *on a moderate pace* strolling along.

4–5. *you might have saved me my pains* Malvolio is clearly annoyed at having been brought into this business. It must seem quite beneath the dignity of his office to have to go running after a young page – especially one so unmoved by these bullying tactics. However, he delivers his message faithfully, though we may detect more of Malvolio than Olivia in his final throwing down of the ring.

11. *I'll none of it* 'I'll have nothing to do with it.'

14. *be it his that finds it* 'Whoever finds it is welcome to it.'

15–39. Verse is now used, as it was at the end of the previous scene, to convey more fittingly the profounder thoughts that Viola can share with no one but herself. The whole mood has changed – and with it the language – from outward wrangling, where little of true self needs to be involved, to meditative discussion of deepest needs.

15. It does not take Viola long to see through to the real motive behind the business of the ring. She had noticed Olivia's odd behaviour; and now, with this further bit of evidence, she has no alternative but to believe the worst.

16. A double negative here. We would say 'Heaven (*Fortune*) forbid that my looks (*outside*) should have charmed her.'

17. *She made good view of me* 'She had a good look at me.'

18–19. This is almost the way Olivia described the experience herself. (Act 1, Scene 5, lines 297–8). The meaning here is that Olivia's whole attention is so engrossed in simply gazing at Viola that there is no rational control left for her words – and so she speaks *distractedly*.

20. *cunning* Here the word seems to have more of its modern meaning (unlike its use in Act 1, Scene 5, line 228). Olivia's emotions are so stirred that she will make use even of this most unlikely go-between to further her purpose, and maintain contact with Viola.

21. *churlish* ill-mannered.

22. *None of my lord's ring!* 'This is certainly not my lord's ring.'

23. *I am the man*. 'I am the *one*' might have been enough, but Viola deliberately says 'man' because it is her feigned manhood that is being singled out and pursued.

23. . . . *as 'tis* . . . What a wealth of feeling in this parenthesis!

SCENE 2

A street

[Enter VIOLA and MALVOLIO at several doors]

Malvolio
Were you not ev'n now with the Countess Olivia?
Viola
Even now, sir; on a moderate pace I have since arriv'd
but hither.
Malvolio
She returns this ring to you, sir; you might have saved
me my pains, to have taken it away yourself. She adds, 5
moreover, that you should put your lord into a
desperate assurance she will none of him. And one
thing more: that you be never so hardy to come
again in his affairs, unless it be to report your lord's
taking of this. Receive it so. 10
Viola
She took the ring of me; I'll none of it.
Malvolio
Come, sir, you peevishly threw it to her; and her will
is it should be so return'd. If it be worth stooping for,
there it lies in your eye; if not, be it his that finds it.

[Exit]

Viola
I left no ring with her; what means this lady? 15
Fortune forbid my outside have not charm'd her!
She made good view of me; indeed, so much
That methought her eyes had lost her tongue
For she did speak in starts distractedly
She loves me, sure: the cunning of her passion 20
Invites me in this churlish messenger
None of my lord's ring! Why, he sent her none
I am the man. If it be so – as 'tis—

24. ***She were better love a dream*** 'It would be better for her if she loved a dream.' (Clearly, there would be less attachment then than to a real person, and the subsequent moment of disillusionment less painful.)
26. Viola is reminded that all disguise is potentially evil, since it deceives. The ***pregnant*** (resourceful) ***enemy*** is the Devil.
27. ***proper-false*** prepossessing outwardly but inwardly false.
28. ***waxen hearts***. 'Waxen' because more easily impressed by false charmers (just as wax receives the imprint of a seal).
29–30. A memorable couplet, almost proverbial, and underlined, as it were, by the use of rhyme (which normally is reserved for the ending of a scene or speech). The point of it is that women are frail by nature, so it is not their fault.
31. ***fadge*** turn out.
32. ***monster*** basically (as here) something that is outside the normal pattern of nature. Viola's double role suggests the title.
34. ***As I am man*** 'As long as I must play the part of man.'
35. 'I have no hope that my love for Orsino can have a happy fulfilment.'
36. ***As I am woman***. If and when she resumes her proper role as woman (and she is beginning to wish she had not been born a woman), then it will be Olivia's turn to suffer frustration.
37. ***thriftless sighs*** wasted sighs (since they will be followed by no joy of fulfilment, to make up for their sadness).
38–9. Compare Viola's resignation with Olivia's, when she first recognised her love for Viola. On that occasion there was mostly happy anticipation – however irresponsibly conceived – but with Viola now, heavy despair. (Compare also Act 1, Scene 2, line 60.)

Poor lady, she were better love a dream.
Disguise, I see thou art a wickedness   25
Wherein the pregnant enemy does much.
How easy is it for the proper-false
In women's waxen hearts to set their forms!
Alas, our frailty is the cause, not we!
For such as we are made of, such we be.   30
How will this fadge? My master loves her dearly,
And I, poor monster, fond as much on him;
And she, mistaken, seems to dote on me.
What will become of this? As I am man,
My state is desperate for my master's love;   35
As I am woman – now alas the day!—
What thriftless sighs shall poor Olivia breathe!
O Time, thou must untangle this, not I;
It is too hard a knot for me t' untie!

          [Exit]

SCENE 3

Sir Toby and Sir Andrew again, familiarly enough employed, this time abetted by Feste. The significance now of their roistering is that it brings them into head-on collision with Malvolio who has been sent to remonstrate – a duty he finds highly gratifying. It becomes plain that two ways of life are here in conflict, Sir Toby and his cronies representing irresponsible lightheartedness, and Malvolio standing stubbornly alone in opposition. The upshot is that a plan is conceived for Malvolio's humiliation; and so the 'sub-plot', held back till now, is set in motion.

1–2. *Not to be abed . . . betimes* 'To be still up after midnight is to be up early.'

2. *'diluculo surgere'* This is the first part of a proverb in Latin – 'To get up early' – the part omitted simply adding 'is most healthful'.

6. *an unfill'd can*. This, to drink-loving Sir Toby, is frustration indeed; and so he uses it to illustrate ***A false conclusion***. Both are to be deplored since neither provides what it seems to promise.

9. *the four elements*. The ancient belief, still not discarded entirely in Shakespeare's day, was that all material creation was made up of the four distinct 'elements' – fire, water, earth and air – in varying proportions.

11. *eating and drinking*. This may seem a down-to-earth and quite humorous way to demolish such a theory. But coming from Sir Andrew, we should perhaps take it as a quite serious observation – that life is sustained by food and drink. That he hasn't intentionally made a joke here is borne out by the fact that Sir Toby makes his rejoinder – ***let us therefore eat and drink*** – as the one who is providing the humorous twist to the conversation.

13. *stoup* a drinking vessel.

15–16. *Did you never . . . 'we three'?* Feste, by joining the group, and making the number up to three (probably by popping up between them) recalls an inn-sign, familiar at the time, showing two fools, or logger-heads, with the title 'We Three Loggerheads' – thus implying that the viewer himself becomes the third, as he reads it.

17. *catch* song sung by three or more people, all of them singing the same piece, but each one starting off a line later than the one before.

18. *breast* a term frequently used for 'voice'.

ACT 2 SCENE 3

SCENE 3

Olivia's house

[*Enter* SIR TOBY *and* SIR ANDREW]

Sir Toby
Approach, Sir Andrew. Not to be abed after midnight is to be up betimes; and 'diluculo surgere' thou know'st—

Sir Andrew
Nay, by my troth, I know not; but I know to be up late is to be up late. 5

Sir Toby
A false conclusion! I hate it as an unfill'd can. To be up after midnight and to go to bed then is early; so that to go to bed after midnight is to go to bed betimes. Does not our lives consist of the four elements?

Sir Andrew
Faith, so they say; but I think it rather consists of 10 eating and drinking.

Sir Toby
Th'art a scholar; let us therefore eat and drink. Marian, I say! a stoup of wine.

[*Enter* CLOWN]

Sir Andrew
Here comes the fool, i' faith.

Clown
How now, my hearts! Did you never see the picture of 15 'we three'?

Sir Toby
Welcome, ass. Now let's have a catch.

Sir Andrew
By my troth, the fool has an excellent breast. I had rather than forty shillings I had such a leg, and so sweet a breath to sing, as the fool has. In sooth, thou 20 wast in very gracious fooling last night, when thou

22–3. *Pigrogromitus . . . Vapians . . . Queubus*. Clearly Feste has been putting on a very impressive display of learning, though just so much nonsense in actual fact, but it has achieved its purpose – Sir Andrew is positively dazzled by it.
24. *leman* sweetheart.
25. *impeticos thy gratillity*. More fancy words invented by Feste to impress Sir Andrew. He means that he has put Sir Andrew's gratuity into his pocket.

32. *testril* a coin (=tester) of the same value as a sixpenny piece (=2½p).

35. *I care not for good life* Sir Andrew, as so often, tamely follows Sir Toby's lead. And there is something quite ludicrous in the idea of Sir Andrew playing the hardened cynic.
36–49. The songs in *Twelfth Night* are highly effective, and to be valued in their own right. This one certainly seems to have been in existence before Shakespeare made use of it in his play. Its theme – that pleasure is fleeting, and therefore to be snatched while offered – is one we would expect to find in favour with Sir Toby and his kind.

ACT 2 SCENE 3

spok'st of Pigrogromitus, of the Vapians passing the
equinoctial of Queubus; 'twas very good, i' faith. I sent
thee sixpence for thy leman; hadst it?
Clown
I did impeticos thy gratillity; for Malvolio's nose is no   25
whipstock. My lady has a white hand, and the
Myrmidons are no bottle-ale houses.
Sir Andrew
Excellent! Why, this is the best fooling, when all is
done. Now, a song.
Sir Toby
Come on, there is sixpence for you, Let's have a   30
song.
Sir Andrew
There's a testril of me too; if one knight give a—
Clown
Would you have a love-song, or a song of good life?
Sir Toby
A love-song, a love-song.
Sir Andrew
Ay, ay; I care not for good life.   35

[CLOWN *sings*]

O mistress mine, where are you roaming?
O, stay and hear; your true love's coming,
   That can sing both high and low.
   Trip no further, pretty sweeting;
   Journeys end in lovers meeting,   40
   Every wise man's son doth know.
Sir Andrew
Excellent good, i' faith!
Sir Toby
Good, good!

[CLOWN *sings*]

What is love? 'Tis not hereafter;
Present mirth hath present laughter;   45
   What's to come is still unsure.
In delay there lies no plenty,

50. ***mellifluous*** literally 'flowing with honey', i.e. 'sweetly flowing'.
51. ***A contagious breath*** Sir Toby praises the moving, affecting quality of the singing, in his own peculiar way.
52. Sir Andrew has already made a perfectly apposite comment (***mellifluous voice***), but the moment Sir Toby adds something different, then he seems to distrust his own choice, as if his only hope of social acceptability lies in slavishly copying Sir Toby.
53. ***To hear by the nose*** Sir Toby is deliberately mixing words up in a nonsensical way to mock Sir Andrew's strange use of language. ***dulcet in contagion*** 'sweetly stinking'.
54. ***welkin*** sky.
55–6. ***draw three souls out of one weaver.*** Weavers, especially perhaps those who were Calvinist refugees from the Continent, seem to have had a reputation for hearty singing (with 'heart' and 'soul') of hymns and psalms. But to move them so deeply in a drinking-song would be a great achievement.
57. ***dog at a catch.*** To be 'dog' at anything simply meant to be good at it.
58. ***some dogs will catch well.*** Feste, as so often, takes the literal meaning of 'dog' and 'catch', suggesting a dog biting someone.
60. ***Hold thy peace*** keep quiet.

62–3. ***'Tis not the first time . . . call me knave.*** What a pathetic delight Sir Andrew gets if he can at all convince anyone (including himself) of some instance of roguishness in his life! (Compare line 35.)

66. Maria does her best to forewarn them of Malvolio's approach, by hurrying to them, ahead of Malvolio, whom she knows to be on his way. Though when she arrives and catches them at the height of their rowdiness, her instinctive reaction is as disapproving as Malvolio's. ***caterwauling*** the noise cats make at mating time. ***keep*** make.

Then come kiss me, sweet and twenty;
Youth's a stuff will not endure.
Sir Andrew
A mellifluous voice, as I am true knight. 50
Sir Toby
A contagious breath.
Sir Andrew
Very sweet and contagious, i' faith.
Sir Toby
To hear by the nose, it is dulcet in contagion. But shall we make the welkin dance indeed? Shall we rouse the night-owl in a catch that will draw three souls out of 55 one weaver? Shall we do that?
Sir Andrew
An you love me, let's do't. I am dog at a catch.
Clown
By'r lady, sir, and some dogs will catch well.
Sir Andrew
Most certain. Let our catch be 'Thou knave'.
Clown
'Hold thy peace, thou knave' knight? I shall be 60 constrain'd in't to call thee knave, knight.
Sir Andrew
'Tis not the first time I have constrained one to call me knave. Begin, fool: it begins 'Hold thy peace'.
Clown
I shall never begin if I hold my peace.
Sir Andrew
Good, i' faith! Come, begin. 65

[Catch sung. Enter MARIA*]*

Maria
What a caterwauling do you keep here! If my lady have not call'd up her steward Malvolio, and bid him turn you out of doors, never trust me.

69. Sir Toby is now more than a little drunk, but, as drunkards often do, concentrates a great deal of colourful vehemence into his choice of language. *Cataian* someone from Cathay, i.e. China. Used thus in Elizabethan times, this would mean 'cheat'.

70. *Peg-a-Ramsey* There was a contemporary song of this name. It may mean something like 'scarecrow' here.

70. *Three merry men be we* another contemporary song.

71. *consanguineous*. This is explained in the next sentence, *of her blood*, related to her. Sir Toby is resentful that his own niece should feel she has to call in a servant, even if her steward, to reprimand him, her uncle.

72. *Tilly-vally* a term of scorn and reproof – 'nonsense!'

73. *There dwelt a man in Babylon*. A line from a contemporary ballad.

75. *Beshrew me* a plague on me. *in admirable fooling* 'playing the fool most successfully.'

76–7. *so do I too*. Sir Andrew does so want to share, if only a little, in Sir Toby's success.

77–8. *more natural*. He means this as in such a modern expression as 'a natural games-player'; but a regular Elizabethan meaning was 'idiotic' or 'half-witted'.

79. *O' the twelfth day of December* another ballad, probably.

81. We have to admit that Malvolio's protest is entirely justified – in any case, he has to voice his mistress's opinion. Yet the four are convinced that he is putting into it far too much of his own kill-joy attitude. It is as if they have been waiting for just such an occasion, to make a stand against him. But they have to wait for Sir Toby to shake himself clear of his drunkenness sufficiently to rally them to the cause of gaiety and good humour, before they discover their solidarity.

82. *wit* good sense. *honesty* decency.

83. *tinkers* These wandering, gipsy-like people had a reputation for drunken chattering.

84–5. *cozier's catches* cobblers' songs.

85. *without any mitigation or remorse of voice* 'at the top of your voices, without stopping'.

88. *We did keep time*. The other meaning of 'time' – rhythm. *Sneck up!* 'be hanged!'

ACT 2 SCENE 3

Sir Toby
My lady's a Cataian, we are politicians, Malvolio's a
Peg-a-Ramsey, and *[Sings]*
                  Three merry men be we.
Am not I consanguineous? Am I not of her blood?
Tilly-vally, lady. *[Sings]*
                  There dwelt a man in Babylon,
                  Lady, lady.
Clown
Beshrew me, the knight's in admirable fooling.
Sir Andrew
Ay, he does well enough if he be dispos'd, and so do
I too; he does it with a better grace, but I do it more
natural.
Sir Toby [Sings]
O' the twelfth day of December—
Maria
For the love o' God, peace!

[Enter MALVOLIO*]*

Malvolio
My masters, are you mad? Or what are you? Have
you no wit, manners, nor honesty, but to gabble like
tinkers at this time of night? Do ye make an ale-house
of my lady's house, that ye squeak out your coziers'
catches without any mitigation or remorse of voice?
Is there no respect of place, persons, nor time, in
you?
Sir Toby
We did keep time, sir, in our catches. Sneck up!

89. *round* outspoken.

91. *she's nothing allied to your disorders* 'she entirely dissociates herself from your unruly conduct.'

92. *separate yourself and your misdemeanours* 'separate yourself from your bad deeds.'

96. The next bit of dialogue, interspersed with snatches of songs, is most effective. This oblique way of answering has an insolence about it more intolerable than a plain statement of opposition. Sir Toby and Feste are ignoring Malvolio, by simply conversing, however unsoberly, with each other, but they are talking *about* him. Their very flippancy is meant to show how little they care for his reproof. (The lines they sing are taken, but altered somewhat, from a contemporary ballad.)

107–13. Drunkenness may accentuate views already held, but it slows down the reactions; and Sir Toby's mind seems up to now to have done little to cope with the crisis. Even now it is Malvolio's earlier remark (line 87), and then not correctly remembered – Malvolio spoke of 'time' but to Sir Toby it has become 'tune' – that finally 'needles' him. It has taken till now to penetrate. But when he does turn and address Malvolio, it is as though he had, all through the small-talk, been simply priming himself for it. As he rises to his feet, however unsteadily, his whole person seems in that instant to overtop Malvolio. We could hardly imagine a more telling line of confrontation.

107. *Art any more than a steward?* Even at his drunken worst, Sir Toby is what Malvolio can never be – blood-relation to the Countess – and at this moment he intends that Malvolio shall have that fact thrust down his throat.

108–9. That other half of Malvolio – his intolerance of all merry-making – is equally hateful to Sir Toby. In lines perhaps more memorable than any others in the whole play, he demolishes the entire case for censoriousness. Malvolio's virtue (even if it has a valid existence), cannot possibly justify his dictating how the rest of the world shall amuse itself. 'Cakes and ale' (typical Elizabethan holiday fare) neatly suggests the simple pleasures of simple folk, especially during the 'twelve days of Christmas'. Feasting at that time was particularly opposed by the Puritans.

Malvolio
  Sir Toby, I must be round with you. My lady bade me tell you that, though she harbours you as her kinsman, she's nothing allied to your disorders. If you can separate yourself and your misdemeanours, you are welcome to the house; if not, and it would please you to take leave of her, she is very willing to bid you farewell.
Sir Toby *[Sings]*
  Farewell, dear heart, since I must needs be gone.
Maria
  Nay, good Sir Toby.
Clown *[Sings]*
  His eyes do show his days are almost done.
Malvolio
  Is't even so?
Sir Toby *[Sings]*
  But I will never die.

[Falls down]

Clown *[Sings]*
  Sir Toby, there you lie.
Malvolio
  This is much credit to you.
Sir Toby *[Sings]*
  Shall I bid him go?
Clown *[Sings]*
  What an if you do?
Sir Toby *[Sings]*
  Shall I bid him go, and spare not?
Clown *[Sings]*
  O, no, no, no, no, you dare not.
Sir Toby *[Rising]*
  Out o' tune, sir! Ye lie. Art any more than a steward? Dost thou think, because thou art virtuous, there shall be no more cakes and ale?

110–11. *ginger shall be hot i' th' mouth, too*. Feste is quick to side with Sir Toby in his stand against Malvolio, but we may feel that his enthusiasm at this moment is stimulated more by the taste he recalls of good fare, than by any principle involved. (Ginger was often used to add flavour to ale.)

112. *rub your chain with crumbs*. Malvolio's chain of office would normally be cleaned by being rubbed with breadcrumbs. By asking Maria for yet more wine, Sir Toby gives the finishing touch to his scornful defiance of Malvolio.

114–17. By addressing his parting remarks to Maria, Malvolio is virtually accepting temporary defeat. His invective against Sir Toby has bounced back upon himself, and he recognises that he can get no further in that direction in the present encounter. All he can do is turn and blame Maria for supplying them with intoxicants, and thus enencouraging their drunken rowdiness.

115–16. *give means for this uncivil rule* 'provide opportunity for this uncivilised behaviour.'

118. An expression of contempt, possibly addressed usually to a dog. Maria is careful to keep back her comment till Malvolio is out of hearing.

119–20. *as good a deed . . . ahungry*. Sir Andrew means that the device he is about to suggest would exasperate Malvolio as much as offering a man drink when he was hungry for solid food.

124–30. Maria has a better plan, and urges them to delay or abandon any other ideas.

126. *out of quiet* restless.

127. *gull* trick. ('Gullible' means 'easy to trick', 'easily deceived'.) ***nayword*** byword; so ***gull him into a nayword*** means 'go on fooling him until he becomes a famous ass'.

128. *common recreation* a figure of fun, laughed at by everybody.

131. *Possess us* inform us. ***Tell us something of him***. Sir Toby isn't just asking for general information about Malvolio, but for that particular point on which he imagines she will be basing her plan.

132. *Puritan* The word then included all that it still does, of opposition to ordinary human joys and jollity. Originally this attitude was but part of a larger religious attitude – the Puritans were a substantial party in the contemporary Church. But it seems that when Maria uses it of Malvolio she is thinking only of the kill-joy aspect of Puritanism. (We must not see in her remark any sort of crusade by Shakespeare against the Puritans as such.)

Clown
    Yes, by Saint Anne; and ginger shall be hot i' th' mouth   110
    too.
Sir Toby
    Th'art i' th' right. Go, sir, rub your chain with crumbs.
    A stoup of wine, Maria!
Malvolio
    Mistress Mary, if you priz'd my lady's favour at anything
    more than contempt, you would not give means for   115
    this uncivil rule; she shall know of it, by
    this hand.

                    [Exit]

Maria
    Go shake your ears.
Sir Andrew
    'Twere as good a deed as to drink when a man's
    ahungry, to challenge him the field, and then to break   120
    promise with him and make a fool of him.
Sir Toby
    Do't, knight. I'll write thee a challenge; or I'll deliver
    thy indignation to him by word of mouth.
Maria
    Sweet Sir Toby, be patient for to-night; since the youth
    of the Count's was to-day with my lady, she is much   125
    out of quiet. For Monsieur Malvolio, let me alone
    with him; if I do not gull him into a nayword, and
    make him a common recreation, do not think I have
    wit enough to lie straight in my bed. I know I can
    do it.   130
Sir Toby
    Possess us, possess us; tell us something of him.
Maria
    Marry, sir, sometimes he is a kind of Puritan.

133–5. When Sir Andrew seems to be making this very mistake, and to vow vengeance on Malvolio for being one of the Puritan party – this is what he thinks Maria is saying – then Sir Toby at once checks him. He knows that he is simply echoing popular sentiment, with never a thought for what is really at stake; and Sir Toby has no time for that.
134. *exquisite* ingeniously devised.
138–9. *The devil a Puritan . . . time-pleaser* 'He's no Puritan (in the regular, religious sense), or anything else that requires selfless loyalty to a cause. He is simply one who judges every situation by its potential advantage to himself.'
139. *affection'd* affected. *cons state* learns matters of state, theories of state-craft.
140. *without book* by heart (as actors in a play, who have to dispense with their written lines). *swarths.* A swath, or swarth, is that quantity of grass or hay cut by a mower with one sweep of his sickle.
140–1. *the best persuaded of himself* always thinking most favourably about himself; having the highest opinion of himself.
142. *his grounds of faith* This certainty about his own attractiveness is as fundamental to Malvolio's whole character as a religious person's faith is.
143. *that vice in him* his conviction that people cannot help admiring him.
146. *epistles* letters.
148. *expressure* expression.
150. *feelingly* accurately. *personated* described. By including descriptions that so obviously must refer to himself, Maria will convince Malvolio that the letter is intended for him, but from one who is at present unable to name himself, or herself, openly and in writing. The subtlety of the letter, with many more such hints of identity, is that it is Malvolio's vanity that is played upon every time. He can identify himself progressively as the addressee only by entertaining more and more outrageous notions of his own charms.
151. *forgotten* unimportant.
153. *I smell a device* An unusual way of describing the detecting of a plot, but just as logical in fact as to speak of 'seeing' it. (We have the saying 'to smell a rat' – to detect something deceptive or unfavourable.)
154. Once again, Sir Andrew feels he must echo the very metaphor Sir Toby has used.
158. *a horse of that colour* 'something like that.'
159. *your horse . . . an ass* Rather unexpected, perhaps, from Sir Andrew, but we must not begrudge him his occasional small joke.

Sir Andrew
  O, if I thought that, I'd beat him like a dog.
Sir Toby
  What, for being a Puritan? Thy exquisite reason, dear
  knight? 135
Sir Andrew
  I have no exquisite reason for't, but I have reason good
  enough.
Maria
  The devil a Puritan that he is, or anything constantly
  but a time-pleaser; an affection'd ass that cons state
  without book and utters it by great swarths; the best 140
  persuaded of himself, so cramm'd, as he thinks, with
  excellencies that it is his grounds of faith that all that
  look on him love him; and on that vice in him will
  my revenge find notable cause to work.
Sir Toby
  What wilt thou do? 145
Maria
  I will drop in his way some obscure epistles of love;
  wherein, by the colour of his beard, the shape of his
  leg, the manner of his gait, the expressure of his eye,
  forehead, and complexion, he shall find himself most
  feelingly personated. I can write very like my lady, 150
  your niece; on a forgotten matter we can hardly make
  distinction of our hands.
Sir Toby
  Excellent! I smell a device.
Sir Andrew
  I have't in my nose too.
Sir Toby
  He shall think, by the letters that thou wilt drop, that 155
  they come from my niece, and that she's in love with
  him.
Maria
  My purpose is, indeed, a horse of that colour.
Sir Andrew
  And your horse now would make him an ass.

162. *Sport royal* first-rate entertainment.

164–5. *observe his construction of it* watch what he makes of it.

166. *event* outcome.

167. *Penthesilea* Queen of the Amazons (a legendary race of warlike females). The thought of the tiny Maria having conceived this impressive strategy no doubt prompts Sir Toby to make his humorous comparison.
169. *beagle* a small type of hunting dog. Here the term is used affectionately, and with reference to Maria's size.

171. Sir Andrew is again feebly imitative, but on this occasion there is something quite pathetic about his timid reminiscence. It certainly forms a contrast to what we see in Sir Toby in a moment – a side usually obscured by his outward good humour – when he callously presses Sir Andrew for more money, promising him a success in his wooing of Olivia which he knows to be out of the question.
174. *a foul way out* in a desperate state.

176. *Cut* a common name for a working horse. The phrase ***call me Cut*** here simply means that Sir Toby will accept blame and insult if he is proved wrong about Sir Andrew and Olivia.

178. *burn some sack*. Sack was a white wine from Spain or the Canary Islands which was sometimes heated.

Maria
Ass, I doubt not. 160
Sir Andrew
O, 'twill be admirable!
Maria
Sport royal, I warrant you. I know my physic will work with him. I will plant you two, and let the fool make a third, where he shall find the letter; observe his construction of it. For this night, to bed, and dream 165 on the event. Farewell.

[Exit]

Sir Toby
Good night, Penthesilea.
Sir Andrew
Before me, she's a good wench.
Sir Toby
She's a beagle true-bred, and one that adores me. What o' that? 170
Sir Andrew
I was ador'd once too.
Sir Toby
Let's to bed, knight. Thou hadst need send for more money.
Sir Andrew
If I cannot recover your niece, I am a foul way out.
Sir Toby
Send for money, knight; if thou hast her not i' th' end, 175 call me Cut.
Sir Andrew
If I do not, never trust me; take it how you will.
Sir Toby
Come, come, I'll go burn some sack; 'tis too late to go to bed now. Come, knight; come, knight.

[Exeunt]

SCENE 4

The lapse of time needed for the maturing of the plot against Malvolio is put to good use on the stage. We are now for a while to be more subtly entertained by the shifting fortunes of Viola and the Duke, whom we find in characteristic setting, with appropriate music and discourse to soothe – or more likely stimulate – his love-sick mood. (There is the added interest that the singing now is provided by Feste.)

1. *Give me some music*. This is exactly how the play began; and we may well feel that nothing that has happened since to the Duke has had the slightest effect on him. There is something very affected about his 'loveliking'. Here, we feel, is a love-sick noble, attentive primarily to his own emotional state. It is only incidentally that Olivia has been singled out as the object of his desire – it could just as easily have been any other lady of noble birth.

3. *old and antique song*. An interesting comparison follows, between the merits of old-fashioned, 'nostalgic' music, and contemporary compositions. Orsino prefers the former, finding the modern pieces too contrived.

5. *recollected terms* suggests unnatural striving after effect.

14. *Come hither, boy*. Viola is brought into the Duke's reverie with little thought at first for her own independent existence. It is not long, however, before Orsino finds himself taking note of her as a person in her own right, whose forthrightness involves him soon in discussion with her on equal terms. His own emotional problems, till now filling all his thoughts, are pushed into the background, as his curiosity about Viola grows. At the end of the scene (line 122) he has forgotten all about Olivia; and it is only when Viola asks him, practically enough – or mischievously – ***shall I to this lady?***, that he brings himself to a not very convincing ***Ay, that's the theme***. (Almost, 'that's the general idea'.)

17. *skittish* fickle. ***motions*** emotions.

18. *Save in the constant image* except in the unchanging picture I have in my mind.

20–1. We are to think of Viola as speaking these lines with deep feeling. She has good reason now to be as moved as Orsino by evocative music.

ACT 2 SCENE 4

SCENE 4

The Duke's palace

[*Enter* DUKE, VIOLA, CURIO *and* OTHERS]

Duke
Give me some music. Now, good morrow, friends,
Now, good Cesario, but that piece of song
That old and antique song we heard last night,
Methought it did relieve my passion much
More than light airs and recollected terms 5
Of these most brisk and giddy-paced times
Come, but one verse.

Curio
He is not here, so please your lordship, that should sing it.

Duke
Who was it? 10

Curio
Feste, the jester, my lord; a fool that the Lady Olivia's father took much delight in. He is about the house

Duke
Seek him out, and play the tune the while

[*Exit* CURIO. *Music plays*]

Come hither, boy. If ever thou shalt love,
In the sweet pangs of it remember me; 15
For such as I am all true lovers are,
Unstaid and skittish in all motions else
Save in the constant image of the creature
That is belov'd. How dost thou like this tune?

Viola
It gives a very echo to the seat 20
Where Love is thron'd.

22. **My life upon't** 'I'll stake my life on it.'
23. **stay'd upon some favour** 'gazed for a long time at the face of someone.'

24. **by your favour** 'with your permission.' A mere convention of politeness. (We often insert the phrase 'if you please' into a simple narrative, in much the same way.) But there is a play on the two meanings of 'favour'. Orsino will have taken it to mean 'permission' – the simple convention. Viola knows this, but also has in mind Orsino's face (the other meaning of *favour* he himself has just used), on which she has gazed many times.
25. **Of your complexion** 'like you in appearance.'
26. **worth** good enough for.
27. **About your years**. Here again, note the delicate humour inherent in this false encounter. The audience knows why Viola describes the person she loves, in this way – Orsino's features are thus singled out because Orsino *is* the man! But he has no idea of this, and pursues the discussion deliberately, pointing out what would be in fact sensible advice if Viola *were* a young man with his heart set on a woman with Orsino's looks and age.
28. **still** always.
29. **so wears she to him** 'in this way she grows to him.'
30. **So sways she level** 'in this way she maintains a steady course.'
31–4. Orsino's argument seems to be that, since men are more likely to be unfaithful, they should not put undue strain on the relationship by union with not-so-young women who have lost their earlier charms.
34. **I think it well, my lord**. Another fine touch of irony. Orsino has been speaking, though not over-discreetly, against his own sex, with which Viola can heartily agree – which may well surprise Orsino.
36. **hold the bent** stand the strain (as of a bow-string).

39. Viola can regret this quite properly in her male role, but how much more feelingly when she identifies – as of course she must – with womanly frailty! The sudden deepening of emotion is brought out most effectively by the second half of the line – using virtually the same words as in the first half, but neatly rearranged.

ACT 2 SCENE 4

Duke
                    Thou dost speak masterly.
My life upon't, young though thou art, thine eye
Hath stay'd upon some favour that it loves;
Hath it not, boy?
Viola
                    A little, by your favour.
Duke
What kind of woman is't?
Viola
                    Of your complexion,   25
Duke
She is not worth thee, then. What years, i' faith?
Viola
About your years, my lord.
Duke
Too old, by heaven! Let still the woman take
An elder than herself; so wears she to him
So sways she level in her husband's heart.   30
For, boy, however we do praise ourselves,
Our fancies are more giddy and unfirm,
More longing, wavering, sooner lost and won,
Than women's are.
Viola
                    I think it well, my lord.
Duke
Then let thy love be younger than thyself,   35
Or they affection cannot hold the bent;
For women are as roses, whose fair flow'r
Being once display'd doth fall that very hour.
Viola
And so they are; alas, that they are so!
To die, even when they to perfection grow!   40

            [Re-enter CURIO *and* CLOWN*]*

43. *spinsters*. This is simply the feminine of 'spinners'.

44. *bones* bobbins made of bone, used often in spinning.
45. *silly sooth* simple truth.
46. *dallies* deals lightly. It is easy to see why Feste's song, with its theme of broken-heartedness, has made such an appeal to Orsino. He can perfectly identify – so he persuades himself – with the betrayed lover who welcomes death.

51. *cypress*. The wood of the cypress tree was used for coffins.

54. *shroud* sheet in which a corpse was wrapped before burial. *stuck all with yew* with sprigs of yew fastened on it. (The yew tree was for centuries associated with funerals, and is still often found in churchyards.)

60. *greet* weep for.

Duke
  O, fellow, come, the song we had last night.
  Mark it, Cesario; it is old and plain;
  The spinsters and the knitters in the sun,
  And the free maids that weave their thread with
    bones,
  Do use to chant it; it is silly sooth,   45
  And dallies with the innocence of love,
  Like the old age.
Clown
  Are you ready, sir?
Duke
  Ay; prithee, sing.

          [Music. FESTE'S *song]*

    Come away, come away, death;   50
  And in sad cypress let me be laid;
    Fly away, fly away, breath,
  I am slain by a fair cruel maid.
  My shroud of white, stuck all with yew,
      O, prepare it!   55
  My part of death no one so true
      Did share it.
    Not a flower, not a flower sweet,
  On my black coffin let there be strown;
    Not a friend, not a friend greet   60
  My poor corpse where my bones shall be thrown;
  A thousand thousand sighs to save,
      Lay me, O, where
  Sad true lover never find my grave,
      To weep there!   65

Duke
  There's for thy pains.
Clown
  No pains, sir; I take pleasure in singing, sir.
Duke
  I'll pay thy pleasure, then.

69–70. *pleasure will be paid one time or another*. This time, Feste means it in the sense, rather regretfully, that we have to pay for our pleasure, sooner or later – that a life of self-indulgence eventually brings its own discomfiture.

71. *Give me now leave* (permission) ***to leave you*** a courteous form of dismissal – the Duke is telling Feste to go.

73. *changeable taffeta*. Taffeta is a thin silk which changes colour when looked at from another angle; as it is *changeable*, it suits the moody Orsino. This is the point also of *opal* (line 74), a precious stone that seems to have shades of all the other jewels in itself. Feste sees Orsino as someone who is so 'beside himself' with love-sickness that all manner of thoughts and moods light upon his mind, and as quickly leave. His use, then, of *constancy* (line 74) is in gentle irony – he means just the opposite.

77. *makes a good voyage of nothing*. Such a person's imagination is so active that the smallest thing is given a disproportionate significance. (The clown is the only one who would be allowed to speak so frankly to the Duke.)

80. *sovereign cruelty*. Olivia is thus described because her 'cruelty' is 'sovereign' (all-powerful) – she will allow nothing to soften her attitude towards Orsino.

80–5. Orsino here insists that he loves her for herself, and not for any of her material possessions.

82. *dirty* contemptible.

83. 'Those possessions that happen to be hers through no virtue of her own.'

84. *giddily* inconstantly (in this case, with complete indifference to their material value). ***as Fortune*.** Because Fortune is equally indifferent in the way she distributes her blessings.

86. *pranks* dresses up. The 'miracle' that Orsino is attracted by is Olivia's real self.

87. This is Viola's way of gradually bringing Orsino to face the truth she knows he will sooner or later have to accept.

88. *I cannot be so answer'd* 'I refuse to accept this explanation.'

88–92. Viola suggests that the Duke should picture a parallel situation, in which he might have to tell someone who was desperately in love with him, but for whom he felt no affection, that he couldn't love her. When Viola speaks of ***some lady, as perhaps there is***, she is, as we know, meaning herself. She is, in this oblique way, going as far as she dares, in declaring her love for the Duke. Even this slight emotional release is better for her than nothing.

Clown
   Truly, sir, and pleasure will be paid one time or
   another.   70
Duke
   Give me now leave to leave thee.
Clown
   Now the melancholy god protect thee; and the tailor
   make thy doublet of changeable taffeta, for thy mind
   is a very opal. I would have men of such constancy
   put to sea, that their business might be everything,   75
   and their intent everywhere: for that's it that always
   makes a good voyage of nothing. Farewell.
                    [Exit CLOWN]
Duke
   Let all the rest give place.
            [Exeunt CURIO and ATTENDANTS]
                         Once more, Cesario,
   Get thee to yond same sovereign cruelty.   80
   Tell her my love, more noble than the world,
   Prizes not quantity of dirty lands;
   The parts that fortune hath bestow'd upon her,
   Tell her I hold as giddily as Fortune;
   But 'tis that miracle and queen of gems   85
   That Nature pranks her in attracts my soul.
Viola
   But if she cannot love you, sir?
Duke
   I cannot be so answer'd.
Viola
                     Sooth, but you must.
   Say that some lady, as perhaps there is,
   Hath for your love as great a pang of heart   90
   As you have for Olivia. You cannot love her;
   You tell her so. Must she not then be answer'd?

93–103. But Viola's comparison is unacceptable, for Orsino insists that women love far less intensely than men. (He is inconsistent: he said men were fickle in lines 32–4; now it is women who have no stability). It is ironic that he says this as one who is completely confident that his hearer will of necessity share his masculine viewpoint. Viola cannot ignore this attack upon her own sex. But see how neatly she refutes him, without in any way disclosing her identity! (lines 103–9).

94. *bide* endure.

98. *liver* It was popularly believed that the liver was the seat of love. Orsino, seeking to discredit the love felt by women, says that it doesn't originate in the liver (where true love should) but in the *palate*, simply as a 'taste'.

99. *surfeit* and *cloyment* are synonymous, both meaning 'excess'. *revolt* revulsion of appetite.

100–101. Compare what Orsino says in Act 1, Scene 1, lines 10–11.

101. *compare* comparison. (We sometimes use the phrase 'beyond compare'.)

104. Notice how quick Orsino is here. What might he be thinking Viola is about to say?

105. All that Viola says now has double meaning – Orsino takes the one superficial sense of her description of her supposed sister's love; but we, the audience, know she is describing her own affections. In lines 107–9 the second meaning almost breaks through to the surface. We may wonder why Orsino doesn't detect the heightened emotion which must surely be apparent in Viola as she says this.

107–9. 'My father had a daughter who loved a man in the same way that I might love you, if I were a woman.'

109. *what's her history?* 'What happened to her?'

110. *A blank* nothing.

111. *concealment* the keeping to herself of her true feelings.

112. *damask* rose-coloured. The comparison between the disfiguring effect of wrongly concealed emotion, and the grub eating away the rose-bud, from inside, is very effective, *pin'd in thought* grieved secretly.

113. *green and yellow* sickly (as the colours suggest).

114. *Patience on a monument.* It is not known whether any particular statue of Patience is here recollected.

115. *Smiling at grief* enduring it cheerfully.

117. *Our shows are more than will* 'We lack the determination to put our good intentions into effect.' *still* always.

ACT 2 SCENE 4

Duke
    There is no woman's sides
    Can bide the beating of so strong a passion
    As love doth give my heart; no woman's heart   95
    So big to hold so much; they lack retention.
    Alas, their love may be call'd appetite—
    No motion of the liver, but the palate—
    That suffer surfeit, cloyment, and revolt;
    But mine is all as hungry as the sea,   100
    And can digest as much. Make no compare
    Between that love a woman can bear me
    And that I owe Olivia.
Viola
              Ay, but I know—
Duke
    What dost thou know?
Viola
    Too well what love women to men may owe.   105
    In faith, they are as true of heart as we.
    My father had a daughter lov'd a man,
    As it might be perhaps, were I a woman,
    I should your lordship.
Duke
              And what's her history?
Viola
    A blank, my lord. She never told her love,   110
    But let concealment, like a worm i' th' bud,
    Feed on her damask cheek. She pin'd in thought;
    And with a green and yellow melancholy
    She sat like Patience on a monument,
    Smiling at grief. Was not this love indeed?   115
    We men may say more, swear more, but indeed
    Our shows are more than will; for still we prove
    Much in our vows, but little in our love.

119. This is perhaps the first point at which we feel that the Duke is becoming sufficiently forgetful of himself to feel genuine concern for the imaginary sister's fate.

120. *I am all the daughters*. Viola knows this to be true, and can affirm it without betraying her secret.

121. *And all the brothers, too*. She still thinks that Sebastian is probably dead *and yet I know not* But she is not certain; she retains some hope.

125. *can give no place* will not surrender; *denay* denial, refusal.

ACT 2 SCENE 4

Duke
  But died thy sister of her love, my boy?
Viola
  I am all the daughters of my father's house,   120
  And all the brothers too – and yet I know not.
  Sir, shall I to this lady?
Duke
                        Ay, that's the theme.
  To her in haste. Give her this jewel; say.
  My love can give no place, bide no denay.   125
              [Exeunt.]

SCENE 5

This scene provides what many people regard as the funniest episode in the play. It is probably the most ingenious. The plot to humiliate Malvolio has not yet matured – this happens later when he has outraged his mistress with his new mood of confidence, and is put in custody for it – but it is here at its most entertaining stage. For, thinking himself to be alone, Malvolio displays the whole range of his conceitedness. (Maria's carefully-worded letter sees to it that no single trait is overlooked.) Every soliloquy gives to the audience this 'unfair advantage' – of seeing without being seen, and of prying unobserved into secret thoughts. But this particular one we share with some of the players – hidden viewers of the results of their plot – and our own amusement is increased by theirs. The group of Malvolio-baiters is joined by Fabian, another of Olivia's household, who from now on associates himself with them.

2. *scruple* a very small part.

4. *niggardly* mean.

5. *sheep-biter* a term of abuse, literally a dog that worries sheep, and metaphorically, perhaps, a man who chases women. ***notable*** public.

6. Fabian has the same cause, basically, as the others, for wanting to 'get his own back' on Malvolio. He has been faulted by him for indulging in disreputable pastimes. (Bear-baiting, like theatre-going, was frowned upon by the Puritan element in England.)

11. *little villain*. We have already been reminded of Maria's small stature, some of the jokes depending upon the fact (e.g., Act 1, Scene 5, line 195).

metal precious metal, gold.

15. *practising behaviour to his own shadow this half hour*. It is not the letter that turns Malvolio into such a conceited ass – he is this already. The letter simply accentuates the characteristic. So Maria's observation serves as one more reminder that his vanity is unrelieved and inexcusable; the blame cannot be laid at anyone else's door.

17. *a contemplative idiot*. His foolishness will become the more apparent, as the letter prompts him to indulge his imagination further and further. ***Close*** 'Be still.' (We often describe a person as 'close' when he shows a tendency to 'keep himself to himself', and not talk freely.)

19–20. *trout that must be caught with tickling* This is an actual method of catching fish in shallow water. What Maria means is that Malvolio's humiliation will be best effected by subtle means.

ACT 2 SCENE 5

SCENE 5

Olivia's garden

[Enter SIR TOBY, SIR ANDREW, and FABIAN]

Sir Toby
Come thy ways, Signior Fabian.
Fabian
Nay, I'll come; if I lose a scruple of this sport let me
be boil'd to death with melancholy.
Sir Toby
Wouldst thou not be glad to have the niggardly rascally
sheep-biter come by some notable shame?   5
Fabian
I would exult, man; you know he brought me out o'
favour with my lady about a bear-baiting here.
Sir Toby
To anger him we'll have the bear again; and we will
fool him black and blue – shall we not, Sir Andrew?
Sir Andrew
And we do not, it is pity of our lives.   10

[Enter MARIA]

Sir Toby
Here comes the little villain. How now, my metal of
India!
Maria
Get ye all three into the box-tree. Malvolio's coming
down this walk. He has been yonder i' the sun
practising behaviour to his own shadow this half hour.   15
Observe him, for the love of mockery, for I know this
letter will make a contemplative idiot of him. Close,
in the name of jesting! *[As the men hide she drops a
letter]* Lie thou there; for here comes the trout that
must be caught with tickling.   20

[*Exit. Enter* MALVOLIO]

21. *'Tis but fortune; all is fortune* Malvolio seems to be ascribing his growing success with Olivia (so he regards it) to pure chance, where we might have expected him to accept it as a quite natural result of his own charm. How should we interpret his comment – how will he say it? Malvolio is already highly optimistic about his chances with Olivia. Even before he sees the letter, he discloses enough of his conceitedness to warrant a pretty severe reprimand from somebody. Nowhere else in the play are his thoughts and motives laid quite so bare as in this scene. There is a degree of concentration here upon his innate character – his 'humour' – that occurs with no one else. Thus when Viola, for example, speaks her thoughts aloud in soliloquy, or half-disguises them before Olivia or the Duke, the focus is not upon her character as something already formulated, but upon her reactions to the present situation. We are never required to assume anything about her – only to take in what she is at that moment experiencing. She will no doubt emerge as an entirely credible person at the end. But the picture is initially blank; and all that there is, virtually, of Viola, has come into being during the course of the play. But with Malvolio, the process is just the opposite. His character is never in question, having been completely defined from the start. The interest this time is what happens to such a character when it meets determined opposition. It is the sheer spectacle of collision that provides the entertainment. This sort of thing takes up only part of Shakespeare's play, whereas it forms the chief theme in that other type of comedy, called 'Comedy of Humours', for which Ben Jonson is famous.
22. *affect* feel affection for.
24. *complexion* appearance (see Scene 4, line 25); *uses* treats.
27. *overweening* thinking too highly of himself.
28. *O, peace!* Throughout the ensuing dialogue, one or other of the hidden observers has the job of keeping the others quiet, in case Malvolio should notice them, and the whole plot be ruined. This is simply a dramatic convention. They will in fact be speaking loud enough all the time for Malvolio to have heard every word. But to preserve some semblance of realism or to make the ridiculous situation even funnier, there are these frequent requests for silence. *Contemplation* see note on line 17. *turkey-cock* The male turkey, like most male birds, makes a great and colourful display with its feathers, to attract the hen, or frighten off rival males.
29. *jets* struts pompously. *advanc'd* raised. Malvolio's self-confidence grows noticeably, the more he dwells upon what seems to him clear evidence of Olivia's favour. The turkey-cock description would, then, come readily to mind.

Malvolio
  'Tis but fortune; all is fortune. Maria once told me she did affect me; and I have heard herself come thus near, that, should she fancy, it should be one of my complexion. Besides, she uses me with a more exalted respect than any one else that follows her. What should I think on't? 25
Sir Toby
  Here's an overweening rogue!
Fabian
  O, peace! Contemplation makes a rare turkey-cock of him; how he jets under his advanc'd plumes!

30. 'Slight 'By God's light.'

32. Count Malvolio his title, as Olivia's husband. Even Malvolio needs some slight reassurance before he can hold out this hope! So he recalls an instance of a notable lady who married a member of her household staff. (There is no clear evidence of any actual lady of this name, but there was a story in existence, on which Webster's *Duchess of Malfi* was based, of a noble lady who married her steward.)

38. Jezebel wife of Ahab, an Israelite King. She has become proverbial for shamelessness – in women, however, not men.
39. he's deeply in 'he has succeeded in deceiving himself completely.'
40. blows him inflates him. (We still sometimes describe a self-opinionated person as 'puffed-up'.)

42. state Malvolio is probably about to say 'state-chair' (but the word *state* by itself could mean 'throne').
43. stone-bow a cross-bow using stones as missiles.

44. branch'd decorated with a branch-like pattern.
45. day-bed sofa.

49. humour disposition. **state** power. The whole phrase **humour of state** means 'whim of a man of authority'.
49–50. after a demure travel of regard 'after gazing gravely round.'
52. kinsman. If he married Olivia, he would become Sir Toby's relative. But Sir Toby clearly doesn't relish the idea, nor the omission of 'Sir'.

Sir Andrew
  'Slight, I could so beat the rogue— 30
Sir Toby
  Peace, I say.
Malvolio
  To be Count Malvolio!
Sir Toby
  Ah, rogue!
Sir Andrew
  Pistol him, pistol him.
Sir Toby
  Peace, peace! 35
Malvolio
  There is example for't: the Lady of the Strachy married the yeoman of the wardrobe.
Sir Andrew
  Fie on him, Jezebel!
Fabian
  O, peace! Now he's deeply in; look how imagination blows him. 40
Malvolio
  Having been three months married to her, sitting in my state—
Sir Toby
  O, for a stone-bow to hit him in the eye!
Malvolio
  Calling my officers about me, in my branch'd velvet gown, having come from a day-bed – where I have left 45 Olivia sleeping—
Sir Toby
  Fire and brimstone!
Fabian
  O, peace, peace!
Malvolio
  And then to have the humour of state; and after a demure travel of regard, telling them I know my 50 place as I would they should do theirs, to ask for my kinsman Toby—

53. Bolts and shackles! Both mean 'fetters', used to chain up offenders; together they make an effective exclamation.
55. Seven of my people Malvolio's new dignity would call for no fewer than seven servants to carry out his wishes.

57. play with my – some rich jewel Malvolio is about to say 'chain of office', as his hand lights upon it, but then recalls that, in his new exalted state, it will no longer be there, to remind him of his subordinate status, but will be replaced by 'some rich jewel'.
58. curtsies. The word is the same as 'courtesy' and means 'to show proper respect by bowing'. It applied to either sex, and not just to women, as it does today.
60. cars carts, or other horse-drawn vehicles. The sense is that their silence will be as painful as if it was having to be dragged forcibly out, yet they must maintain it. (We have the expression, 'wild horses won't drag it out of him', to indicate someone's determination not to divulge information – though there the pressure is to produce words, whereas in Fabian's image, the pressure is for silence.)
62. extend my hand i.e., to be kissed (a regal gesture of condescension).
62–3. familiar smile. If Malvolio is miming all this – and he almost certainly has to – then how do we picture this 'familiar smile'?
63. austere regard of control 'stern look of authority.'
66. give me this prerogative of speech 'give me leave to address you in this way.' (How significant, that Sir Toby's drunkenness is the first thing to be reproved!)

69. scab contemptible fellow.

ACT 2 SCENE 5

Sir Toby
　Bolts and shackles!
Fabian
　O, peace, peace, peace! Now, now.
Malvolio
　Seven of my people, with an obedient start, make out   55
　for him. I frown the while, and perchance wind up
　my watch, or play with my – some rich jewel. Toby
　approaches; curtsies there to me—
Sir Toby
　Shall this fellow live?
Fabian
　Though our silence be drawn from us with cars, yet   60
　peace.
Malvolio
　I extend my hand to him thus, quenching my familiar
　smile with an austere regard of control—
Sir Toby
　And does not Toby take you a blow o' the lips then?
Malvolio
　Saying 'Cousin Toby, my fortunes having cast me on   65
　your niece give me this prerogative of speech'—
Sir Toby
　What, what?
Malvolio
　'You must amend your drunkenness'—
Sir Toby
　Out, scab!
Fabian
　Nay, patience, or we break the sinews of our plot.   70
Malvolio
　'Besides, you waste the treasure of your time with a
　foolish knight'—
Sir Andrew
　That's me, I warrant you.
Malvolio
　'One Sir Andrew.'

75. *many do call me fool* How different Sir Andrew's reaction is from Sir Toby's, to Malvolio's insults! He has been just as outspoken as the others against Malvolio's presumptuousness; and he has forgotten about himself in his enthusiasm. But the moment Malvolio slights him personally, all the fight is knocked out of him. Instead of countering insult with insult, as Sir Toby has done, he becomes once again his old, diffident self, and meekly accepts Malvolio's low opinion of him.

76. 'What's this business?'

77. *woodcock* a game-bird that is supposed to be stupid; ***gin*** a bird snare.

78–9. *the spirit of humours . . . to him!* Sir Toby fondly hopes that Malvolio will be moved to read the letter aloud – so that they may miss none of the fun. ***Intimate*** is a verb expressing a wish: 'may ***the spirit of humours*** (his inclination) suggest to him that he read it aloud.'

82. *in contempt of question* beyond question. ***hand*** handwriting The careful wording of the letter is so devised as to seem exactly the kind of message Olivia would compose, if she wished to tell him of her love, but at the same time preserve just that degree of anonymity that modesty and security might demand. She would not be expected, in such a rare situation, to commit openly to writing, with her own plain signature, such strong feelings for her steward – not in the opening stages, anyway, when she would need first to ascertain his feelings in the matter. Lovers have commonly used a kind of code in the early stages of contact; and so, to Malvolio now, it seems the most likely thing in the world that Olivia would choose to compose her first love-letter to him in such riddles.

84. *this* that is, the letter itself.

85. *By your leave, wax.* In exaggerated politeness – or quite genuine homage – Malvolio asks the wax seal on the letter for permission to open it. ***Soft!*** Normally this is a request for silence. Here, it indicates more of the hushed mood of intense concentration Malvolio now adopts – he is saying it to himself.

85–6. *the impressure her Lucrece* the impression (on the wax) is of her seal (or brooch) with an engraving of Lucretia upon it. (Lucretia was the wife of one of the Tarquins of legendary Rome, who took her own life after having been raped by another Tarquin. Her modesty was legendary) ***with which she uses to seal*** with which she normally seals.

Sir Andrew
I knew 'twas I; for many do call me fool. 75
Malvolio
What employment have we here? *[Taking up the letter]*
Fabian
Now is the woodcock near the gin.
Sir Toby
O, peace! And the spirit of humours intimate reading aloud to him!
Malvolio
By my life, this is my lady's hand: these be her very 80
C's, her U's, and her T's; and thus makes she her great
P's. It is, in contempt of question, her hand.
Sir Andrew
Her C's, her U's, and her T's. Why that?
Malvolio *[Reads]*
'To the unknown belov'd, this, and my good wishes.'
Her very phrases! By your leave, wax. Soft! And the 85
impressure her Lucrece with which she uses to seal;
'tis my lady. To whom should this be?

88. *liver* thought of as the seat of love, in the human anatomy.
93–4. *The numbers alter'd*. This probably refers to the changed length of line in the next four verses of the letter.
96. *brock* a badger. Used as a term of contempt (possibly on account of its strong smell).
98–9. Having to keep silent, up to now, about her love has been as painful as the knife-wound with which Lucretia committed suicide, only in this case there has been no ensuing death to end the suffering.
100. Maria's choice of these letters from Malvolio's name gives rise to much amusement, not least because Malvolio seems slow to apply the 'code' to himself. Thus the others can laugh at him for his lack of astuteness, as well as for his vanity. (Though there is no suggestion elsewhere in the play that Malvolio is, in normal circumstances, at all lacking in intelligence.)
101. *fustian* ridiculously pompous. (Literally, fustian was a coarse kind of cloth.)
104. Malvolio's agitation is well brought out here.
105. *dress'd him* prepared for him. Maria's bogus letter is likened to an attractive-looking meal which, in fact, contains deadly poison.
106. *staniel* an inferior kind of hawk. ***checks*** a hawking term. When a hawk 'checks', it turns from pursuing the quarry it is meant to follow, and instead goes after some other bird that chances to cross its path. So here is Malvolio, simply not reacting the way he should have done, to the suggestion of his own name in the four letters. There would have been (and will in a few moments be) ample satisfaction for them, in the way they have anticipated, when he succeeds in identifying himself with the 'code'. But his apparent stupidity at first is something they have not anticipated – but find amusing enough, nevertheless. They watch fascinated, as we do, as Malvolio laboriously works his way through the puzzle.
109. *formal capacity* logical reasoning.
110. *obstruction* difficulty.
110. *the end* the end of the verses.
111–12. *If I could make that resemble something in me*. It is hard perhaps here, not to feel a momentary pity for Malvolio. He would dearly love to believe that Olivia does care for him, and the entire plot leads him on, subtly but inevitably, to feel convinced that she does. Yet all the while we know how desperately mistaken he is, and how ludicrous he will be made to appear in the end. We can enjoy the situation only if we regard him more as the stereotyped villain of melodrama or pantomime, for whom no sort of compassion is seriously expected.

Fabian
  This wins him, liver and all.
Malvolio [Reads]
    'Jove knows I love,
      But who?
    Lips, do not move;
    No man must know.'
  'No man must know.' What follows? The numbers
  alter'd! 'No man must know.' If this should be thee,
  Malvolio?
Sir Toby
  Marry, hang thee, brock!
Malvolio [Reads]
    'I may command where I adore;
      But silence, like a Lucrece knife,
    With bloodless stroke my heart doth gore;
      M. O. A. I. doth sway my life.'
Fabian
  A fustian riddle!
Sir Toby
  Excellent wench, say I.
Malvolio
  'M. O. A. I. doth sway my life.'
  Nay, but first let me see, let me see, let me see.
Fabian
  What dish o' poison has she dress'd him!
Sir Toby
  And with what wing the staniel checks at it!
Malvolio
  'I may command where I adore.' Why, she may
  command me: I serve her; she is my lady. Why, this
  is evident to any formal capacity; there is no
  obstruction in this. And the end – what should that
  alphabetical position portend? If I could make that resemble
  something in me. Softly! M. O. A. I.—

113. O, ay. We may imagine Sir Toby emphasising this, as a pun on the letters 'O' and 'I' that Malvolio has just repeated. ***cold scent.*** The metaphor is now of hounds following the scent of the creature they are trying to catch. A 'cold' scent is one that is hard to find, because time has gone by since the animal passed.

114. *Sowter* cobbler, or clumsy workman – but here, simply the name of a hound. Fabian means that Malvolio will 'give tongue', or ***cry upon*** the false scent when he finds it – which, being a not very good hound, he will – even though it is as strong, and therefore as utterly distinctive, as a fox's scent. (It is to be assumed that this imagined hound is supposed to be hunting something else!)

118. *faults* wrong trails. (Though, in fact, of course, Malvolio is beginning to get on to the right trail.)

119. *consonancy* agreement; ***the sequel*** the end bit (of the 'code').

120. *suffers under probation* 'doesn't fit in when put to the test.'

122. Fabian's pun – if it is such – on 'O' is not obvious (like Sir Toby's in the next line). In the Book of Revelation in the Bible, God is described as 'Alpha and Omega' (the first and last letters of the Greek alphabet), because He is the 'Beginning and the End'. Perhaps Fabian simply hopes that this is going to be the end of Malvolio's riddle-solving.

125–7. Fabian is clearly punning here, however. The ***I . . . behind*** becomes the 'eye', and the ***detraction*** it would see means the loss of reputation that will shortly overtake Malvolio. Fabian probably also refers to the threatening antics going on behind Malvolio's back, or at least out of his sight.

128. *This simulation is not as the former* 'This disguise is not the same as the one used before' – that is, the actual words which seemed to describe, so unmistakably to Malvolio, Olivia's situation and his own.

129. *to crush this a little* 'to force things a bit,' meaning to change the order of the letters in the 'code'. ***bow to me*** 'fit in with my needs,' 'do what I want it to do.'

132. *revolve* consider.

132–3. *In my stars I am above thee* 'Fortune has made me superior to you.'

135. *open their hands* 'make a generous offer' ('open-handed' means 'generous').

136. *inure* accustom.

137. *like* likely.

137–8. *cast . . . slough* A snake 'casts its slough' when it gets rid of its old skin, to make way for the new skin underneath. Malvolio's ***humble slough*** is the subordinate role he has up to now filled, as her steward.

Sir Toby
  O, ay, make up that! He is now at a cold scent.
Fabian
  Sowter will cry upon't for all this, though it be as
  rank as a fox.   115
Malvolio
  M – Malvolio; M – why, that begins my name.
Fabian
  Did not I say he would work it out? The cur is
  excellent at faults.
Malvolio
  M – But then there is no consonancy in the sequel;
  that suffers under probation: A should follow, but O   120
  does.
Fabian
  And O shall end, I hope.
Sir Toby
  Ay, or I'll cudgel him, and make him cry 'O!'
Malvolio
  And then I comes behind.
Fabian
  Ay, an you had any eye behind you, you might see   125
  more detraction at your heels than fortunes before
  you.
Malvolio
  M. O. A. I. This simulation is not as the former; and
  yet, to crush this a little, it would bow to me, for every
  one of these letters are in my name. Soft! here follows 130
  prose.
  [*Reads*] 'If this fall into thy hand, revolve. In my stars I
  am above thee; but be not afraid of greatness. Some
  are born great, some achieve greatness, and some have
  greatness thrust upon 'em. Thy Fates open their hands;135
  let thy blood and spirit embrace them; and, to inure
  thyself to what thou art like to be, cast thy humble

138. Be opposite 'be unfriendly.'
138. kinsman meaning, of course, Sir Toby; **tang** clang (sound like a bell).
140. put thyself into the trick of singularity 'start behaving in an eccentric way.'
141–2. Remember who commended . . . cross-garter'd From Malvolio's comment, a little later, on this part of the letter, it is clear that there was an occasion when his mistress had apparently spoken favourably about this leg-wear. But Maria makes it clear, at the end of the scene, that any such remark by Olivia could have been no more than a polite gesture to cover up her very strong dislike of this mode of dress, which was probably old-fashioned at that time.
143–4. thou art made 'your success is assured'
147. alter services with thee 'Olivia' would gladly change places with him, and offer willing service to him, because she loves him so helplessly.
Fortunate-Unhappy A love-sick person is both elated and despairing, almost in the same moment.
148. champain flat, open country; **discovers** reveals.
150. baffle publicly disgrace; **wash off gross acquaintance** 'break off acquaintance with unworthy people'
151. point-devise correct in every detail.
152. jade deceive.
153. excites to this 'drives me to this conclusion.
156–7. with a kind of injunction . . . of her liking 'almost commands me to adopt this way of dress that she so much admires.'
158. strange aloof; **stout** haughty.
159–60. even with the swiftness of putting on 'and I'll be no longer than it takes just to put them on.'
163. let it appear in thy smiling. Believing that Olivia is thus inviting him to show his feelings for her by smiling continuously, Malvolio is tricked into what will be perhaps his most ludicrous exhibition.
165. still all the time.

169. Sophy Shah of Persia.

slough and appear fresh. Be opposite with a kinsman,
surly with servants; let thy tongue tang arguments of
state; put thyself into the trick of singularity. She thus   140
advises thee that sighs for thee. Remember who
commended thy yellow stockings, and wish'd to see
thee ever cross-garter'd. I say, remember. Go to, thou
art made, if thou desir'st to be so; if not, let me see
thee a steward still, the fellow of servants, and not   145
worthy to touch Fortune's fingers. Farewell. She that
would alter services with thee,
                    THE FORTUNATE-UNHAPPY.'
Daylight and champain discovers not more. This is
open. I will be proud, I will read politic authors, I will
baffle Sir Toby, I will wash off gross acquaintance, I   150
will be point-devise the very man. I do not now fool
myself to let imagination jade me; for every reason
excites to this, that my lady loves me. She did
commend my yellow stockings of late, she did praise
my leg being cross-garter'd; and in this she manifests   155
herself to my love, and with a kind of injunction
drives me to these habits of her liking. I thank my
stars I am happy. I will be strange, stout, in yellow
stockings, and cross-garter'd, even with the swiftness
of putting on. Jove and my stars be praised! Here is   160
yet a postscript.
[Reads] 'Thou canst not choose but know who I am. If
thou entertain'st my love, let it appear in thy smiling;
thy smiles become thee well. Therefore in my presence
still smile, dear my sweet, I prithee.'   165
Jove, I thank thee. I will smile; I will do everything
that thou wilt have me.
                        [Exit]

Fabian
I will not give my part of this sport for a pension of
thousands to be paid from the Sophy.
Sir Toby
I could marry this wench for this device.   170

171. *So could I too* Sir Andrew has been so overawed by the brilliance of Maria's trick, that he is reduced to a tame kind of repetition of each of Sir Toby's remarks – he does it four more times before the end of this scene. This is a characteristic we have noticed before, but it has never been quite so pronounced. Any independent Sir Andrew there may have been has now been frightened out of sight, and we are simply left with feeble echoes of Sir Toby.

175. *gull-catcher* This was a recognised term for a cheat or someone who preyed on fools. (In this instance, to cheat Malvolio is regarded by Fabian as something commendable.)

176. *set thy foot o' my neck* The victor in a combat would, by tradition, place his foot on the neck of his vanquished opponent, as a sign of his supremacy. By asking Maria to do this to himself, Sir Toby is signifying that her success with the letter has been outstanding.

178. *tray-trip* a game with dice, in which the winner had to throw a 'three' (*tray*). Sir Toby means that he would willingly wager his ***freedom*** in such a game, and very cheerfully lose it, to become Maria's bond-slave, so impressed is he by her cleverness.

181–2. Sir Toby has summed it up well – this is the very essence of the 'torture' Maria has devised; ***dream*** and ***image*** in fact both mean the same thing, namely, the false notion (of Olivia's love for him) that Maria has so successfully implanted in Malvolio's mind. (This notion does keep him going for a long time, in the face of pretty solid evidence to the contrary, making the moment of disenchantment the more painful when it comes.)

183. *Nay, but say true* 'No, but honestly now . . .'

184. *aqua-vitae* alcoholic stimulant; spirits. This probably refers to a reputation midwives had for functioning efficiently only when supplied with intoxicants.

187–8. *abhors . . . detests* See note on line 142.

190. *melancholy* Not the original mood of grief for her brother, but her recent love-sickness for Viola.

191. *notable contempt* a laughing-stock.

193. *Tartar* hell, the right place for a devil!

ACT 2 SCENE 5

Sir Andrew
  So could I too.
Sir Toby
  And ask no other dowry with her but such another jest.

  [Enter MARIA]

Sir Andrew
  Nor I neither.
Fabian
  Here comes my noble gull-catcher. 175
Sir Toby
  Wilt thou set thy foot o' my neck?
Sir Andrew
  Or o' mine either?
Sir Toby
  Shall I play my freedom at tray-trip, and become thy bond-slave?
Sir Andrew
  I' faith, or I either? 180
Sir Toby
  Why, thou hast put him in such a dream that when the image of it leaves him he must run mad.
Maria
  Nay, but say true; does it work upon him?
Sir Toby
  Like aqua-vitae with a midwife.
Maria
  If you will then see the fruits of the sport, mark his 185 first approach before my lady. He will come to her in yellow stockings, and 'tis a colour she abhors, and cross-garter'd, a fashion she detests; and he will smile upon her, which will now be so unsuitable to her disposition, being addicted to a melancholy as she is, 190 that it cannot but turn him into a notable contempt. If you will see it, follow me.
Sir Toby
  To the gates of Tartar, thou most excellent devil of wit!
Sir Andrew
  I'll make one too.

  [Exeunt]

TWELFTH NIGHT

ACT 3 SCENE 1

This scene shows us, for the first time, how Viola handles Feste, Sir Toby and Sir Andrew. She 'holds her own' admirably, and answers them in their own language – resiliently enough but not unkindly. Then, with Olivia, she has a much more serious part to play. Olivia's love for her, at first hinted, then almost defiantly affirmed, presents her with perhaps the greatest challenge yet, to her self-possession. Fortunately she is primed for this, having already diagnosed Olivia's feelings accurately (Act 2, Scene 2). More than anyone else in the play, Viola seems unsubdued by her circumstances, acutely distressing though they are. She is able to remain detached sufficiently to greet each new face and situation freshly and with genuine interest.

1. ***Save thee*** 'God save thee.' Viola's greeting, and her appreciation of his music, are warm and sincere.
2. ***tabor*** a small drum, often used by professional jesters.
3. A simple enough pun on the two meanings of '***live by***' – 'to make a living out of', and 'to live near to'.
11. ***To see this age*** Feste professes admiration – but does he mean it for 'the present day' (and the wonderful things that are happening), or for the 'youthfulness' of Viola, whose wit Feste pretends, or really believes, to be a challenge to his own? This kind of ironical praise, by the professional for the amateur, is a familar comic device – though the irony is not always as gentle as on this occasion.
11–12. ***A sentence is . . . a good wit*** A cheveril glove is one made of kid-leather which can easily be turned inside out. Feste means that a witty person can easily find a double meaning in the simplest of sentences.
14. Viola enjoys this 'sharpening of wits' with Feste. ***dally*** 'trifle,' and also 'to play amorously'. ***nicely*** with close attention to the finer points of meaning. (This is the proper meaning of the word 'nice' – much more than its modern use, indicating vague approval.)
15. ***wanton*** 'going beyond the bounds of convention', and also 'lascivious'. Viola had pointed out cleverly that, if you play with words, you'll land yourself in dubious meanings
19–20. ***words are . . . disgrac'd them***. Feste pretends to deplore the corrupting effect which the writing down of a word (as in a legal agreement) has upon its meaning. There is a pun on the word 'bond' – a person is disgraced by imprisonment, and probably remains lawless at heart ever after; and words, having been 'disciplined' by formal writing, never again recover their intrinsic liveliness – which was their best guarantee of integrity.

ACT 3

SCENE 1

Olivia's garden

[Enter VIOLA, *and* CLOWN *with a tabor]*

Viola
Save thee, friend, and thy music!
Dost thou live by thy tabor?
Clown
No, sir, I live by the church.
Viola
Art thou a churchman?
Clown
No such matter, sir: I do live by the church; for I do 5
live at my house, and my house doth stand by the
church.
Viola
So thou mayst say the king lies by a beggar, if a beggar
dwell near him; or the church stands by thy tabor, if
thy tabor stand by the church. 10
Clown
You have said, sir. To see this age! A sentence is but a
chev'ril glove to a good wit. How quickly the wrong
side may be turn'd outward!
Viola
Nay, that's certain; they that dally nicely with words
may quickly make them wanton. 15
Clown
I would, therefore, my sister had had no name, sir.
Viola
Why, man?
Clown
Why, sir, her name's a word; and to dally with that
word might make my sister wanton. But indeed words
are very rascals since bonds disgrac'd them. 20
Viola
Thy reason, man?

22–4. Another quibble – Feste protesting that he cannot explain his reason, since he would have to use discredited words. He then uses *reason* in a more basic sense, where *false* words would be even further out of place.

32–6. Another play on the two meanings of *fool* – 'professional jester' and 'foolish person'.

34. *pilchers* another spelling, then, of 'pilchards' – fish not unlike a small herring.

38. *orb* world.

39–41. Feste is suggesting, not over-politely, that there is as much scope for his work with Orsino as with his own mistress.

41. *your wisdom*. A playful irony at Viola's expense, for having matched her wits against his. (See note on line 11.)

42. *an thou pass upon me* 'if you are getting the better of me.'

43. *expenses* pay (for having entertained her with his wit).

44. *commodity* consignment. Feste may quite seriously think that Viola ought to have a beard and look more manly; for her actual manner, towards himself and everyone else, is much too self-assertive and poised for any young man who looks as smooth-faced and immature physically as she does. The fact that the sexes mature physically and psychologically at different ages, and how this expresses itself, is made great use of in the play, and provides much of its subtler humour.

46–8. Viola's reply has a double meaning: for Feste, she simply endorses his wish, but for herself, she is expressing her longing for the bearded Orsino.

Clown
Troth, sir, I can yield you none without words, and words are grown so false I am loath to prove reason with them.

Viola
I warrant thou art a merry fellow and car'st for nothing. 25

Clown
Not so, sir; I do care for something; but in my conscience, sir, I do not care for you. If that be to care for nothing, sir, I would it would make you invisible. 30

Viola
Art not thou the Lady Olivia's fool?

Clown
No, indeed, sir; the Lady Olivia has no folly; she will keep no fool, sir, till she be married; and fools are as like husbands as pilchers are to herrings – the husband's the bigger. I am indeed not her fool, but her corrupter 35 of words.

Viola
I saw thee late at the Count Orsino's.

Clown
Foolery, sir, does walk about the orb like the sun – it shines everywhere. I would be sorry, sir, but the fool should be as oft with your master as with my mistress: 40 I think I saw your wisdom there.

Viola
Nay, an thou pass upon me, I'll no more with thee. Hold, there's expenses for thee. *[Giving a coin]*

Clown
Now Jove, in his next commodity of hair, send thee a beard! 45

Viola
By my troth, I'll tell thee, I am almost sick for one; *[Aside]* though I would not have it grow on my chin. – Is thy lady within?

49. Before Feste will answer Viola's question, he holds out his hand for another coin – with the saucy excuse that two coins (he already has the one she has just given him) will be able to breed, and so make more money.

51–2. Pandarus . . . Cressida . . . Troilus These are characters from the ancient legend of the Trojan War. Pandarus has been developed in literature as a 'Go-between', who brought Troilus and Cressida together and assisted their love. (He has given his name to the word 'pander', which means to encourage a low desire.) Superficially, Feste calls the coin in his hand, **Troilus**, and the one he hopes to add to it, **Cressida**. But he may well also be thinking of Viola as **this Troilus**, and wondering what sort of a **Cressida** he could be introducing to her.

53. 'tis well begg'd Feste's 'begging' has been effective.

54. The matter the thing he has begged for.

55. Cressida was a beggar In one version of the legend Cressida became a leper and begged from door to door.

57. welkin usually means 'sky'; here something like 'world'. Perhaps Feste is humorously suggesting that Viola is 'above and beyond' him.

59–67. Viola, now alone, gives us a fairly general observation on professional jesting, which she can do after such a first-hand experience. She speaks in blank verse, appropriately, for her comment is meant to stand out from the haphazard exchanges that precede and follow it. (See note, Act 1, Scene 5, lines 32–3.)

59. This line sums up the whole case, which clearly sides with the clown, and appreciates the insight and shrewdness he must possess.

60. craves demands.

62. time appropriate moment, occasion.

63. haggard a wild female hawk caught when adult and therefore difficult to train properly to concentrate on its quarry; it **check** (s), or turns aside, to follow every **feather** (or bird) that comes into its view. The idea is that a clown should be quick enough to change his tactics from moment to moment. He must not decide beforehand on the person or subject to mock.

66. 'His jesting, if it is introduced tactfully, and with real understanding of his audience, is most valuable and acceptable.'

67. folly-fall'n fallen into folly. (Here meaning foolishness in its general sense, and not as in the previous line.) Note the rhyme in the last two lines, to mark the ending of the passage.

70. Sir Andrew's greeting is the same as Sir Toby's but in French. It might surprise us that he has now mastered enough of the language to conduct at least this bit of conversation, in view of his earlier confession of ignorance (Act 1, Scene 3, line 85). But it seems that he has been busy with phrase-book and pencil since then, picking up whatever scraps of sophistication he can, in English or French. (See lines 85 and 88.)

ACT 3 SCENE 1

Clown
  Would not a pair of these have bred, sir?
Viola
  Yes, being kept together and put to use. 50
Clown
  I would play Lord Pandarus of Phrygia, sir, to bring a
  Cressida to this Troilus.
Viola
  I understand you, sir; 'tis well begg'd. *[Giving another
  coin]*
Clown
  The matter, I hope, is not great, sir, begging but a
  beggar: Cressida was a beggar. My lady is within, sir. I 55
  will construe to them whence you come; who you are
  and what you would are out of my welkin – I might
  say 'element' but the word is overworn.

   [Exit]

Viola
  This fellow is wise enough to play the fool;
  And to do that well craves a kind of wit. 60
  He must observe their mood on whom he jests,
  The quality of persons, and the time;
  And, like the haggard, check at every feather
  That comes before his eye. This is a practice
  As full of labour as a wise man's art; 65
  For folly that he wisely shows is fit;
  But wise men, folly-fall'n, quite taint their wit.

   [Enter SIR TOBY *and* SIR ANDREW*]*

Sir Toby
  Save you, gentleman!
Viola
  And you, sir.
Sir Andrew
  Dieu vous garde, monsieur. 70
Viola
  Et vous aussi; votre serviteur.

73. encounter the house a deliberately pompous way of saying, simply, 'go in'. (***taste your legs***, in line 77 meaning 'put them to the test', 'try them out', and so simply 'go', is in the same exaggerated style.)
74. trade business.
75. bound to on my way to. (See Act 2, Scene 1, line 39.)
75–6. list of my voyage limit of my journey (and therefore, 'destination'.) The word ***voyage*** was not restricted to a journey by sea

78. understand ... understand When Viola says this first, she means 'under-stand' or 'stand underneath', – which is, of course, what one's legs do! The second meaning she gives is the normal one, 'to comprehend'.

81. gait and entrance The first ('way of walking') answers Sir Toby's ***go***, the second answers his ***enter***.
82. prevented forestalled. (This was a common meaning of the word.)

87. pregnant receptive, ***vouchsafed*** To vouchsafe means to 'allow', usually with some idea of condescension. So here, Viola means that her message is for Olivia alone, if she will be gracious enough to listen to it.
88–9. See note on line 70, ***get 'em all three all ready*** Sir Andrew is going to learn the words so that he can use them later on as his own

93. This is pointedly formal. The last thing Viola wants is that Olivia shall imagine that she is in the slightest degree identifying herself with the Duke's enthusiasm. She is still trying, almost instinctively, to keep Olivia at arm's length; and she is virtually saying to her, 'I am speaking and acting like this solely out of duty to my master; but nothing could be further from my own personal inclinations.'

Sir Andrew
  I hope, sir, you are; and I am yours.
Sir Toby
  Will you encounter the house? My niece is desirous you should enter, if your trade be to her.
Viola
  I am bound to your niece, sir; I mean, she is the list of my voyage.   75
Sir Toby
  Taste your legs, sir; put them to motion.
Viola
  My legs do better understand me, sir, than I understand what you mean by bidding me taste my legs.
Sir Toby
  I mean, to go, sir, to enter.   80
Viola
  I will answer you with gait and entrance. But we are prevented.

  [Enter OLIVIA *and* MARIA*]*

  Most excellent accomplish'd lady, the heavens rain odours on you!
Sir Andrew
  That youth's a rare courtier – 'Rain odours' well!   85
Viola
  My matter hath no voice, lady, but to your own most pregnant and vouchsafed ear.
Sir Andrew
  'Odours', 'pregnant', and 'vouchsafed' – I'll get 'em all three all ready.
Olivia
  Let the garden door be shut, and leave me to my   90
  hearing. *[Exeunt all but* OLIVIA *and* VIOLA*]* Give me your hand, sir.
Viola
  My duty, madam, and most humble service.
Olivia
  What is your name?

96. *My servant, sir* Olivia is clearly riled by Viola's behaviour. She can at least see that, whatever her purpose, Viola is not being 'straight' with her. The fact that she is being so effusive, but clearly means none of it, is particularly hard for Olivia to accept or understand, when she so desperately needs to be treated sincerely. ***'Twas never merry world*** 'Things have never been happy and right.'

97. *Lowly feigning* is better put as 'feigned lowliness', meaning 'false humility', which Olivia hates to see made use of in the paying of compliments. Not that she imagines that Viola is trying to compliment her! (If she did think so, then Olivia would be the last person to criticise her method!) But she detects an unmistakable opposition in Viola's present tactics, and she cannot disguise her feeling of injury. We can imagine how infuriating Olivia will find this 'clever' talk, not least because it studiously avoids any indication of Viola's personal feelings, which alone are what Olivia is now concerned about. Notice the changed motive behind her protestation of indifference to Orsino. Earlier, this could have been a simple statement of fact, which would, she hoped, have ended further courtship from that quarter. But now she has a far more pressing reason for disclaiming any fondness for the Duke; for as long as there appears even a slight chance of winning her for her master, Viola can entertain no thought that Olivia may have set her heart on someone else. (At least, this is how Olivia sees it, for she can have no idea yet that Viola both knows of her feelings for her, and is in no position ever to reciprocate them.) Viola started out on her 'mission' with little to inspire her except loyalty to the Duke. But she is now beginning to warm to her task, if only to 'draw Olivia off' from pursuing her. So she must indeed hope to succeed in 'whetting' Olivia's thoughts towards Orsino, to give them greater keenness. (***to whet*** is to sharpen.)

104. Olivia's irritated '***O, by your leave, I pray you***' is almost our modern 'Oh, for goodness sake, shut up!'

106. *another suit* The look on Olivia's face, perhaps more than her voice, will make it clear that she wishes to be courted by Viola, and not by the Duke.

108. *music from the spheres* There was a theory that the movement of the stars in the sky was accompanied by a heavenly music normally beyond the hearing of human beings, because of their imperfection. To hear 'the music of the spheres' (transparent globes, each with a star fixed in it) was thus regarded as a privilege indeed.

ACT 3 SCENE 1

Viola
   Cesario is your servant's name, fair Princess.   95
Olivia
   My servant, sir! 'Twas never merry world
   Since lowly feigning was call'd compliment.
   Y'are servant to the Count Orsino, youth.
Viola
   And he is yours, and his must needs be yours:
   Your servant's servant is your servant, madam.   100
Olivia
   For him, I think not on him; for his thoughts,
   Would they were blanks rather than fill'd with me!
Viola
   Madam, I come to whet your gentle thoughts
   On his behalf.
Olivia
              O, by your leave, I pray you:
   I bade you never speak again of him;   105
   But, would you undertake another suit,
   I had rather hear you to solicit that
   Than music from the spheres.
Viola
                     Dear lady—

109. Olivia again cuts Viola short.
110. *enchantment* An over-expressive word, if simply to describe Orsino's love-messages dutifully presented by Viola. But by her use of it Olivia is betraying her own reaction to Viola, whose visits have, quite irrespective of the Duke's addresses, cast a kind of spell upon her.
111–20. Olivia now has the painful task of admitting her foolish in discretion over the ring. She appears entirely conscience-stricken. Is it perhaps, that her very genuine love (however misguided) for Viola has begun to drive out the inferior motives of deception and pride?
111. *abuse* treat badly.
113. *construction* judgment.
115. *Which you knew none of yours* 'which you knew didn't belong to you.' ***What might you think?*** 'What must you have thought?'
116–17. *stake ... baited ... unmuzzled* The image Olivia is using is from bear-baiting (a contemporary entertainment in which a bear was fastened to a ***stake***, and ***baited*** or teased by dogs using their fangs and teeth to harass the bear). It seems to her a very appropriate way to describe what she is convinced Viola must have been thinking about her and her ***honour***, ever since the ring was 'planted' for her to take up. The savagery of the illustration indicates more of Olivia's vexation with herself than with Viola.
118. *To one of your receiving* 'to someone as receptive, and as hard to deceive, as you are.' There is little left now of Olivia's self-possession. Viola certainly does have these characteristics; but it is resentment that makes Olivia refer to them now. She feels cruelly humiliated, and wants to put the blame, irrationally, on Viola, for having seen through her trick. (In her embarrassment, she feels certain that Viola has seen through it, though Viola has said nothing to suggest this.)
119–20. *a cypress, not a bosom, Hides my heart* In fine imagery, she makes some amends for her unfair bitterness, by admitting that her love-sickness must be obvious not only to Viola but to everyone else – just as someone wearing cypress (the black mourning crepe-cloth, rather than part of the tree) could not expect to keep his grief secret from other people.
120. *So, let me hear you speak* What reply does Olivia expect? Her question almost implies that she is prepared for the worst, and thinks she has ruined all her chances with Viola.
121. Viola replies in all sincerity – in contrast to her deliberate uninvolvement up to this point. Olivia notes the compassion in her voice, and takes it as a step in the right direction (***degree to love***). She has no idea that it is the sheer hopelessness of her quest that excites Viola's pity.

ACT 3 SCENE 1

Olivia
  Give me leave, beseech you. I did send,
  After the last enchantment you did here,   110
  A ring in chase of you; so did I abuse
  Myself, my servant, and, I fear me, you.
  Under your hard construction must I sit,
  To force that on you in a shameful cunning
  Which you knew none of yours. What might you
     think?   115
  Have you not set mine honour at the stake,
  And baited it with all th' unmuzzled thoughts
  That tyrannous heart can think? To one of your
     receiving
  Enough is shown: a cypress, not a bosom,
  Hides my heart. So, let me hear you speak.   120
Viola
  I pity you.
Olivia
           That's a degree to love.

122. *grize* step; ***vulgar proof*** common experience. Viola really pities Olivia; but to save herself from Olivia's eagerness, which refuses to be checked, she has to 'pass it off' now as a kind of scorn. But even this is gladly accepted by Olivia.

125. ***poor*** Olivia sees herself as ***poor***, in begging for Viola's affection, and so she is really reminding herself not to be too proud to submit to Viola's scorn.

126–7. If she is to be treated cruelly, she would rather it were at the hands of Viola than anyone else. Viola, in her present imperious mood, suggests a ***lion*** to Olivia, any other suitor seeming a ***wolf*** by contrast.

128. ***upbraids*** blames. The chiming clock gives her the chance, which she seizes, of recovering some shred of dignity. She attempts to dissociate herself from what has just taken place, dismissing it as a ***waste of time***.

129. This is said patronisingly; and the subsequent reference to Viola's youthfulness is in the same vein. It is as if Olivia is trying to detach herself from the whole affair without 'losing face'. She would like to convince Viola momentarily – herself even – that she couldn't possibly have had any serious thoughts about anyone so young.

130. But she can't keep this up, nor refrain from further personal involvements. ***when wit and youth is come to harvest*** 'when you have reached maturity, in years and wisdom.' (The use of the singular verb ***is*** after the double subject, is quite common in Shakespeare.)

131. ***like*** likely. ***reap*** The word is used to keep up the harvest image. ***proper*** with all the appropriate qualities of a man.

132. The moment Olivia suggests leaving, Viola almost leaps to it, heartily relieved to escape from her ordeal. Her leave-taking is entirely formal, and Orsino is mentioned only as an afterthought.

135–6. Seeing her go is too much for Olivia. She puts the question she has been longing to ask ever since they were alone together – for this may be her last chance.

137. Nothing could be more to the point – yet Viola manages to dodge the issue once again. Instead of giving, as one might expect, a straightforward opinion of Olivia's womanly qualities, Viola simply says that Olivia is not being honest with herself, or is deluding herself. (It is only through hints like this that Viola can come anywhere near the plain truth. Olivia is hopelessly mistaken in thinking that she can ever be in love with Viola; but to explain why would mean divulging the whole secret.)

138. 'If I am not being honest with myself, then no more are you.'

139. With this, Viola can heartily agree – she knows only too well how self-contradictory her own position is.

Viola
   No, not a grize; for 'tis a vulgar proof
   That very oft we pity enemies.
Olivia
   Why, then, methinks 'tis time to smile again.
   O world, how apt the poor are to be proud! 125
   If one should be a prey, how much the better
   To fall before the lion than the wolf! *[Clock strikes]*
   The clock upbraids me with the waste of time.
   Be not afraid, good youth; I will not have you;
   And yet, when wit and youth is come to harvest, 130
   Your wife is like to reap a proper man.
   There lies your way, due west.
Viola
                    Then westward-ho!
   Grace and good disposition attend your ladyship!
   You'll nothing, madam, to my lord by me?
Olivia
   Stay. 135
   I prithee tell me what thou think'st of me.
Viola
   That you do think you are not what you are.
Olivia
   If I think so, I think the same of you.
Viola
   Then think you right: I am not what I am.
Olivia
   I would you were as I would have you be! 140

142. *I am your fool* 'I am being used simply to provide your entertainment (as a Clown).' There is a note of peevishness here, as if Viola's self-control suddenly breaks down. But whatever her motive, it becomes, for Olivia, yet one more side of Viola's character for her to idolise. And so, however hard Viola tries to alienate Olivia, she simply increases her own attractiveness in Olivia's eyes. Olivia believes that Viola's display of vexation is simply a 'cover-up' for her love, which she cannot, however, conceal, any more than a murderer can hide his guilt.
146 *love's night is noon* An excellent example of how, in few words, poetry can say so much more, and with far greater effectiveness, than prose. 'The most secret thoughts (***night***) of those in love are as conspicuous as the noonday sun.'
147 *roses of the spring* Why does Olivia think of roses? Perhaps because the rare beauty of roses, like youthful love, is both exquisite and brief. (See Act 2, Scene 4, lines 37–8.)
148 *maidhood* virginity
149 *maugre* in spite of
150 *wit* and ***reason***. Olivia has just tried both of these, but has had to come out at last with the truth.
151–2 'Do not try to justify yourself (***extort thy reasons***) on the grounds that (***from this clause***), because (***For that***) I have made the first move, there is no need for you to do anything in response.'
153. *fetter* is the verb here. Viola is to control (***fetter***) one reason (namely, the false argument that Olivia has just rejected) with another (namely, the one she gives in the next line).
154. Olivia is trying to convince Viola that the conventional kind of wooing – when the man takes the initiative (***love sought***) – has less to commend it than when the lady actually offers herself first (***given unsought***).
155–8. Equally earnest now, it is Viola's turn for solemn oaths.
156. *truth* loyalty. By great dexterity, as on previous occasions, she manages to speak truthfully – and therefore with obvious sincerity – but without in any way revealing her secret. (Compare Act 2, Scene 4, lines 105–9.)
157. *no woman has* 'no woman possesses these things of mine' (as a lover).
157. *nor never none* We often find double negatives in Elizabethan English, for extra emphasis (they do not, as today, 'cancel out'); but a triple negative, again for emphasis, is rare. This is dramatic irony at its most effective. The audience knows what Viola means. No other woman can ever be in love with her – her own womanhood precludes it – but Olivia thinks she is stubbornly protesting that she will 'have nothing to do with the opposite sex'.
160. *deplore* tell, with grief.
162. *That heart* Namely, Olivia's own. ***abhors to like his love*** 'shrinks from responding to his (the Duke's) love.'

Viola
   Would it be better, madam, than I am?
   I wish it might, for now I am your fool.
Olivia
   O, what a deal of scorn looks beautiful
   In the contempt and anger of his lip!
   A murd'rous guilt shows not itself more soon   145
   Than love that would seem hid: love's night is noon.
   Cesario, by the roses of the spring,
   By maidhood, honour, truth, and every thing,
   I love thee so that, maugre all thy pride,
   Nor wit nor reason can my passion hide.   150
   Do not extort thy reasons from this clause,
   For that I woo, thou therefore hast no cause;
   But rather reason thus with reason fetter:
   Love sought is good, but given unsought is better.
Viola
   By innocence I swear, and by my youth,   155
   I have one heart, one bosom, and one truth,
   And that no woman has; nor never none
   Shall mistress be of it, save I alone.
   And so adieu, good madam; never more
   Will I my master's tears to you deplore.   160
Olivia
   Yet come again; for thou perhaps mayst move
   That heart which now abhors to like his love.

              [Exeunt]

TWELFTH NIGHT

SCENE 2

This scene brings a kind of progress report, from Maria, of the plot against Malvolio. But before this, Sir Toby and Fabian begin to hatch a second plot, a slightly gentler version, against Sir Andrew (and involving Viola), this time with no justification except to provide themselves (and the audience) with a good laugh. As before, the humour consists in talking Sir Andrew into a course of action that is entirely out of character. (It is almost as if, with Malvolio satisfactorily disposed of, they cast about for a second victim.)

1. *jot* a moment, 'jot' is from the Greek letter 'i' (iota), the smallest in the alphabet, and hence refers to the smallest part of anything.

2. *dear venom* A playful touch of irony. Sir Andrew is showing more spirit than is his custom, but nothing that could seriously be described as ***venom*** (the poison of a snake). (Compare Feste's ***your wisdom*** in Scene 1, lines 39–41.)

9. *a great argument* clear evidence.

11. *prove it legitimate* 'show that I am right.'

13–14. Sir Toby says this sarcastically, implying that people have regularly appealed to good sense and reason even when their cause was undeserving.

14. *Noah . . . sailor* Refers to the Biblical story of the Flood, from which Noah and his family escaped by building the Ark. Here it simply means 'from earliest times'.

16. *dormouse valour* A most expressive description of Sir Andrew's timidity. The dormouse is one of the tiniest animals – when asleep, virtually invisible, and, when awake, hardly ferocious!

17. *liver* See note, Act 2, Scene 4, line 98.

18. *accosted* How well did Sir Andrew understand this word previously?

19. *fire-new from the mint* original, like genuine coins that have just been made. (Unoriginal jests would be like counterfeit coins.)

20. *bang'd* thumped, or beaten.

20–1. *look'd for* expected. ***baulk'd*** avoided.

21. *gilt* gold paint.

ACT 3 SCENE 2

SCENE 2

Olivia's house

[Enter SIR TOBY, SIR ANDREW, and FABIAN]

Sir Andrew
  No, faith, I'll not stay a jot longer.
Sir Toby
  Thy reason, dear venom, give thy reason.
Fabian
  You must needs yield your reason, Sir Andrew.
Sir Andrew
  Marry, I saw your niece do more favours to the Count's
  serving man than ever she bestow'd upon me; I saw't   5
  i' th' orchard.
Sir Toby
  Did she see thee the while, old boy? Tell me that.
Sir Andrew
  As plain as I see you now.
Fabian
  This was a great argument of love in her toward you.
Sir Andrew
  'Slight! will you make an ass o' me?   10
Fabian
  I will prove it legitimate, sir, upon the oaths of
  judgment and reason.
Sir Toby
  And they have been grand-jurymen since before
  Noah was a sailor.
Fabian
  She did show favour to the youth in your sight only   15
  to exasperate you, to awake your dormouse valour, to
  put fire in your heart and brimstone in your liver. You
  should then have accosted her; and with some
  excellent jests, fire-new from the mint, you should have
  bang'd the youth into dumbness. This was look'd for   20
  at your hand, and this was baulk'd. The double gilt of
  this opportunity you let time wash off, and you are

23. ***north*** the colder, and therefore less friendly part.

26. ***policy*** diplomacy.
27. ***An't*** if it.
28. ***had as lief be*** would as willingly be. ***Brownist*** Brownists were followers of Robert Brown, a Puritan. (We have already seen how strongly Sir Andrew disapproved of Puritans – Act 2, Scene 3, lines 132–7.)
29–30. ***build me thy fortunes . . . Challenge me the Count's youth.*** The word ***me*** here is an old grammatical form which adds little to the meaning.
32. ***love-broker*** someone who acts as an agent between lovers; a match-maker.
33–4. ***man's commendation with woman*** 'man's reputation in the eyes of woman.'

37. ***curst*** sharp.
39. ***with the licence of ink*** One is much less inhibited writing things, than saying them to a person's face.
40. ***thou'st***. To 'thou' a person meant to address him as 'thou', which was taken as a sign of contempt. (It still is, sometimes, in modern French).
42. ***bed of Ware***. An actual bed, reputed to be the biggest in existence, formerly housed at the Saracen's Head Inn, in Ware, Hertfordshire, and now in the Victoria and Albert Museum, in London. It could accommodate twelve people.
43. ***gall*** bitterness.
45. ***goose-pen*** Goose-feathers were used for pens (a 'pen-knife' was originally so called because it was used to shape the end of the feather, or quill, for writing.) A goose was proverbial for its cowardice.
47. ***cubiculo*** a small room. ***Go*** a simple dramatic convenience, to have Sir Andrew out of the way now, so that the others can be more explicit (for our benefit) about their plan to fool Sir Andrew and Viola.
48. ***manakin*** little man. Fabian uses the term derisively rather than with affection.
49. A pun on ***dear***. Sir Toby has cost him two thousand ducats or so, by living off Sir Andrew's generosity.

ACT 3 SCENE 2

now sail'd into the north of my lady's opinion; where
you will hang like an icicle on a Dutchman's beard,
unless you do redeem it by some laudable attempt
either of valour or policy.

Sir Andrew
An't be any way, it must be with valour, for policy I
hate; I had as lief be a Brownist as a politician.

Sir Toby
Why, then, build me thy fortunes upon the basis of
valour. Challenge me the Count's youth to fight with
him; hurt him in eleven places. My niece shall take
note of it; and assure thyself there is no love-broker
in the world can more prevail in man's commendation
with woman than report of valour.

Fabian
There is no way but this, Sir Andrew.

Sir Andrew
Will either of you bear me a challenge to him?

Sir Toby
Go, write it in a martial hand; be curst and brief; it is
no matter how witty, so it be eloquent and full of
invention. Taunt him with the license of ink; if thou
thou'st him some thrice, it shall not be amiss; and as
many lies as will lie in thy sheet of paper, although
the sheet were big enough for the bed of Ware in
England, set 'em down; go about it. Let there be gall
enough in thy ink, though thou write with a
goose-pen, no matter. About it.

Sir Andrew
Where shall I find you?

Sir Toby
We'll call thee at the cubiculo. Go.

[Exit SIR ANDREW]

Fabian
This is a dear manakin to you, Sir Toby.

Sir Toby
I have been dear to him, lad – some two thousand
strong, or so.

53. Never trust me then 'Never trust me again if I don't.' (Though in fact Sir Toby has second thoughts, and in the end thinks it better to deliver the challenge verbally, and in his own words.)
54. oxen. Still used to pull loads. **wainropes** wagon-ropes. (Compare Act 2, Scene 5, line 60, and Note.)
55. hale pull.
55–7. The liver was thought to be the source of blood, and the seat of courage (compare the expression 'lily-livered', i.e. with a bloodless liver, meaning cowardly).
58. opposite opponent.
59. presage indication.

60. youngest wren of nine refers to Maria's slight stature. The wren is one of the smallest birds, and the ninth or last chick to be hatched could be expected to be the weakest and smallest of the whole brood.
61. spleen This organ was thought to be associated with laughter, and to become enlarged through too much mirth. 'To have the spleen' here means to suffer from an enlarged spleen.
62. Yond yonder, over there. (Here the word virtually adds no meaning.)
63. renegado renegade – one who gives up one religion and adopts another. No one, thinks Maria, could go on being a Christian (where right belief is essential) and at the same time believe the outrageous nonsense that Malvolio now entertains.
68. villainously This means little more than 'in shocking taste', **pedant** teacher.
68–9. school i' the church A not unusual practice at the time.
69. dogg'd followed closely (as a dog follows its master).

72. new map with the augmentation of the Indies A new map had been published in 1600, on new principles of projection, which made the Indies look much bigger than on previous maps. (This reference has been used by some scholars to help in dating *Twelfth Night*.)

Fabian
We shall have a rare letter from him; but you'll not deliver't?

Sir Toby
Never trust me then; and by all means stir on the youth to an answer. I think oxen and wainropes cannot hale them together. For Andrew, if he were open'd and you find so much blood in his liver as will clog the foot of a flea, I'll eat the rest of th' anatomy.

Fabian
And his opposite, the youth, bears in his visage no great presage of cruelty.

[Enter MARIA]

Sir Toby
Look where the youngest wren of nine comes.

Maria
If you desire the spleen, and will laugh yourselves into stitches, follow me. Yond gull Malvolio is turned heathen, a very renegado; for there is no Christian that means to be saved by believing rightly can ever believe such impossible passages of grossness. He's in yellow stockings.

Sir Toby
And cross-garter'd?

Maria
Most villainously; like a pedant that keeps a school i' th' church. I have dogg'd him like his murderer. He does obey every point of the letter that I dropp'd to betray him. He does smile his face into more lines than is in the new map with the augmentation of the Indies. You have not seen such a thing as 'tis; I can hardly forbear hurling things at him. I know my lady will strike him; if she do, he'll smile and take't for a great favour.

Sir Toby
Come, bring us, bring us where he is.

[Exeunt]

SCENE 3

A short but useful scene, to explain why Sebastian and Antonio, though still devoted friends, agree to separate for a few hours, and why Sebastian is persuaded to borrow Antonio's purse of money. Both these factors contribute significantly to the plot. The scene is useful, too, in not allowing us to forget about Sebastian, and his close resemblance to his sister – though this will, in a stage production, have to be conveyed chiefly by their wearing of identical attire. They must never be so alike that we, the audience, become confused.

1. *by my will* intentionally.
2. *make your pleasure of* enjoy, *pains* hardships.
3. *chide* reprove – for following him, as the next line makes clear.
6–7. *not all love to see you . . . voyage* 'not simply because I love to see you, though that in itself would make a much longer journey worth while.'
8. *jealousy* anxiety.
9. *skilless* inexperienced.
10. *unfriended* friendless. (We have 'befriended' today.)
11. *willing* freely given.
12. *arguments of* causes for.

14. Being shipwrecked, and therefore penniless, he is in no position to do otherwise.
16. *shuffl'd off* unfairly rewarded. *uncurrent* not valid as coinage. (There is no 'cash value' in thanks.)
17. 'But if my actual wealth matched my sincere intentions.'
18. *What's to do?* 'What is there for us to do?'
19. *reliques* objects (buildings chiefly) of interest because of their age.

21. *'tis long to night* 'it is a long time till night.'

23. *memorials* sights worth remembering.

24. *Would you'd pardon me* 'I wish you would excuse me (from accompanying you).'

SCENE 3

A street

[Enter SEBASTIAN and ANTONIO]

Sebastian
I would not by my will have troubled you;
But since you make your pleasure of your pains,
I will no further chide you.

Antonio
I could not stay behind you: my desire,
More sharp than filed steel, did spur me forth; 5
And not all love to see you – though so much
As might have drawn one to a longer voyage—
But jealousy what might befall your travel,
Being skilless in these parts; which to a stranger,
Unguided and unfriended, often prove 10
Rough and unhospitable. My willing love,
The rather by these arguments of fear,
Set forth in your pursuit.

Sebastian
My kind Antonio,
I can no other answer make but thanks,
And thanks, and ever thanks; and oft good turns 15
Are shuffl'd off with such uncurrent pay;
But were my worth as is my conscience firm,
You should find better dealing. What's to do?
Shall we go see the reliques of this town?

Antonio
To-morrow, sir; best first go see your lodging. 20

Sebastian
I am not weary, and 'tis long to night;
I pray you, let us satisfy our eyes
With the memorials and the things of fame
That do renown this city.

Antonio
Would you'd pardon me.
I do not without danger walk these streets: 25

26. ***the Count his galleys*** the Count's galleys (the old form of the possessive).
27. ***of such note***. Antonio's part in the battle was so conspicuous.
28. ***ta'en*** arrested. ***it would scarce be answer'd*** 'it would be extremely difficult to answer their charges against me.'
29. ***Belike*** Probably.

31–2. 'Though we had occasion enough for fierce fighting.'

33. ***It might have since been answer'd*** 'We might have made amends.'
34. ***for traffic's sake*** 'to re-establish normal relationships.'
36. ***lapsed*** arrested.

37. ***too open*** too openly.

40. ***bespeak our diet*** 'order what meals we shall require.'
41. ***beguile the time*** 'pass the time pleasantly.'

42. ***have me*** find me.

44. ***Haply*** Perhaps. ***toy*** ornament.
45. ***have desire*** would like.
45–6. ***your store, I think, is not for idle markets*** 'what you have, of your own, won't go very far in shopping for luxuries.' So they part – Antonio, a 'marked man' already in considerable jeopardy through his strong loyalty to his friend; and Sebastian, greatly indebted to Antonio, and warmly appreciative. What does this scene gain from being spoken in blank verse? (The previous one with Sebastian and Antonio was chiefly in prose.) Is it to contrast with the comic scenes that precede and follow it? Or because their friendship is to be seen always as a thing of dignity and depth?

ACT 3 SCENE 3

Once in a sea-fight 'gainst the Count his galleys
I did some service; of such note, indeed,
That, were I ta'en here, it would scarce be answer'd.
Sebastian
Belike you slew great number of his people.
Antonio
Th' offence is not of such a bloody nature; 30
Albeit the quality of the time and quarrel
Might well have given us bloody argument.
It might have since been answer'd in repaying
What we took from them; which, for traffic's sake,
Most of our city did. Only myself stood out; 35
For which, if I be lapsed in this place,
I shall pay dear.
Sebastian
                    Do not then walk too open.
Antonio
It doth not fit me. Hold, sir, here's my purse;
In the south suburbs, at the Elephant,
Is best to lodge. I will bespeak our diet, 40
Whiles you beguile the time and feed your knowledge
With viewing of the town; there shall you have me.
Sebastian
Why I your purse?
Antonio
Haply your eye shall light upon some toy
You have desire to purchase; and your store, 45
I think, is not for idle markets, sir.
Sebastian
I'll be your purse-bearer, and leave you for
An hour.
Antonio
To th' Elephant.
Sebastian
                    I do remember.

[Exeunt]

SCENE 4

A long and highly exciting scene, in which the plots against Malvolio and Sir Andrew come to a head. (Whatever happens to either, after this, is bound to seem something of an anti-climax – their mocking has reached saturation-point.) Viola, too, involved in the contrived duel, has to face further embarrassment, and – something new for her – a completely undeserved charge of treachery, which, however, brings with it new hope of her brother's survival.

2. bestow of confer as a gift upon.
3. Does Olivia really feel as cynical towards young people?
4. I speak too loud This suggests that Olivia's opening remarks are really addressed to herself. She has managed to persuade Viola to visit her again, but she doesn't want anyone, not even Maria, to witness her agitation as she considers how best to win her over.
5. sad serious. **civil** well-mannered (not speaking out of turn).
6. with my fortunes 'who has to share my fortunes.'
8–9. Either Maria is 'acting' very convincingly, or else she is genuinely alarmed at the extent to which Malvolio has responded to their 'treatment', and feels that the whole thing has got out of hand.

11–13. This concern for Olivia's personal safety suggests that Maria is really convinced. As the scene progresses, Maria's misgivings increase. Much as she hates Malvolio – perhaps more than all the others do – the thought of him in the power of the Devil is something she has not bargained for, and she begins to panic. She may be feeling more than a little guilty for her own major part in the affair. (A deranged mind was then popularly ascribed to devil-possession.)
13. tainted impaired.

15. Malvolio's madness is **merry**, since he keeps smiling; and Olivia's is **sad** in the sense that she is distraught with grief.

19. upon a sad occasion for a serious purpose.

SCENE 4

Olivia's garden

[Enter OLIVIA and MARIA]

Olivia
I have sent after him; he says he'll come.
How shall I feast him? What bestow of him?
For youth is bought more oft than begg'd or
  borrow'd.
I speak too loud.
Where's Malvolio? He is sad and civil,   5
And suits well for a servant with my fortunes.
Where is Malvolio?

Maria
He's coming, madam; but in very strange manner.
He is sure possess'd, madam.

Olivia
Why, what's the matter? Does he rave?   10

Maria
No, madam, he does nothing but smile. Your ladyship
were best to have some guard about you if he come;
for sure the man is tainted in's wits.

Olivia
Go call him hither.

[Exit MARIA]

I am as mad as he,
If sad and merry madness equal be.   15

[Re-enter MARIA with MALVOLIO]

How now, Malvolio!

Malvolio
Sweet lady, ho, ho.

Olivia
Smil'st thou?
I sent for thee upon a sad occasion.

22. *please the eye of one* Malvolio is referring to Olivia, of course.

26. *black in my mind* without understanding.
27. *to his hands*. Malvolio speaks of himself, but with a coy indirectness.
28. *Roman hand* a sloping Italian-style handwriting, much imitated at the time.
29. Olivia suggests bed for Malvolio as a sick man; but to Malvolio it is an invitation to go to bed with her!

33. *How do you?* 'How are you feeling?'

34. *At your request?* '(Why should I answer simply) because you ask me?' ***nightingales answer daws!*** Malvolio is the 'nightingale', Maria the 'daw' (jackdaw), a mischievous 'undignified' bird; and so, like the nightingale, Malvolio will condescend to reply.

35–52. Now follows a succession of quick exchanges – a well-tried comic device – between Malvolio and Olivia, with Malvolio so convinced of the genuineness of the letter, and of Olivia's eager affection, that none of her protestations deters him. Being Malvolio, he will take longer anyway to give up his delusions of greatness, and to recognise that she has no idea what he is talking about. One by one, her attempts to deflate him are surmounted, by quotations – her own heartfelt sentiments, he believes – from the letter.

Malvolio
   Sad, lady? I could be sad. This does make some   20
   obstruction in the blood, this cross-gartering; but what of
   that? If it please the eye of one, it is with me as the
   very true sonnet is: 'Please one and please all'.
Olivia
   Why, how dost thou, man? What is the matter with
   thee?   25
Malvolio
   Not black in my mind, though yellow in my legs. It
   did come to his hands, and commands shall be
   executed. I think we do know the sweet Roman hand.
Olivia
   Wilt thou go to bed, Malvolio?
Malvolio
   To bed? Ay, sweetheart, and I'll come to thee.   30
Olivia
   God comfort thee! Why dost thou smile so, and kiss
   thy hand so oft?
Maria
   How do you, Malvolio?
Malvolio
   At your request? Yes, nightingales answer daws!
Maria
   Why appear you with this ridiculous boldness before   35
   my lady?
Malvolio
   'Be not afraid of greatness.' 'Twas well writ.
Olivia
   What mean'st thou by that, Malvolio?
Malvolio
   'Some are born great,'—
Olivia
   Ha?   40
Malvolio
   'Some achieve greatness,'—
Olivia
   What say'st thou?

50. *Am I made?* Olivia, not knowing, of course, that his strange remarks are quotations from the letter, assumes that they are meant for her. In this instance, she may well be taking the word as 'maid', which would have some bearing upon herself.

52. *midsummer madness*. Midsummer was popularly thought to be a season in which all manner of strange behaviour ran riot.

56. How relieved Olivia must be to have something to 'break the spell'! Yet, eager as she must be to escape from this present painful encounter, and be with Viola again, she cares enough about Malvolio to give instructions for his welfare.

58–9. *I would not have him miscarry*. For all his irritating ways, Malvolio must hold a high place in Olivia's regard, even in her affection. (Maria confirms this a little later, in line 101.)

61. Malvolio now has the stage to himself – his last opportunity in fact, to speak to us direct. It is, therefore, perhaps as well that he should still be exulting in his supposed success. If we regard this as his last free utterance before the doors of 'justice' close upon him, then we have to admit that he still needs further 'remedial treatment'. His self-confidence shows no signs of weakening – indeed, thanks to Maria's thoroughness, it is more firmly established than ever. The entire conception of his 'one-track' personality, and the ruthlessness that has still to be used to oppose it, would be called into question if we saw signs in him now of normal human affection, to arouse our pity at least. All that has been done to him already, probably, and all that is still to be done, certainly, would begin to strike us as altogether too inhuman. (Is Olivia's concern, then, an inconsistency on Shakespeare's part?) So well has Maria done her work on the letter – too well, she may now think – that even Olivia's desperate request for Sir Toby to look after him in his distraction, is seen by Malvolio as simply confirming what she has already indicated in writing!

61. *do you come near me now?* 'You're beginning to understand me now, aren't you?'

62. *look to* look after.

Malvolio
  'And some have greatness thrust upon them.'
Olivia
  Heaven restore thee!
Malvolio
  'Remember who commended thy yellow stockings,'— 45
Olivia
  'Thy yellow stockings'?
Malvolio
  'And wish'd to see thee cross-garter'd.'
Olivia
  'Cross-garter'd'?
Malvolio
  'Go to, thou art made, if thou desir'st to be so;'—
Olivia
  Am I made? 50
Malvolio
  'If not, let me see thee a servant still.'
Olivia
  Why, this is very midsummer madness.

  [Enter SERVANT]

Servant
  Madam, the young gentleman of the Count Orsino's
  is return'd; I could hardly entreat him back; he attends
  your ladyship's pleasure. 55
Olivia
  I'll come to him. *[Exit SERVANT]* Good Maria,
  let this fellow be look'd to. Where's my cousin Toby?
  Let some of my people have a special care of him; I
  would not have him miscarry for the half of my
  dowry. 60

  [Exeunt OLIVIA and MARIA]

Malvolio
  O, ho! do you come near me now? No worse man than
  Sir Toby to look to me! This concurs directly with the
  letter: she sends him on purpose, that I may appear
  stubborn to him; for she incites me to that in the

69. *reverend carriage* way of movement that will inspire respect.
71. *lim'd* caught. (Lime was used to catch birds.) ***Jove's doing.*** Jove was the pagan equivalent of 'God'. (It probably replaces the 'God' of the original text, to comply with regulations, in James I's reign, prohibiting the use of the name of God on the stage.) It is interesting to note Malvolio's attitude here. To thank God is normally a sign of humble trust; but in this instance it more likely indicates an all-too-willing assumption that his fortunes are of over-riding concern to God. (Understood rightly, this can argue a commendable faith in Divine Providence. But in Malvolio's case, it is his own greatness, probably, rather than God's, that is uppermost in his mind.) See also lines 79–80.
74. '*fellow*.' This can have two meanings. Olivia used it condescendingly, as to an inferior. It can also denote equality of status, even intimacy. Malvolio in his present mood will have extracted only this second meaning.
75. *dram of a scruple* Both are, literally, units of apothecaries' weight; the dram is one eighth of an ounce, the scruple one third of a dram.
76. *incredulous* incredible.
76–7. *no incredulous or unsafe circumstance* 'nothing that could conceivably go wrong.'
78–9. *full prospect of my hopes* 'the fulfilment of all my hopes.'
Malvolio is from now on presented to us virtually through the reactions of the other three. He has never really come near to us, as the others have, however much we have been able to see inside his mind. The character he has been given has, by its very self-centredness, precluded our affection. But at this point he seems to recede to the very edge of things, and to detach from the human scene. The others have, from the start, been united by their detestation of his unloving ways. But now, regarding him as a lunatic – one who, in the common view, had passed beyond the reach of normal human contacts – they are banded together even more instinctively against him, as the herd is when faced with an intruder it wishes to isolate and expel. Insanity in those days, and for a long time after, still belonged to the realm of the unknown. Lunatics stood outside the reach of normal human relationships, largely because they seemed to be so un-human themselves. We should bear this in mind, and not expect a modern, enlightened compassion and understanding in their attitude to Malvolio.
81. *Which way is he . . . ?* 'How is he?'
82. *in little* on a small scale, in miniature. ***Legion*** The name of a man 'possessed by many devils' who was cured by Jesus.

letter. 'Cast thy humble slough' says she. 'Be opposite 65
with a kinsman, surly with servants; let thy tongue
tang with arguments of state; put thyself into the
trick of singularity' and consequently sets down the
manner how, as: a sad face, a reverend carriage, a slow
tongue, in the habit of some sir of note, and so forth. 70
I have lim'd her; but it is Jove's doing, and Jove make
me thankful! And when she went away now – 'Let
this fellow be look'd to'. 'Fellow' not 'Malvolio'
nor after my degree, but 'fellow'. Why, everything
adheres together, that no dram of a scruple, no scruple 75
of a scruple, no obstacle, no incredulous or unsafe
circumstance – What can be said? Nothing that can
be can come between me and the full prospect of my
hopes. Well, Jove, not I, is the doer of this, and he is
to be thanked. 80

    [Re-enter MARIA, *with* SIR TOBY *and* FABIAN*]*

Sir Toby
  Which way is he, in the name of sanctity? If all the
  devils of hell be drawn in little, and Legion himself
  possess'd him, yet I'll speak to him.
Fabian
  Here he is, here he is. How is't with you, sir?
Sir Toby
  How is't with you, man? 85

86. *Go off* Go away. *discard* have nothing more to do with. *private* privacy.
88. *hollow* falsely. *fiend* devil (under whose control Maria thinks he is).
91. *Ah, ha! does she so?* Still quite convinced that Olivia loves him, and quite deaf to their insistence upon his derangement, Malvolio is quick to interpret Olivia's instructions as signs of amorousness.
93. *Let me alone* Sir Toby would like to handle this alone. This is not surprising, for the other two don't seem to be offering much effective help – Maria is by now almost hysterical with alarm, while Fabian's concern is at best mixed with amusement. Sir Toby himself shakes off his habitual carelessness, and at least tries, boldly and with conviction, to grapple with the problem. (The distinctive reactions of all three to this present emergency are well brought out.) How ironic that Malvolio, the suspected lunatic, should be finding the remarks of the others so fantastic – and we can hardly blame him for this!
97. *La you* Simply an exclamation of surprise.
98. *at heart* to heart. Maria, quite genuinely (as throughout this scene) sees in Malvolio's 'touchiness' at mention of the devil, a sign that he is in league with the devil, and resents any opposition to his master.
99. *wise woman* one who was skilled in folk-medicine. The practice referred to, of inspecting a patient's urine, so as to diagnose his illness, was not in favour among qualified doctors.
100. Whether Fabian means this seriously or not, Maria gladly seizes on the suggestion, as at least offering some hope of a cure.
103. *How now, mistress!* As before (line 91), Malvolio reacts at once, and optimistically, to any mention of Olivia's concern for his welfare. And, to judge by Maria's comment (*O Lord!*) of alarm, or pity, or both, we may suppose that his sudden interest has been accompanied by equally sudden gestures in her direction. We know why he reacts in this way; but to Maria it is one more sign of a deranged mind. Maria's present distress has, if only temporarily, made her forget the letter – *her* letter – and the way it was bound to stimulate Malvolio's desires in Olivia's direction. Malvolio is 'running true to form' in all this, and she should have been prepared for just this reaction from him.
105. *this is not the way* This is said to Maria. Sir Toby is beginning to have the situation weighed up, and to assert some kind of control. He may not have the full solution, but at least realises that Maria's hysteria is going to excite Malvolio even more.
108. *us'd* treated.
109. *bawcock* (from the French 'beau coq') fine fellow.
110. *chuck* a term of affection (the same as 'chick', which is still used today as an endearment).

Malvolio
Go off; I discard you. Let me enjoy my private; go off.

Maria
Lo, how hollow the fiend speaks within him! Did not I tell you? Sir Toby, my lady prays you to have a care of him.

Malvolio
Ah, ha! does she so?

Sir Toby
Go to, go to; peace, peace; we must deal gently with him. Let me alone. How do you, Malvolio? How is't with you? What, man, defy the devil; consider, he's an enemy to mankind.

Malvolio
Do you know what you say?

Maria
La you, an you speak ill of the devil, how he takes it at heart! Pray God he be not bewitch'd.

Fabian
Carry his water to th' wise woman.

Maria
Marry, and it shall be done to-morrow morning, if I live. My lady would not lose him for more than I'll say.

Malvolio
How now, mistress!

Maria
O Lord!

Sir Toby
Prithee hold thy peace; this is not the way. Do you not see you move him? Let me alone with him.

Fabian
No way but gentleness – gently, gently. The fiend is rough, and will not be roughly us'd.

Sir Toby
Why, how now, my bawcock!
How dost thou, chuck?

111. *Sir!* Malvolio is carrying out what he believes to be Olivia's injunctions, in reproving Sir Toby for his familiarity.
112. *Biddy* another name for 'chicken' (and so in the same vein as ***bawcock*** and ***chuck***).
112–13. *for gravity* dignified.
113. *cherrypit* a children's game in which cherry-stones were thrown into a small hole; so the expression ***to play at cherrypit*** would mean 'to be on friendly terms with.'
113–14. *Hang him, foul collier!* A miner and the Devil were both black and worked in a pit. Sir Toby, as with a child, is trying to coax Malvolio into renouncing the Devil. ('Don't have anything to do with the Devil, that nasty old thing!')
117. *My prayers, minx!* Malvolio is right in thinking that Maria wants him to pray because she believes that he is in desperate need of spiritual help. It is her reason that he is indignant about, not the idea of praying in itself. (***minx*** = wanton woman.)
118. *he will not hear of godliness*. Maria, however, misunderstands him; in her view, he is so possessed by evil, that he instinctively repudiates 'godliness'.
119–20. *I am not of your element* 'I live in a different world from you.'
122. *Is't possible?* and **124. *improbable fiction*** The conspirators have really surprised themselves by their success – they can hardly believe their eyes, and ears. Fabian's remark has an additional point, a sort of dramatic irony. Shakespeare is in a way putting himself and his play into our hands, and mischievously inviting our criticism of himself, for devising and handling such an ingenious plot.
125. *His very genius* His essential self. ***taken the infection of*** been infected by. Sir Toby is emphasizing the completeness of the deception – Malvolio is beside himself.
127–8. *take air and taint* grow stale. An odd line for Maria, in face of her recent distress on Malvolio's account. Together with her next observation – ***The house will be the quieter*** – it suggests that she is now 'back to normal' and as eager as the others to see the matter through to the end. Perhaps, with Malvolio out of sight, she can put out of her mind the harrowing side of his humiliation, and dwell only on the 'justice' of it.

Malvolio
  Sir!
Sir Toby
  Ay, Biddy, come with me. What, man, 'tis not for gravity to play at cherrypit with Satan. Hang him, foul collier!
Maria
  Get him to say his prayers, good Sir Toby, get him to pray. 115
Malvolio
  My prayers, minx!
Maria
  No, I warrant you, he will not hear of godliness.
Malvolio
  Go, hang yourselves all! You are idle shallow things; I am not of your element; you shall know more hereafter. 120

  [Exit]

Sir Toby
  Is't possible?
Fabian
  If this were play'd upon a stage now, I could condemn it as an improbable fiction.
Sir Toby
  His very genius hath taken the infection of the device, man. 125
Maria
  Nay, pursue him now, lest the device take air and taint.
Fabian
  Why, we shall make him mad indeed.
Maria
  The house will be the quieter. 130

131–7. Sir Toby's closing remarks perhaps come nearest to summing up their common attitude. His words serve, in addition, as a kind of justification – perhaps Shakespeare's own – of the entire Malvolio plot, on moral and dramatic grounds. On moral grounds, the treatment Malvolio is receiving, is designed as a **penance** – to make some amends for his errors. On dramatic grounds, it has given them, and us, **pleasure**. (How significant is it, that they will stop tormenting him only when they are tired of their fun, and not for any reason of compassion?)

136. *to the bar* to be judged. *finder of madmen* In the sense probably of 'certifying' them as insane.

Sir Andrew's arrival, with his challenge for Viola, is most salutary. It smoothes away any misgivings about Malvolio's fate that may still exist, and brings us at once into a fresh situation, where the humour taxes our susceptibilities less.

138. *May morning* morning of May 1st, one of the happiest popular feast-days, on which all manner of entertainment took place to celebrate the coming of spring. Fabian sees Sir Andrew's arrival as providing such entertainment for them.

139–40. *vinegar and pepper* It will need no 'seasoning' to bring out the flavour, which will be piquant enough as it stands.

145. *Good and valiant* Fabian and Sir Toby are making fun of Sir Andrew, in their customary style, by pretending that they think he is fierce and aggressive. Sir Andrew doesn't disappoint them – he drinks in their flattery with never a second thought.

146. *admire* wonder. *nor . . . not* A double negative. Only one of these is needed in modern English.

148–9. *keeps you from the blow of the law* By not making specific charges against Viola, Sir Andrew avoids prosecution for libel.

151. *thou liest in thy throat* What lying does Sir Andrew refer to – her persistent denial of love for Olivia, or when she says (as Sir Andrew assumes she will) that she is being challenged solely because of her attachment to Olivia?

153. *to exceeding good sense* according to very good sense. Fabian's addition of *less* at the end (making 'senseless') will be spoken 'aside', a little game that children often get up to.

ACT 3 SCENE 4

Sir Toby
Come, we'll have him in a dark room and bound. My
niece is already in the belief that he's mad. We may
carry it thus, for our pleasure and his penance, till our
very pastime, tired out of breath, prompt us to have
mercy on him; at which time we will bring the device   135
to the bar and crown thee for a finder of madmen,
But see, but see.

[Enter SIR ANDREW]

Fabian
More matter for a May morning.
Sir Andrew
Here's the challenge; read it. I warrant there's vinegar
and pepper in't.   140
Fabian
Is't so saucy?
Sir Andrew
Ay, is't, I warrant him; do but read.
Sir Toby
Give me. *[Reads]* 'Youth, whatsoever thou art, thou art
but a scurvy fellow.'
Fabian
Good and valiant.   145
Sir Toby [Reads]
'Wonder not, nor admire not in thy mind, why I do
call thee so, for I will show thee no reason for't.'
Fabian
A good note; that keeps you from the blow of the
law.
Sir Toby [Reads]
'Thou com'st to the Lady Olivia, and in my sight she   150
uses thee kindly; but thou liest in thy throat; that is
not the matter I challenge thee for.'
Fabian
Very brief, and to exceeding good sense – less.
Sir Toby [Reads]
'I will waylay thee going home; where if it be thy

158. *th' windy side of the law* the right side of the law. (The metaphor is a nautical one – for a sailing ship, the best side was the one on which it could catch the wind, to propel it over the water, and thus escape from an enemy.)

160–1. *He may have mercy . . . hope is better* an unintentional piece of humour. It sounds as if Sir Andrew hopes for something better than God's mercy! What he actually means, of course, is that he hopes he won't be the loser and die in the forthcoming duel, and thus be needing the mercy of God in the specific way a dead man needs it.

161. *Thy friend* One of many conventional ways of ending a letter; whereas ***thy sworn enemy*** (line 162) expresses Sir Andrew's 'real' sentiments at this moment. The humour is in the juxtaposition of the two opposites.

163. *If this letter . . . legs cannot* Another way of saying that the letter cannot fail to move Viola, any more than her legs can fail to carry her.

165. *fit occasion* favourable opportunity.

165–6. *in some commerce* on some business.

168. *scout* keep a look out. ***me*** This cannot be directly rendered in Modern English. It is the same usage as in Scene 2, lines 29–30.

169. *bum-bailey* sheriff's officer (who would be adept at knowing where to find law-breakers who were trying to escape detection).

172–4. *gives manhood . . . earn'd him* 'is a better way of showing one's manliness than by trying to act courageously.' This is a cynicism that probably passes over Sir Andrew's head. All that comes through to him is that he must swear ferociously, which he claims he can do better than anyone else – ***let me alone for swearing*** (line 175). This might equally mean that Sir Andrew's oaths will be too terrifying for them, or anyone else, to listen to.

chance to kill me'— 155
Fabian
  Good.
Sir Toby
  'Thou kill's me like a rogue and a villain.'
Fabian
  Still you keep o' th' windy side of the law. Good!
Sir Toby [Reads]
  'Fare thee well; and God have mercy upon one of
  our souls! He may have mercy upon mine; but my 160
  hope is better, and so look to thyself. Thy friend, as
  thou usest him, and thy sworn enemy,
                    ANDREW AGUECHEEK.'
  If this letter move him not, his legs cannot. I'll give't
  him.
Maria
  You may have very fit occasion for't; he is now in some 165
  commerce with my lady, and will by and by
  depart.
Sir Toby
  Go, Sir Andrew; scout me for him at the corner of
  the orchard, like a bum-baily; so soon as ever thou
  seest him, draw; and as thou draw'st, swear horrible; 170
  for it comes to pass oft that a terrible oath, with a
  swaggering accent sharply twang'd off, gives manhood
  more approbation than ever proof itself would have
  earn'd him. Away.
Sir Andrew
  Nay, let me alone for swearing. 175
                [Exit]

176–88. Sir Toby is right in surmising that Viola will be far more effectively panicked – and we better entertained – if he personally draws the picture of Sir Andrew's 'ferocity'. Sir Toby is in his element telling tall stories, and he does it superbly. Nothing puts him off his stride, once he has decided on his line of approach, and even this he seems to do with more success, and less effort, than anyone else. It is difficult to imagine a more hilarious scene than the one they are now engineering, between Sir Andrew and Viola. Yet it has cost them virtually no trouble – a few well-chosen untruths are planted in the right places, and all they have to do then is 'sit back' and enjoy the outcome.

177. *gives him out* shows him.

178. *capacity* ability.

180. *excellently* exceedingly. (We tend to limit the word to things that are good.)

181. *clodpole* person without intelligence. It may jolt us a little to see just how much Sir Andrew is despised by his 'friend'. But there have been signs before (Scene 2, line 49) and will be later (Act 5, Scene 1, lines 200–1) of Sir Toby's essential callousness towards him.

183. *set upon Aguecheek . . . valour* 'invent for Aguecheek an outstanding reputation for courage.'

184–5. *as I know his youth will aptly receive it* 'which, being young, and inexperienced in fighting, he will be only too ready to believe.'

185. *hideous* shocking.

188. *cockatrices* A cockatrice was a fabulous reptile, half serpent and half cockerel, thought to kill by its look and breath. (It was also called a basilisk.)

189. *give them way* 'let them alone.'

190. *presently after him* 'follow him at once.'

193–209. This short interlude, in dignified verse, carries us back to the highly-strung atmosphere of the main plot. The Viola who is shortly to step straight into the duelling trap, has to be seen as coming, as it were, straight from her other ordeal, with no time to adjust resourcefully to the new situation.

Viola and Olivia are still at the same impasse as when they last appeared, Olivia having abandoned all attempts to disguise her love for Viola, and Viola still trying to 'redirect' it towards her master.

194. *too unchary* too rashly.

195. *reproves my fault* The fault, that is, of allowing herself to fall for Viola, and of telling her about it.

196–7. But her love is so overpowering that any conscience she has about it has little effect.

198. *haviour* behaviour. The order is: My master's griefs go(es) on with the same (be)haviour as your passions bear – 'My master's suffering in love expresses itself in the same way as yours.' (Note the quite common Shakespearean usage of singular verb with plural subject.)

ACT 3 SCENE 4

Sir Toby
  Now will not I deliver his letter; for the behaviour of
  the young gentleman gives him out to be of good
  capacity and breeding; his employment between his
  lord and my niece confirms no less. Therefore this
  letter, being so excellently ignorant, will breed no terror   180
  in the youth; he will find it comes from a clodpole.
  But, sir, I will deliver his challenge by word of mouth,
  set upon Aguecheek a notable report of valour, and
  drive the gentleman – as I know his youth will aptly
  receive it – into a most hideous opinion of his rage,   185
  skill, fury, and impetuosity, This will so fright them
  both that they will kill one another by the look, like
  cockatrices.
        [Re-enter OLIVIA, *with* VIOLA*]*
Fabian
  Here he comes with your niece; give them way till he
  take leave, and presently after him.   190
Sir Toby
  I will meditate the while upon some horrid message
  for a challenge.
        [Exeunt SIR TOBY, FABIAN, *and* MARIA*]*
Olivia
  I have said too much unto a heart of stone,
  And laid mine honour too unchary out;
  There's something in me that reproves my fault;   195
  But such a headstrong potent fault it is
  That it but mocks reproof.
Viola
  With the same haviour that your passion bears
  Goes on my master's griefs.

201. *no tongue to vex you*. It will be a reminder of her love, but a silent one.

203–4. 'Whatever you ask me for, I'll give you, if I can do so honourably.'

205. '(I ask for) nothing but this.'

207. *I will acquit you* 'I will release you (from any obligation to go on loving me).'

209. Another memorable 'aside' to conclude the encounter. Olivia means that she could quite willingly go to hell if the devil who carried her off there was like Viola. (This has a profounder implication – she is prepared to lose her place in heaven as long as she can have Viola.)

212–17. Notice how, in order to carry off the deception more successfully, Sir Toby plunges straight into the business of the challenge. He pretends to assume that Viola knows what he is referring to. This will also make Viola feel that she is caught up in something that is too far advanced to be halted by her, or anyone else.

212. *That defence thou hast, betake thee to't* 'Be ready to defend yourself, as best you can.'

214. *intercepter* adversary. (Literally, the one who stands in your way.) ***despite*** malice.

215. *Dismount thy tuck* draw your rapier from its sheath.

216. *be yare in* be quick about.

218–20. This present confrontation is probably Viola's most testing experience. In her previous encounters, with Olivia and Orsino, she usually recovers some degree of composure, and even takes the initiative. But here she seems to be nearer the point of feminine panic at the thought of naked steel and bloodshed.

218–19. *quarrel to* quarrel with.

223. *opposite* opponent. (as in Scene 2, line 58.)

223–4. *youth, strength, skill, and wrath*. This is the sort of outrageous lie that Sir Toby loves to slip into the conversation without turning a hair. ***withal*** with.

ACT 3 SCENE 4

Olivia
Here, wear this jewel for me; 'tis my picture.   200
Refuse it not; it hath no tongue to vex you.
And I beseech you come again to-morrow.
What shall you ask of me that I'll deny,
That honour sav'd may upon asking give?
Viola
Nothing but this – your true love for my master.   205
Olivia
How with mine honour may I give him that
Which I have given to you?
Viola
                              I will acquit you.
Olivia
Well, come again to-morrow. Fare thee well;
A fiend like thee might bear my soul to hell.

[Exit. Re-enter SIR TOBY *and* FABIAN*]*

Sir Toby
Gentleman, God save thee.   210
Viola
And you, sir.
Sir Toby
That defence thou hast, betake thee to't. Of what nature
the wrongs are thou hast done him, I know not; but
thy intercepter, full of despite, bloody as the hunter,
attends thee at the orchard end. Dismount thy tuck,   215
be yare in thy preparation, for thy assailant is quick,
skilful, and deadly.
Viola
You mistake, sir; I am sure no man hath any quarrel
to me; my remembrance is very free and clear from
any image of offence done to any man.   220
Sir Toby
You'll find it otherwise, I assure you; therefore, if you
hold your life at any price, betake you to your guard;
for your opposite hath in him what youth, strength,
skill, and wrath, can furnish man withal.

225. *what is he?* 'who is it?'
226. *dubb'd*. To dub a man was to confer knighthood upon him. ***unhatch'd*** not hacked or blunted in battle. A man's own blade was laid upon him in the ceremony of knighting. Sir Toby, therefore, implies that Sir Andrew had seen no fighting when he became a knight.
226–7. *on carpet consideration* a knight dubbed when kneeling on a carpet, not on the ground of a battle-field.
228. *divorc'd* separated – by killing three people. (In death, the soul was thought to be separated from the body.)
229. *incensement* rage.
230–1. *satisfaction can . . . death and sepulchre* 'he will be satisfied with nothing less than a fight to the death.' (***Sepulchre*** is a burial-place.)
231. *Hob-nob* another rendering of 'hab-nab' (a corruption from Latin) meaning 'have or have not', almost in the same sense as ***give't or take't***. Sir Andrew is prepared (says Sir Toby) to gain or lose all in the ensuing fight.
232–3. *desire some conduct of the lady* 'ask the Countess for someone to escort me.' (We speak today of granting someone a 'safe conduct'.) What humiliation for Viola if she had ever gone to Olivia with this request!
236. *quirk* odd trick of behaviour.
237–43. Sir Toby at once blocks this line of escape. We must imagine him doing this literally, barring the way physically himself.
238. *competent* that calls for redress.
238–9. *give him his desire* do what he wants.
239. *Back you shall not to the house* 'You shall not go back to the house.'
239–41. *unless you undertake . . . answer him* 'unless you are prepared to accept the same challenge from me – and it will involve you in no less violence.' In other words, Sir Toby makes it painfully clear that Viola is expected to fight one or the other!
242. *meddle* join battle.
243. *forswear to wear iron about you* 'renounce the right to wear a sword.'
244. *uncivil*. Normally this would mean 'impolite', but it seems here to be used in a stronger sense, almost like our modern 'uncivilised'. ***strange*** aloof, reserved.
244–5. *do me this courteous office* 'do me the favour'
245. *as to know of the knight* 'of finding out from the knight.'
246–7. *something of my negligence, nothing of my purpose* 'caused by some carelessness on my part, and in no way intentional.'

Viola
I pray you, sir, what is he? 225
Sir Toby
He is knight, dubb'd with unhatch'd rapier and on carpet consideration; but he is a devil in private brawl. Souls and bodies hath he divorc'd three; and his incensement at this moment is so implacable that satisfaction can be none but by pangs of death and 230 sepulchre. Hob-nob is his word – give't or take't.
Viola
I will return again into the house and desire some conduct of the lady. I am no fighter. I have heard of some kind of men that put quarrels purposely on others to taste their valour; belike this is a man of 235 that quirk.
Sir Toby
Sir, no; his indignation derives itself out of a very competent injury; therefore, get you on and give him his desire. Back you shall not to the house, unless you undertake that with me which with as much safety 240 you might answer him; therefore on, or strip your sword stark naked; for meddle you must, that's certain, or forswear to wear iron about you.
Viola
This is as uncivil as strange. I beseech you do me this courteous office as to know of the knight what my 245 offence to him is: it is something of my negligence, nothing of my purpose.
Sir Toby
I will do so. Signior Fabian, stay you by this gentleman till my return.

[Exit SIR TOBY*]*

Viola
Pray you, sir, do you know of this matter? 250

251–2. *even to a mortal arbitrement* 'to the point of deciding the matter in mortal combat.' (***Arbitrement*** means settlement of a dispute.) Can we detect any difference between Fabian's treatment here of Viola, and Sir Toby's?

252–3. *but nothing of the circumstance more* 'but no further details.'

255–7. 'There is nothing that you can deduce (***read***) from his appearance (***form***) that suggests what you will discover when his valour is put to the test (***in the proof of his valour***).'

261. *bound* obliged.

262. *with sir priest than sir knight*. Does Viola imply more than a general contrast between a non-violent way of life, and a warlike one?

262–3. *I care not who knows*. Said in defiance, or desperation?

263. *mettle* basic quality. (Of a man, it would normally denote his courage.)

264–9. Alone now with Sir Andrew, Sir Toby subjects him to the same treatment as he dealt to Viola, thus building up to the crowning situation where the two unwilling 'combatants', each terrified of the other, each expecting the roughest handling, are gradually coaxed together, into some kind of duelling stance.

265. *firago* (usually virago) a violent, fierce woman. (Sir Toby is simply describing the only kind of ferocity he can imagine in connection with Viola.) ***pass*** bout (of fencing).

266. *stuck in* a term from fencing, no doubt used by Sir Toby with some relish.

266. *mortal motion* deadly action.

267. *is inevitable* cannot be avoided. (We rarely use the word today in its physical sense.)

267. *on the answer, he pays you* 'he makes his return stroke.'

269. *Sophy* Shah of Persia.

As Sir Toby enlarges upon Viola's swordsmanship, he will almost certainly be miming it, over-emphatically, to make quite sure that Sir Andrew has a clear picture of what could be in store for him.

270. But Sir Andrew reacts too thoroughly, and tries to call the whole thing off, so that Sir Toby has to do some quick thinking, or their joke will 'misfire'.

273–6. Sir Andrew is refreshingly honest – he is quite prepared to bribe Viola to drop the matter, and he doesn't mind who knows about it. (What ingenious excuses would Sir Toby have invented, if he had been caught in a similar dilemma?)

ACT 3 SCENE 4

Fabian
　I know the knight is incens'd against you, even to a
　mortal arbitrement; but nothing of the circumstance
　more.
Viola
　I beseech you, what manner of man is he?
Fabian
　Nothing of that wonderful promise, to read him by　255
　his form, as you are like to find him in the proof of
　his valour. He is indeed, sir, the most skilful, bloody,
　and fatal opposite that you could possibly have found
　in any part of Illyria. Will you walk towards him? I
　will make your peace with him if I can.　260
Viola
　I shall be much bound to you for't. I am one that
　would rather go with sir priest than sir knight. I care
　not who knows so much of my mettle.

　　　[Exeunt. Re-enter SIR TOBY *with* SIR ANDREW*]*

Sir Toby
　Why, man, he's a very devil; I have not seen such a
　firago. I had a pass with him, rapier, scabbard, and all,　265
　and he gives me the stuck in with such a mortal motion
　that it is inevitable; and on the answer, he pays you
　as surely as your feet hit the ground they step on. They
　say he has been fencer to the Sophy.
Sir Andrew
　Pox on't, I'll not meddle with him.　270
Sir Toby
　Ay, but he will not now be pacified; Fabian can scarce
　hold him yonder.
Sir Andrew
　Plague on't; an I thought he had been valiant, and so
　cunning in fence, I'd have seen him damn'd ere I'd
　have challeng'd him. Let him let the matter slip, and　275
　I'll give him my horse, grey Capilet.

277. ***I'll make the motion*** 'I'll pass on your proposal' (about the horse)

278. ***this shall end without the perdition of souls***. This is put as an assurance, by Sir Toby, that no lives will be lost.

279–80. ***as well as I ride you*** Sir Toby is boasting about the way he has Sir Andrew completely under his control (as a rider has his horse).

281–2. ***I have his horse to take up the quarrel. I have*** simply implies Sir Toby's part in the arrangement – the offer was put to him as the intermediary.

283. ***as horribly conceited*** 'has an equally horrible impression.' (To be 'conceited' here means to have a conceit, or idea, about someone or something.)

286. ***better bethought him*** thought better.

288–9. ***for the supportance of his vow*** 'to enable him to discharge his vow.'

289. ***protests*** declares.

291. ***how much I lack of a man*** 'how little manliness I really possess.'

293–7. Notice the neat way in which Sir Toby repeats to Sir Andrew what he has just said, by way of explanation, to Viola. The words are almost identical, except that with Sir Andrew, it was an 'oath' to be kept, whereas, in Viola's case, it is 'honour' to be observed. The humour of this, and the barefaced trickery, is for our benefit, and Fabian's, not theirs.

295. ***the duello*** the laws of duelling.

297. The antics of Fabian and Sir Toby at this point must be imagined, as they try to get the other two into effective swordplay with each other. (This is a good example of how little the simple text, and stage directions, may indicate of the actual goings-on on the stage.)

300. Here the confusions start, between Viola and Sebastian – both humorous and distressing (as this one is). Antonio at once rushes to the defence of Viola, thinking her to be his friend Sebastian.

ACT 3 SCENE 4

Sir Toby
I'll make the motion. Stand here, make a good show
on't; this shall end without the perdition of souls.
[Aside] Marry, I'll ride your horse as well as I ride
you.   280

[Re-enter FABIAN and VIOLA]

[To FABIAN] I have his horse to take up the quarrel; I
have persuaded him the youth's a devil.
Fabian *[To SIR TOBY]*
He is as horribly conceited of him; and pants and looks
pale, as if a bear were at his heels.
Sir Toby *[To VIOLA]*
There's no remedy, sir: he will fight with you for's oath   285
sake. Marry, he hath better bethought him of his
quarrel, and he finds that now scarce to be worth
talking of. Therefore draw for the supportance of his
vow; he protests he will not hurt you.
Viola *[Aside]*
Pray God defend me! A little thing would make me   290
tell them how much I lack of a man.
Fabian
Give ground if you see him furious.
Sir Toby
Come, Sir Andrew, there's no remedy; the gentleman
will, for his honour's sake, have one bout with you;
he cannot by the duello avoid it; but he has promis'd   295
me, as he is a gentleman and a soldier, he will not
hurt you. Come on; to't.
Sir Andrew
Pray God he keep his oath!

[They draw. Enter ANTONIO]

Viola
I do assure you 'tis against my will.
Antonio
Put up your sword. If this young gentleman   300
Have done offence, I take the fault on me:
If you offend him, I for him defy you.

306. *undertaker* one who takes upon himself a task. (Here it is used rather scathingly, implying that Antonio should 'mind his own business'.)

308. *anon* presently, i.e. in a little while. ('Anon', like 'presently', originally meant 'at once'.) Notice that Sir Toby, normally a great talker, says nothing from now until the departure of the law officers. Probably he is afraid of being arrested for debt.

310. *for that I promis'd you* 'as regards the promise I made you' – namely, the gift of Sir Andrew's horse, Capilet.

313. *office* duty.

314. *at the suit* on the instruction.

315. *You do mistake me* 'You are confusing me with someone else.'

316. *favour* face. (Compare Act 2, Scene 4, lines 23–4.)
319. *This comes with seeking you*. This will not be said resentfully. It is only later, when Viola claims complete ignorance of his meaning, that Antonio gives way to bitter reproach.
320. *answer it* answer their charge.
321. *necessity* need. (In his present situation, he will need money, and he has already lent it to his friend.)
322–4. This is characteristic of Antonio – he is more concerned about having to deprive his friend of material help (by asking for the return of his purse) than about his own fate.
324. *You stand amaz'd*. Antonio imagines that Viola is amazed at his sudden arrest – he has no idea of the true reason.

ACT 3 SCENE 4

Sir Toby
  You, sir! Why, what are you?
Antonio
  One, sir, that for his love dares yet do more
  Than you have heard him brag to you he will. 305
Sir Toby
  Nay, if you be an undertaker, I am for you.

  [They draw. Enter OFFICERS*]*

Fabian
  O good Sir Toby, hold! Here come the officers.
Sir Toby [To ANTONIO*]*
  I'll be with you anon.
Viola
  Pray, sir, put your sword up, if you please.
Sir Andrew
  Marry, will I, sir; and for that I promis'd you, I'll be 310
  as good as my word. He will bear you easily and reins
  well.
First Officer
  This is the man; do thy office.
Second Officer
  Antonio, I arrest thee at the suit
  Of Count Orsino.
Antonio
             You do mistake me, sir. 315
First Officer
  No, sir, no jot; I know your favour well,
  Though now you have no sea-cap on your head.
  Take him away; he knows I know him well.
Antonio
  I must obey. *[To* VIOLA*]* This comes with seeking you;
  But there's no remedy; I shall answer it. 320
  What will you do, now my necessity
  Makes me to ask you for my purse? It grieves me
  Much more for what I cannot do for you
  Than what befalls myself. You stand amaz'd;
  But be of comfort. 325

TWELFTH NIGHT

327. *entreat of you* 'beg you to give me.'
Viola's spontaneous offer of help is quite moving, and helps to bring out the tragic element in the ensuing encounter. If she had not been so generously motivated, the injustice of her fate at Antonio's hands would not weigh so heavily.
329. Viola refers to his rescue of her from the duelling.
330. *part* partly. Either reason – her gratitude or his need – is cogent enough to solicit her willing help.
331. *my lean and low ability* 'the little that I possess.' (Probably no more than she would have received up to now in her service to the Duke.)
332. *My having* 'what I have.'
333. *my present* 'all that I have with me.'
334. *coffer* treasure-chest. Viola is being ironical. *deny* refuse.
335–6. 'Can you possibly be unmoved by your obligations to me?' (*my deserts to you* 'what I deserve of you.')
336. *tempt* 'put too much strain upon.'
337–9. Antonio is afraid that it will sour their entire relationship. To **upbraid** with the **kindnesses** done means to remind 'him' of them, and to point out that 'he' has not been duly grateful – and Antonio has taken his friendship with Sebastian far too seriously to do this sort of thing except as a last desperate remedy.
341–4. Viola's attitude towards ingratitude seems to have been Shakespeare's own. It is worth noting that the 'lesser' faults she lists, by comparison, are the very ones that the play was written ostensibly to expose.
342–3. *vice . . . our frail blood*. This looks like a reference to 'Original Sin', a theological doctrine that all members of the human race inherit a tendency to evil (**strong corruption**) which they are too weak to master (**frail blood**) without the help of God. Viola's list, then, represents some of the ways in which this basic tendency shows itself.
344. We can well sympathise with Antonio's bewilderment – how could anyone so guilty of ingratitude (as he believes 'Sebastian' to be) speak so feelingly against it?
347. *one half out of the jaws of death* already half-dead.
349. *image* what Antonio believed to be Sebastian's true nature, but he now thinks he was mistaken.
350. *did I devotion* 'I gave my devoted service.' The use of **sanctity**, **image, venerable** and **devotion** – all of them having a religious flavour – brings out the essence of Antonio's earlier attitude to Sebastian. We may disapprove of the intensity of his affection, we may even call it an obsession, perhaps, but its singlemindedness and sincerity are undeniable. It is his excessive devotion which is hurt the more deeply by what is seen as a betrayal, and recoils more bitterly from it.

ACT 3 SCENE 4

Second Officer
  Come, sir, away.
Antonio
  I must entreat of you some of that money.
Viola
  What money, sir?
  For the fair kindness you have show'd me here,
  And part being prompted by your present trouble, 330
  Out of my lean and low ability
  I'll lend you something. My having is not much;
  I'll make division of my present with you;
  Hold, there's half my coffer.
Antonio
                    Will you deny me now?
  Is't possible that my deserts to you 335
  Can lack persuasion? Do not tempt my misery,
  Lest that it make me so unsound a man
  As to upbraid you with those kindnesses
  That I have done for you.
Viola
                    I know of none,
  Nor know I you by voice or any feature, 340
  I hate ingratitude more in a man
  Than lying, vainness, babbling drunkenness,
  Or any taint of vice whose strong corruption
  Inhabits our frail blood.
Antonio
                    O heavens themselves!
Second Officer
  Come, sir, I pray you go, 345
Antonio
  Let me speak a little. This youth that you see here
  I snatch'd one half out of the jaws of death,
  Reliev'd him with such sanctity of love,
  And to his image, which methought did promise
  Most venerable worth, did I devotion, 350

351. Quite understandably, the Officer is not interested in all this – his job is to arrest Antonio. ***The time goes by*** 'We're wasting time.'
352–7. But Antonio is so consumed with indignation that he hardly hears him.
352. *vile* of no value.
353. *good feature* outward appearance of goodness. Antonio means that 'Sebastian' has, by his conduct, discredited the whole concept of beauty.
354. Antonio himself now proceeds to reject outward beauty – it has lost all value for him. The only ugliness (***blemish***) he now considers is that of the mind, or character.
356. *Virtue is beauty* Compare 'Beauty is truth, truth beauty,' from Keats' *Ode on a Grecian Urn*.
356–7. *the beauteous evil . . . by the devil* 'wicked people with beautiful looks are like hollow trees, overgrown (***o'erflourished***) with another plant, or weed, which may look nice, but is in fact deadly.'
360. When Antonio does finally consent to go along with them, we can well imagine that his arrest has become a matter of little concern to him, compared with his present mental distress.
361–4. It is now Viola's turn to be nonplussed. But Antonio's very sincerity leads her to think that he must believe that there is someone – obviously (to her) not herself – who has treated him like this. So she goes on to hope (***Prove true, imagination***) that Antonio has in fact mistaken her for her brother (which would be strong evidence that he was still alive).
365–6. The approach of the other three passes without notice.

First Officer
  What's that to us? The times goes by; away.
Antonio
  But, O, how vile an idol proves this god!
  Thou hast, Sebastian, done good feature shame.
  In nature there's no blemish but the mind:
  None can be call'd deform'd but the unkind. 355
  Virtue is beauty; but the beauteous evil
  Are empty trunks, o'erflourish'd by the devil.
First Officer
  The man grows mad. Away with him. Come, come, sir.
Antonio
  Lead me on. 360
              [Exit with officers]
Viola
  Methinks his words do from such passion fly
  That he believes himself; so do not I.
  Prove true, imagination, O, prove true,
  That I, dear brother, be now ta'en for you!
Sir Toby
  Come hither, knight; come hither, Fabian; we'll whisper 365
  o'er a couplet or two of most sage saws.

367–8. *I my brother know Yet living in my glass* Every time Viola looks at herself in a mirror she can imagine that she is looking at her brother.
369. *favour* looks.
369–71. *he went still . . . I imitate* 'the clothes he was wearing were like those I now have on – for I chose them in imitation.' Sebastian and Viola have to be in the same attire (a simple enough matter for the wardrobe mistress), if their being mistaken for each other is to be at all credible on the stage. To make their faces look alike is a much less simple business, one which will have to depend virtually upon the audience's imagination.
371. *if it prove* if it proves true.
372. 'Storms and waves (like the ones that nearly drowned them both) will have shown themselves to be entirely friendly.'
There is something appropriate in the use of prose to end the scene. It suits the detached, unemotional, almost callous attitude of the three as they 'dissect' Viola's character – just as the verse she has just used was the best way to express her intense emotion. Sir Toby and the others have no sympathy now for Viola, and are conscious only of her cowardice and apparent disloyalty. It is part of the irony of Viola's present situation that she should be suspected of such faithlessness, when in fact she is the most loyal of creatures.
373–4. *more a coward than a hare* 'a greater coward than a hare' (noted for its timorousness).
377. *devout coward, religious in it*. An obvious contradiction, and laughable for that reason. We can, however, understand why Fabian describes her attitude thus. He is emphasising her preoccupation with her fear; it fills all her thoughts, as one's religion should, and produces a state of intense emotion.
378. What can one think of Sir Andrew for suggesting this now? *'Slid* 'By God's lid' (eye-lid); a contemporary oath, like ''sblood' (God's blood) and 'zounds' (God's wounds).
381. *event* outcome.

ACT 3 SCENE 4

Viola
    He nam'd Sebastian. I my brother know
    Yet living in my glass; even such and so
    In favour was my brother; and he went
    Still in this fashion, colour, ornament,   370
    For him I imitate. O, if it prove,
    Tempests are kind, and salt waves fresh in love!
                      [Exit]

Sir Toby
    A very dishonest paltry boy, and more a coward than
    a hare. His dishonesty appears in leaving his friend here
    in necessity and denying him; and for his cowardship,   375
    ask Fabian.

Fabian
    A coward, a most devout coward, religious in it.

Sir Andrew
    'Slid, I'll after him again and beat him.

Sir Toby
    Do; cuff him soundly, but never draw thy sword.

Sir Andrew
    An I do not—   380
                      [Exit]

Fabian
    Come, let's see the event.

Sir Toby
    I dare lay any money 'twill be nothing yet.
                      [Exeunt]

ACT 4 SCENE 1

This scene is virtually a continuation of the previous one. The confusion over the identity of Sebastian and Viola, which produced harrowing effects before, is the subject once again, only this time the outcome is entirely laughable. The main humour of the scene (to us) is prefaced by some typical 'clown-wit' – perhaps as a kind of appetiser. The source is still the same – Sebastian is mistaken for Viola – but this is the first occasion on which he is made aware of the confusion, and is touched personally by it. Unlike his sister, who could only wonder and suffer, he is able to fight back, and at the end of it all there is a prize for him that he can gladly accept.

So in this first encounter, it is Feste really who is thrown on to the defensive, having to justify himself, and prove to Sebastian that he is talking sense, and that his request is genuine – both of which he fails to do.

1. 'How can you possibly convince me that I have not been sent to fetch you?'

4. **Well held out, i'faith** (ironically) 'that's a fine show you're putting up.' The rest of Feste's speech is also ironical – he quotes all the things that to him are plain facts (at least they would be if Sebastian were in fact 'Cesario', and Feste believes he is), and says that they are all untrue.

7. **nor this is not my nose neither**. A triple negative. We only need a single one!

9. **vent** discharge. This use of the word was still probably somewhat unfamiliar. Feste picks upon it and repeats it mockingly. (Is Feste beginning to lose his customary self-possession? We could hardly blame him in the circumstances.)

13. **lubber** loutish person.

13. **cockney** foppish, effeminate person. Sebastian's use of such language makes Feste begin to wonder whether the whole world, for all its roughness, will soon be adopting similar affectations of speech (**will prove a cockney**).

14. **ungird thy strangeness** 'stop pretending not to know me.'

17. **Greek**. Often used then to describe a merry person.

22. **after fourteen years' purchase** The value of land was calculated at twelve annual rentals. One was paying dearly at fourteen rentals. Feste is probably despising Sebastian for giving him such a large 'bribe' – he takes it as a sign of weakness in Sebastian, almost as an admission of defeat. (Feste's observation will be spoken as an 'aside'.)

ACT 4
SCENE 1

Before Olivia's house

[Enter SEBASTIAN *and* CLOWN*]*

Clown
Will you make me believe that I am not sent for you?
Sebastian
Go to, go to, thou art a foolish fellow; let me be clear of
thee.
Clown
Well held out, i' faith! No, I do not know you;
nor I am not sent to you by my lady, to bid you come   5
speak with her; nor your name is not Master Cesario;
nor this is not my nose neither. Nothing that is so is
so.
Sebastian
I prithee vent thy folly somewhere else. Thou know'st
not me.   10
Clown
Vent my folly! He has heard that word of some great
man, and now applies it to a fool. Vent my folly! I am
afraid this great lubber, the world, will prove a cockney.
I prithee now, ungird thy strangeness, and tell me what
I shall vent to my lady. Shall I vent to her that thou   15
art coming?
Sebastian
I prithee, foolish Greek, depart from me;
There's money for thee; if you tarry longer
I shall give worse payment.
Clown
By my troth, thou hast an open hand. These wise men   20
that give fools money get themselves a good
report – after fourteen years' purchase.

[Enter SIR ANDREW, SIR TOBY, *and* FABIAN*]*

24. There's for you 'Take that!'

27. Hold stop.

28–9. in some of your coats. Today we say, 'in your shoes'.

31–2. I'll go another way to work with him Sir Andrew realises that he must try something else, having come off the worse in this latest encounter.
32. battery The legal term for 'physical assault on the person'.
33–4. it's no matter for that 'it doesn't matter.'

37. iron sword. **well flesh'd** experienced in fighting.

42. malapert impudent.

Sir Andrew
  Now, sir, have I met you again?
  [Striking SEBASTIAN*]* There's for you.
Sebastian
  Why, there's for thee, and there, and there. 25
  Are all the people mad?
Sir Toby
  Hold, sir, or I'll throw your dagger o'er the house.
                              [Holding SEBASTIAN*]*
Clown
  This will I tell my lady straight. I would not be in some
  of your coats for two-pence.
                [Exit]
Sir Toby
  Come on, sir; hold. 30
Sir Andrew
  Nay, let him alone. I'll go another way to work with
  him; I'll have an action of battery against him, if there
  be any law in Illyria; though I struck him first, yet it's
  no matter for that.
Sebastian
  Let go thy hand. 35
Sir Toby
  Come, sir, I will not let you go. Come, my young
  soldier, put up your iron; you are well flesh'd. Come
  on.
Sebastian
  I will be free from thee. What wouldst thou now?
  If thou dar'st tempt me further, draw thy sword. 40
                              [Draws]
Sir Toby
  What, what? Nay, then I must have an ounce or two
  of this malapert blood from you.   *[Draws]*
                [Enter OLIVIA*]*
Olivia
  Hold, Toby; on thy life, I charge thee hold.

45. *Will it ever be thus?* Olivia says this with almost weary resignation – 'Will you never change your ways?' The rhetorical outburst that follows must make Sir Toby feel even more rejected than if Olivia had remonstrated with him in everyday terms. It is as if she has been offering hospitality to her uncle only out of charity, perhaps keeping up some sort of pretence to herself that his grossness might be cured. But this pretence is now shattered, and Olivia casts him off almost as if she could never have seriously regarded him as a kinsman. (This incident may suggest, in a small way, the rejection of Falstaff by Prince Hal, in the second part of *Henry IV*.)

48. How effective that, in the middle of her fiery dismissal of the others, Olivia should show such tender concern for 'Cesario'!

49. *Rudesby* lout.

49–57. Perhaps Olivia is secretly glad of an opportunity – which she has not had to initiate – for fresh and close contact with 'Viola'. There is little reason for her suggestion – to make amends for Sebastian's rough treatment – that they should return to the house, and even less that they should pass the time hearing of Sir Toby's other misdemeanours.

50. *sway* influence (you).

51. *uncivil* discourteous; ***extent*** assault (a legal term).

53. *fruitless* 'pointless' probably, rather than 'unsuccessful'.

54. *botch'd up* 'put together anyhow' (in a rough way).

56. *deny* refuse. ***Beshrew*** Curse. The shrew was commonly held to possess malevolent qualities.)

57. A difficult line – the meaning probably is that Sir Toby, by his rough treatment of Sebastian ('Cesario', of course, in Olivia's mind), **started** or startled Olivia. Being so in love, Olivia would feel the outrage as if levelled against herself.

58. *What relish is in this?* 'What does this taste like?' 'What am I to make of this?' ***How runs the stream?*** has much the same significance.

59. *Or . . . or* We would say 'Either . . . or.'

60. *Lethe* a river of the Underworld in ancient Greek mythology. To drink its water induced forgetfulness of one's past life on earth, ***steep*** immerse. ***still*** is used adverbially here; the modern order of words would be: 'Let fancy steep my senses in Lethe still' – 'Let my imagination continue to lull my senses, so that I forget reality.'

61. *If it be thus to dream* 'If this is what dreaming is like.'

62. *Would thou'dst be rul'd by me* 'I wish you would accept my advice.' 'Would' (or more usually 'Would that') was a common way of introducing a wish, and meant 'I wish that . . .'

Sir Toby
  Madam!
Olivia
  Will it be ever thus? Ungracious wretch, 45
  Fit for the mountains and the barbarous caves,
  Where manners ne'er were preach'd! Out of my sight!
  Be not offended, dear Cesario—
  Rudesby, be gone!
      [Exeunt SIR TOBY, SIR ANDREW, *and* FABIAN*]*
              I prithee, gentle friend,
  Let thy fair wisdom, not thy passion, sway 50
  In this uncivil and unjust extent
  Against thy peace. Go with me to my house,
  And hear thou there how many fruitless pranks
  This ruffian hath botch'd up, that thou thereby
  Mayst smile at this. Thou shalt not choose but go; 55
  Do not deny. Beshrew his soul for me!
  He started one poor heart of mine in thee.
Sebastian
  What relish is in this? How runs the stream?
  Or I am mad, or else this is a dream.
  Let fancy still my sense in Lethe steep; 60
  If it be thus to dream, still let me sleep!
Olivia
  Nay, come, I prithee. Would thou'dst be rul'd by me!
Sebastian
  Madam, I will.
Olivia
          O, say so, and so be!
          [Exeunt]

SCENE 2

The sequel to this promising encounter between Olivia and Sebastian is delayed, in order to make way for a scene of a very different kind. Perhaps it is only the pleasurable anticipation that has just been aroused that tides us over this next shabby piece of Malvolio-baiting. By this time, with Olivia's (and Sebastian's) fortunes so obviously drawing to a climax, we may have begun to lose interest in Malvolio's fate. With his humiliation already effected, he has little further to do dramatically. The inclusion, therefore, of this scene may strike us as a forcing of the humour of the Malvolio plot – little more than a concession to the cruder elements in the audience. This is perhaps a good illustration of the intrinsic contrast between the two kinds of comedy brought together in *Twelfth Night* – the Comedy of Humours seems to have exhausted itself, while Shakespeare's 'character-development' approach has not yet reached its prime.

2. Sir Topas the curate The title 'Sir' was commonly applied to a priest. (Viola says she would rather 'go with sir priest than sir knight', in Act 3, Scene 4.) The name 'Thopas' was chosen by Chaucer for the knight in the tale he ascribes to himself, in *The Canterbury Tales*. Also, the precious stone, the topaz, was used in treating lunacy. Malvolio is to be treated, as before, as one possessed by a devil; and, dressed as a priest, Feste will drive the point home more convincingly. Whereas earlier, the thought that Malvolio might really be devil-possessed, threw Maria into a certain panic, she has no qualms now about initiating this latest torment.

3. the whilst in the meantime.

5. Feste plays on the two meanings of **dissemble**. He uses it first simply as 'disguise', but then in an unfavourable sense – 'behave deceptively'. He is having a 'dig' at the clergy, who, by very reason of their high calling, must always run the risk of being termed hypocritical.

6. tall good; **become** suit.

7. function i.e. of the priest. **lean enough** A hard-working student would have little time or money to live comfortably or grow fat.

8. to be said to be called.

9. housekeeper Either 'one who stays at home (leading a quiet, law-abiding life)', or 'a hospitable person'. **goes as fairly as to say** 'is as good as being called.' Feste seems to mean that, for all his ordinariness, he is just as good as the scholarly parson he is impersonating.

10. competitors partners.

11. Jove bless thee For this use of 'Jove' instead of 'God', see note on Act 3, Scene 4, line 71.

SCENE 2

Olivia's house

[Enter MARIA and CLOWN]

Maria
Nay, I prithee, put on this gown and this beard; make him believe thou art Sir Topas the curate; do it quickly. I'll call Sir Toby the whilst.

[Exit]

Clown
Well, I'll put it on, and I will dissemble myself in't; and I would I were the first that ever dissembled in such a gown. I am not tall enough to become the function well nor lean enough to be thought a good student; but to be said an honest man and a good housekeeper goes as fairly as to say a careful man and a great scholar. The competitors enter.

[Enter SIR TOBY and MARIA]

Sir Toby
Jove bless thee, Master Parson.

12. *Bonos dies* good day. ***old hermit of Prague*** a typical Feste invention, which sounds almost authentic.

14. *King Gorboduc*. A legendary British King. (The first English tragedy in blank verse was about him.) Feste clearly enjoys playing this part, in which he can positively revel in pseudo-scholarship, interlaced, however, with enough genuine learning to convince Malvolio that he is a bona-fide priest.

21–2. *Malvolio the lunatic*. Malvolio's chief fault was in thinking too highly of himself, and in this way welcoming untruth. It was a sort of 'sin against the light', as all self-conceit must be in some measure. The mental torture to which he is now subjected – being made to feel that he can no longer rely on the plain evidence of his senses, and that his very reasoning powers are false – is therefore highly appropriate, if excessively severe. The effect it actually has upon Malvolio is, however, to throw him entirely upon the resources of his own reason. There is nothing else for him to grasp except the plain functioning of reason. And this, we may like to believe, is the beginning of his cure – whether Maria and the others intended that it should turn out like this, or were simply out for one final laugh at his expense. (We have to admire Malvolio for his heroic defiance of what to most of us would have seemed unanswerable opposition.)

24. *hyperbolical* excessively bad. The expected word would be 'diabolical' – devilish. But Feste's use of ***hyperbolical*** is not entirely out of place. (Literally, Feste's phrase means 'excessive fiend').

25. *Talkest thou nothing but of ladies?* This kind of wilful misunderstanding is a familiar humorous device, and particularly effective if it substitutes something that is as inappropriate as in this instance. (Malvolio is the last person we would describe as a lady's man!)

30. *dishonest*. Satan is referred to in the Bible as the 'Father of Lies'. Feste's humour here consists in claiming to speak with restraint, but in fact, addressing 'the Devil' quite bluntly.

32–3. *Say'st thou that house is dark?* Feste's simple plan is to contradict Malvolio flatly at every point, in such a way as to persuade him that he must be quite out of his mind ('seeing things' as we say). The darkness of Malvolio's 'prison' was to him the one central fact of his life just then. So this is the reality that Feste proceeds to deny. But he goes further – he mixes sense with nonsense in such a way as to shatter, if possible, Malvolio's very hold upon sanity. A less tough victim would have surrendered to such nightmarish treatment.

ACT 4 SCENE 2

Clown
  Bonos dies, Sir Toby; for as the old hermit of Prague,
  that never saw pen and ink, very wittily said to a niece
  of King Gorboduc 'That that is is'; so I, being Master
  Parson, am Master Parson; for what is 'that' but that, 15
  and 'is' but is?
Sir Toby
  To him, Sir Topas.
Clown
  What ho, I say! Peace in this prison!
Sir Toby
  The knave counterfeits well; a good knave.
Malvolio [*Within*]
  Who calls there? 20
Clown
  Sir Topas the curate, who comes to visit Malvolio the
  lunatic.
Malvolio
  Sir Topas, Sir Topas, good Sir Topas, go to my lady.
Clown
  Out, hyperbolical fiend! How vexest thou this man!
  Talkest thou nothing but of ladies? 25
Sir Toby
  Well said, Master Parson.
Malvolio
  Sir Topas, never was man thus wronged. Good Sir Topas,
  do not think I am mad; they have laid me here in
  hideous darkness.
Clown
  Fie, thou dishonest Satan! I call thee by the most 30
  modest terms, for I am one of those gentle ones that
  will use the devil himself with courtesy. Say'st thou
  that house is dark?
Malvolio
  As hell, Sir Topas.

35. *barricadoes* barricades. This is intentional nonsense; a barricade is designed solely to block up an opening, and seal it off – not to let in the light!
36. *clerestories* windows set high up in the walls of a church or hall, their chief purpose being to let in plenty of light. ***south north*** An impossible compass direction, of course, but, again, delivered with apparent authority.
37. *lustrous as ebony*. The third of Feste's paradoxes – ebony is black, so what sort of light shines through them?
38. *obstruction* i.e. of the light.
41–2. *no darkness but ignorance*. Part of the effect of this valid observation is to imply to Malvolio that the darkness he experiences is simply the projection of his own inner darkness or ignorance.
43. *Egyptians in their fog*. Probably a reference to the 'plague' of darkness that afflicted the Egyptians at the time of the Israelites' exodus (see *Exodus*, Chapter 10).
44. Malvolio's mental powers show no weakening – the old intractable spirit is still active.
47. He will welcome any opportunity to prove, in honest argument, that he is as sane as they are. ***constant question*** is a question of hard fact, not just opinion, which Feste could twist to suit himself.
48. *Pythagoras* a philosopher of Ancient Greece, who taught the doctrine of Transmigration of Souls – that, at death, the soul entered the body of some other living creature, human or otherwise. (He is chiefly remembered today for his mathematical propositions.)
50. *Grandam* grandmother. ***haply*** by chance.

53. A reasonable and tactful reply!

56–7. But Feste is adamant – Malvolio must accept Pythagoras' theory before Feste will admit that he is in his right mind (***allow of thy wits***).

60. Sir Toby says this teasingly, but with admiration for Feste's success in 'bringing off' the deception.

ACT 4 SCENE 2

Clown
   Why, it hath bay windows transparent as barricadoes, 35
   and the clerestories toward the south north are as
   lustrous as ebony; and yet complainest thou of
   obstruction?

Malvolio
   I am not mad, Sir Topas, I say to you this house is
   dark. 40

Clown
   Madman, thou errest. I say there is no darkness but
   ignorance; in which thou art more puzzled than the
   Egyptians in their fog.

Malvolio
   I say this house is as dark as ignorance, though
   ignorance were as dark as hell; and I say there was never 45
   man thus abus'd. I am no more mad than you are;
   make the trial of it in any constant question.

Clown
   What is the opinion of Pythagoras concerning wild
   fowl?

Malvolio
   That the soul of our grandam might haply inhabit a 50
   bird.

Clown
   What think'st thou of his opinion?

Malvolio
   I think nobly of the soul, and no way approve his
   opinion.

Clown
   Fare thee well. Remain thou still in darkness: thou 55
   shalt hold th' opinion of Pythagoras ere I will allow
   of thy wits; and fear to kill a woodcock, lest thou
   dispossess the soul of thy grandam. Fare thee well.

Malvolio
   Sir Topas, Sir Topas!

Sir Toby
   My most exquisite Sir Topas! 60

61. ***for all waters*** 'ready for anything'.

62–3. Maria's comment is perfectly true; but the disguise was really for the audience's entertainment.

65–9. We can well understand Sir Toby's misgivings. This treatment of Olivia's steward would have been a risky thing to attempt in any circumstances, but quite foolhardy in view of Sir Toby's present low standing with his niece.

66. ***deliver'd*** set free.

67. ***I am now so far in offence with my niece*** 'I'm now so much in my niece's bad books,' 'I've done so much which has offended her.'

68–9. ***to the upshot*** to its conclusion, ***by and by*** shortly.

70–7. Feste's song has the same mocking effect on Malvolio as the one sung earlier by Sir Toby and himself, in Act 2, Scene 3. In each case the intention is to treat Malvolio as if he isn't there, or at least doesn't matter. In this present instance, it is particularly hurtful, for Malvolio is in great desperation, and yet he can get no response or reaction of any kind from Feste till the end of his song. The words of the song itself are not going to help either – Malvolio's pursuit of Olivia has been ill-fated enough already, and he doesn't need a song to remind him that women can be unfaithful.

73. ***perdy*** 'par Dieu.' (A softer version, since it's in a foreign language, of the literal 'By God,' which was too profane for common usage.)

79. ***help me to*** 'please fetch me.'

80. ***thankful*** deserving of thanks. If Feste will do him this kindness, then Malvolio (***as I am a gentleman***) will, by rewarding him, deserve his thanks (for the reward).

81. Feste pretends that he has only just recognised the voice.

Clown
  Nay, I am for all waters.
Maria
  Thou mightst have done this without thy beard and
  gown: he sees thee not.
Sir Toby
  To him in thine own voice, and bring me word how
  thou find'st him. I would we were well rid of this 65
  knavery. If he may be conveniently deliver'd, I would
  he were; for I am now so far in offence with my niece
  that I cannot pursue with any safety this sport to the
  upshot. Come by and by to my chamber.

        [Exeunt SIR TOBY *and* MARIA*]*

Clown [Sings]
  Hey, Robin, jolly Robin, 70
  Tell me how thy lady does.
Malvolio
  Fool!
Clown [Sings]
  My lady is unkind, perdy.
Malvolio
  Fool!
Clown [Sings]
  Alas, why is she so? 75
Malvolio
  Fool I say!
Clown [Sings]
  She loves another – Who calls, ha?
Malvolio
  Good fool, as ever thou wilt deserve well at my hand,
  help me to a candle, and pen, ink, and paper; as I am
  a gentleman, I will live to be thankful to thee for't. 80
Clown
  Master Malvolio?
Malvolio
  Ay, good fool.

83. *'Alas, sir, how is it that you are out of your mind?'* **besides** out of. **five wits** normal faculties. The Elizabethans listed them as follows: commonsense, imagination, fancy, estimation and memory.

86. **But** Only. Feste is getting his own back now, for Malvolio's earlier scorn of him and of all professional fools (Act 1, Scene 5). So there is more in his reply here than just a play on the two meanings of 'fool'.

88. **propertied** used as their property, for their own ends.

89–90. **face me out of my wits**. A most apt description of the way Feste has, by barefaced lies, tried to convince Malvolio that he must be mad.

91. **Advise you** Take care. ('Advisedly' means 'after due consideration.')

92–4. The sudden change of voice and manner is a well-used comic device, and parsonical tones have always been 'good for a laugh'. The artificial order (object-subject-verb) of **thy wits the heavens restore**, and the stilted **Endeavour thyself to sleep** stress further the contrast Feste wants to make between himself as Clown and himself as Sir Topas.

94. **bibble-babble** senseless talk.

96–8. Feste pretends to be now himself, now Sir Topas, changing his voice (and possibly – for our benefit, since Malvolio can see none of this – his position on the stage, and even part of his disguise) in rapid alternation. This bit of lightning conversation with himself can be very amusing.

Maintain . . . fellow is by Sir Topas.

Who, I . . . Sir Topas by Feste.

Marry, amen – Sir Topas.

I will, sir, I will – Feste.

100. **shent** blamed. Feste means that he shouldn't really be talking to someone like Malvolio.

105. **Well-a-day** Alas. **that** if. 'It would be a bad look-out if you were' (that is to say if other people were as mad as Malvolio!).

ACT 4 SCENE 2

Clown
  Alas, sir, how fell you besides your five wits?
Malvolio
  Fool, there was never man so notoriously abus'd; I am
  as well in my wits, fool, as thou art.   85
Clown
  But as well? Then you are mad indeed, if you be no
  better in your wits than a fool.
Malvolio
  They have here propertied me; keep me in darkness,
  send ministers to me, asses, and do all they can to face
  me out of my wits.   90
Clown
  Advise you what you say: the minister is here. *[Speaking
  as* SIR TOPAS*]* Malvolio, Malvolio, thy wits the heavens
  restore! Endeavour thyself to sleep, and leave thy vain
  bibble-babble.
Malvolio
  Sir Topas!   95
Clown
  Maintain no words with him, good fellow. – Who, I,
  sir? Not I, sir. God buy you, good Sir Topas. – Marry,
  amen. – I will, sir, I will.
Malvolio
  Fool, fool, fool, I say!
Clown
  Alas, sir, be patient. What say you, sir? I am shent for 100
  speaking to you.
Malvolio
  Good fool, help me to some light and some paper.
  I tell thee I am as well in my wits as any man in
  Illyria.
Clown
  Well-a-day that you were, sir!   105

107. *convey what I will set down* 'take what I am going to write.'

110–11. Perhaps Feste's most ingenious question – 'Are you mad, or just pretending to be?'

113. *till I see his brains*. This could mean several things: 'Till I see some evidence of his intelligence,' or 'Till he is dead' (in other words, 'never'), or most likely, 'Till I have the unmistakable medical proof in front of me.'
115. *requite* repay.

117. Feste's song refers to the old morality plays, in which 'Vice' – probably the prototype of the professional jester, and similarly portrayed – would, as part of his routine, leap upon the Devil and beat him with a wooden (***of lath***) dagger till he cried out. He would also make a show of cutting the Devil's nails with the dagger (***Pare thy nails***).

128. *goodman*. This word, followed by the name of a person's occupation, served as a term of address.

Malvolio
By this hand, I am. Good fool, some ink, paper, and light; and convey what I will set down to my lady. It shall advantage thee more than ever the bearing of letter did.
Clown
I will help you to't. But tell me true, are you not mad indeed, or do you but counterfeit?
Malvolio
Believe me, I am not; I tell thee true.
Clown
Nay, I'll ne'er believe a madman till I see his brains. I will fetch you light and paper and ink.
Malvolio
Fool, I'll requite it in the highest degree; I prithee be gone.
Clown *[Singing]*
  I am gone, sir,
  And anon, sir,
 I'll be with you again,
  In a trice,
  Like to the old Vice,
 Your need to sustain;
 Who with dagger of lath,
 In his rage and his wrath,
  Cries, Ah, ha! to the devil,
 Like a mad lad,
 Pare thy nails, dad.
  Adieu, goodman devil.

[Exit]

SCENE 3

The fresh air and sunshine, which tally so exactly with Sebastian's hopefulness, are in strong contrast with Malvolio's darkness and frustration. What dramatic purpose is served by this? Is it solely for our benefit, to cheer us up after the questionable goings-on in the last scene?

1–2. By using his senses, Sebastian seeks to convince himself that he is not just imagining his present good fortune. (Is this intended as a further contrast? – Malvolio was almost brow-beaten into giving up all trust in *his* senses.)

6. there he was 'he had been there.' *credit* general opinion.

8. counsel advice. *golden service* 'service so valuable as to deserve generous (golden) reward.' As he goes on to say, Sebastian needs Antonio's clear-headedness to help him out of his confusion.

9–21. The argument here is involved – which is not inappropriate, since Sebastian is extremely confused by what is happening to him, and not likely to express himself over-simply.

9–10. soul . . . sense. The higher and the lower human faculties. *disputes well.* They are both in agreement, that Sebastian's present situation may be the result of a misunderstanding (*error*) but it does not mean that he has gone mad (*no madness*).

11. accident that which has actually happened. *flood* fulness, 'the wonderful way things have turned out.'

12. instance example, precedent. *discourse* reasoning, 'normal experience, both outward and inward.' This seems to take us back to *soul* and *sense* in line 9, and is repeated by *eyes* and *reason* in lines 13 and 14.

14–16. persuades me . . . the lady's mad 'persuades me that neither I nor the lady is mad.' (Literally, 'persuades me to believe anything else except that I and the lady are mad.') In other words, what is happening is so 'out of this world' that Sebastian is inclined to distrust his common-sense when it tells him that this is probably just a case of misunderstanding.

16–19. But the alternative is not satisfactory either, for Sebastian cannot wholly believe that Olivia *is* mad, because of the obviously sane way she manages her household.

17. sway her house 'run her house' is how we would put it today.

18. 'Handle business matters, making sure things are properly carried out.'

21. deceivable 'not what it seems.'

ACT 4 SCENE 3

SCENE 3

Olivia's garden

[Enter SEBASTIAN*]*

Sebastian
    This is the air; that is the glorious sun;
    This pearl she gave me, I do feel't and see't;
    And though 'tis wonder that enwraps me thus,
    Yet 'tis not madness. Where's Antonio, then?
    I could not find him at the Elephant;   5
    Yet there he was; and there I found this credit,
    That he did range the town to seek me out.
    His counsel now might do me golden service;
    For though my soul disputes well with my sense
    That this may be some error, but no madness,   10
    Yet doth this accident and flood of fortune
    So far exceed all instance, all discourse,
    That I am ready to distrust mine eyes
    And wrangle with my reason, that persuades me
    To any other trust but that I am mad,   15
    Or else the lady's mad; yet if 'twere so,
    She could not sway her house, command her followers,
    Take and give back affairs and their dispatch
    With such a smooth, discreet, and stable bearing,
    As I perceive she does. There's something in't   20
    That is deceivable. But here the lady comes.

[Enter OLIVIA *and* PRIEST*]*

22. Blame not this haste of mine It seems to be Olivia's fate to be landed in situations where, for all her would-be dignity and poise, she finds herself doing all the wrong things. It is not surprising that she feels she must apologise for acting with such indecent haste, and producing a priest so precipitately to officiate at their betrothal.
24. chantry a small private chapel, with a priest permanently resident. (People of means often endowed a chantry and priest, so that Mass could be said regularly on their behalf.) *by* nearby.
26. Plight pledge, solemnly promise. *of your faith* 'that you will be faithful.'
27–8. That my most jealous and too doubtful soul May live at peace. Olivia's jealousy and uncertainty would make her suspicious and anxious, but once he is 'secured' by betrothal she can relax. Though not complete wedlock, betrothal was solemnly binding, much more so than our modern 'engagement'.
28. He the priest.
29. Whiles until ('While'='until' in North of England conversation still.) *come to note* be made public.
30. What time At which time.
31. According to my birth 'As befits my social status.'
34. father a traditional term of address for a priest.
35. fairly note 'look favourably upon.'

Olivia
    Blame not this haste of mine. If you mean well,
    Now go with me and with this holy man
    Into the chantry by; there, before him
    And underneath that consecrated roof,   25
    Plight me the full assurance of your faith,
    That my most jealous and too doubtful soul
    May live at peace. He shall conceal it
    Whiles you are willing it shall come to note,
    What time we will our celebration keep   30
    According to my birth. What do you say?
Sebastian
    I'll follow this good man, and go with you;
    And, having sworn truth, ever will be true.
Olivia
    Then lead the way, good father; and heavens so shine
    That they may fairly note this act of mine!   35

        [Exeunt]

ACT 5 SCENE 1

The resolving of all the confusions that have been building up since the play began – *Twelfth Night* has more than most – is the inevitable business of this final act. Traditionally, this must take place in the presence of someone of highest rank (in this case the Duke Orsino). He alone will be in a position to administer whatever is required of justice and reconciliation, and to guarantee permanence and stability. Orsino has this further reason to be present at the dénouement, since he is as closely implicated in the confusion as anyone else. Apart from some initial clowning, the whole of the action serves this end – to gather together the whole company, introducing, explaining and reconciling. Malvolio alone stands outside the final happy reunion (from choice, however) though Sir Toby's and Sir Andrew's leave-taking is under almost as heavy a cloud.

1. *as* if. *his letter*. i.e. the one Malvolio has written, from 'prison'.
3. *anything* 'Whatever you ask.'

5–6. *desire my dog again* i.e. want to have it back.

8. *trappings* literally, 'trivial ornaments.' (Why does Feste so describe himself and Fabian?)
9. *I know thee well*. When did Orsino and Feste first meet?

10. *for* because of.

ACT 5
SCENE 1

Before Olivia's house

[*Enter* CLOWN *and* FABIAN]

Fabian
Now, as thou lov'st me, let me see his letter.
Clown
Good Master Fabian, grant me another request.
Fabian
Anything.
Clown
Do not desire to see this letter.
Fabian
This is to give a dog, and in recompense desire my   5
dog again.

[*Enter* DUKE, VIOLA, CURIO *and* LORDS]

Duke
Belong you to the Lady Olivia, friends?
Clown
Ay, sir, we are some of her trappings.
Duke
I know thee well. How dost thou, my good fellow?
Clown
Truly, sir, the better for my foes and the worse for my   10
friends.
Duke
Just the contrary: the better for thy friends.
Clown
No, sir, the worse.
Duke
How can that be?
Clown
Marry, sir, they praise me and make an ass of me. Now   15
my foes tell me plainly I am an ass; so that by my
foes, sir, I profit in the knowledge of myself, and by

18. *abused* deceived.

19. *your . . . your* 'the ones we are talking about.'

26–7. A neat pun – *double-dealing* normally means 'acting dishonestly', but here Feste also uses it to mean 'making the gift twice as large.'

29. *grace* (God's special help) is a theological antithesis to *flesh and blood* (man's natural, unrefined instincts). Since Orsino has described Feste's argument (about what he should give him) as *ill counsel*, and therefore not to be listened to, Feste, in order to win his point, has to urge him to ignore conscience (*Put your grace in your pocket*) and obey his natural instincts – and Feste's request at the same time! This is all purely in fun; neither of them is taking any of it seriously.

33–6. Quick as ever, Feste calls to mind four separate examples of 'threes', to cajole Orsino into adding yet another coin to the two already given. (When he first met Viola, Feste followed the same tactics. How much did he scrounge from her?)

33. *Primo, secundo, tertio* First, second, third. Probably refers to a contemporary schoolboys' game. *play* 'throw', probably, rather than 'game'.

35. *Saint Bennet* a well-known church (probably one that used to stand near the Globe Theatre, and was destroyed in the Great Fire of London), and with an obviously familiar triple chime.

37. *throw* (literally 'throw of the dice'), attempt.

39–40. *awake my bounty*. Orsino's metaphor here is almost unconscious – it simply adds a certain graciousness to his half-promise.

41–5. But Feste's reply is perhaps his best demonstration of quick-thinking in the whole play. He won't let it be just a conventional turn of speech, but at once develops the idea of sleep and waking, to serve as a slight but ingenious reminder that he hopes for Orsino's undivided generosity. For if the Duke's bounty will need to be awakened, this implies that it will have gone to sleep – which will suit Feste admirably, since he doesn't want it to be exercised in any other direction but his own! So *lullaby to your bounty* he says, 'keep a tight hold on your money – till I come back!' (*I will awake it anon*).

my friends I am abused; so that, conclusions to be as
kisses, if your four negatives make your two
affirmatives, why then, the worse for my friends, and the   20
better for my foes.
Duke
Why, this is excellent.
Clown
By my troth, sir, no; though it please you to be one
of my friends.
Duke
Thou shalt not be the worse for me. There's gold.   25
Clown
But that it would be double-dealing, sir, I would you
could make it another.
Duke
O, you give me ill counsel.
Clown
Put your grace in your pocket, sir, for this once, and
let your flesh and blood obey it.   30
Duke
Well, I will be so much a sinner to be a double-dealer.
There's another.
Clown
Primo, secundo, tertio, is a good play; and the old
saying is 'The third pays for all'. The triplex, sir, is a
good tripping measure; or the bells of Saint Bennet,   35
sir, may put you in mind – one, two, three.
Duke
You can fool no more money out of me at this throw;
if you will let your lady know I am here to speak with
her, and bring her along with you, it may awake my
bounty further.   40
Clown
Marry, sir, lullaby to your bounty till I come again. I
go, sir; but I would not have you to think that my
desire of having is the sin of covetousness. But, as you
say, sir, let your bounty take a nap; I will awake it
anon.   45

46. Serious things now take over, with the arrival, under escort, of Antonio, to answer his charge before the Duke. The dialogue, then, is continued in verse, which is sustained until, as a timely relaxation, Sir Andrew appears with news of less dignified happenings. Antonio's affairs, interesting enough in themselves, have always subserved dramatically the fortunes of first, Sebastian, and now, Viola. To extract the full flavour from Viola's plight – a necessary prelude to the happy ending – there must be an intensifying of her ordeal, a 'piling-up', as never before, of undeserved suffering. (Many heroines are seen on the very brink of disaster and disgrace before their final rescue!) So she must once again bear the brunt of Antonio's scorn, and then (a worse ordeal, we may imagine) the hatred of her dearly loved Orsino, the cause in each case being the unfaithfulness they so wrongly suspect. To this we can add the bewilderment she suffers when Olivia insists that she had already become her husband, and when Sir Toby and Sir Andrew insist that it is she who has just assaulted them. But if Viola is to be reinstated with the full acclaim of the whole company – and this is the chief point now – she must submit to this public scrutiny.

Notice how Viola's greeting of Antonio's appearance brings out her innate warm-heartedness. She recalls his kindness only – nothing of his fierce incriminations.

47–72. But now, for a while, all thought is for Antonio for his own sake. Courtly matters recede, and the man's world of battle and violence takes over.

49. *Vulcan* the Roman god of fire.
50. *baubling* trifling, insignificant.
51. *unprizable* of no value.
52. *scathful* harmful. *grapple* joining in battle.
53. *bottom* ship. (The figure of speech used here – a part of something when the whole of it is meant – is called synecdoche. Ships are also referred to as 'sails', in the same way.) The fact that Antonio took on a much more powerful opponent emphasised his courage.
54. 'Even those who resented his victory and bewailed their losses.'
55. *What's the matter?* 'Come to the point.'
57. *Phoenix* the ship's name. *fraught* cargo. *Candy* Candia, the old name for Crete.
60. *desperate of shame and state* An involved phrase, which loses much in prosaic rendering. The impression gained is of someone who has 'come down in the world' and has stopped caring what other people think – just the sort of person to fall foul of the authorities!
61. *brabble* brawl. *apprehend* arrest.

ACT 5 SCENE 1

[Exit. Enter ANTONIO *and* OFFICERS*]*

Viola
   Here comes the man, sir, that did rescue me.
Duke
   That face of his I do remember well;
   Yet when I saw it last it was besmear'd
   As black as Vulcan in the smoke of war.
   A baubling vessel was he captain of,   50
   For shallow draught and bulk unprizable,
   With which such scathful grapple did he make
   With the most noble bottom of our fleet
   That very envy and the tongue of loss
   Cried fame and honour on him. What's the matter?   55
First Officer
   Orsino, this is that Antonio
   That took the Phoenix and her fraught from Candy;
   And this is he that did the Tiger board
   When your young nephew Titus lost his leg.
   Here in the streets, desperate of shame and state,   60
   In private brabble did we apprehend him.

62. Ever generous, Viola intervenes on Antonio's behalf, pointing out he took her part in the 'duel' (***drew on my side***) and attributing even his highly offensive charges against her to some temporary mental aberration (***distraction***).
65. ***Notable*** Well-known, notorious.
66–8. Which concerns Orsino most, Antonio's piracy and his disorderly conduct, or his foolhardiness in putting himself right into his enemies' hands?
67. ***dear*** dire.
69. ***Be pleas'd that I . . .*** 'Please let me . . .'
71. ***on base and ground enough*** 'with good enough reason.' Having cleared up this point of honour, Antonio goes on to voice his indignation against Viola. (It is clear that his sense of betrayal still dominates all other feelings.)
72. ***A witchcraft*** In Antonio's mind, the whole episode, from his rescue of Sebastian, to this present bitter experience, must have been brought about by some evil power working against him – otherwise how could his own single-minded generosity have provoked such an inhuman reaction in the one he has befriended?
75. ***redeem*** The word implies rescue of someone from a situation from which he could not have saved himself – in this case, certain death from drowning.
77. ***retention*** holding back. (Almost the same as ***restraint***).
78. ***All his in dedication*** 'Entirely out of devotion to him.'
79. ***pure*** purely. ***of*** because of. ***his love*** my love for him.
80. ***adverse*** hostile.
81. ***drew*** drew my sword.
84. ***face me out of his acquaintance*** Malvolio accused Feste and the others of trying to 'face him out of his wits'. The meaning is the same here – when Viola protested (the audience, but not Antonio, know how sincerely) that she had no idea who he was, Antonio took it to be a particularly barefaced piece of deception.
85–6. A most effective expression. In a moment (***While one would wink***) Antonio felt he had become a complete stranger. This feeling of separation we tend to describe in spatial terms (e.g., 'miles apart') but Antonio's ***twenty years removed*** is perhaps more effective. ***denied me*** 'refused to give me.'
87. ***to*** for.

Viola
　He did me kindness, sir; drew on my side;
　But in conclusion put strange speech upon me.
　I know not what 'twas but distraction.
Duke
　Notable pirate, thou salt-water thief! 65
　What foolish boldness brought thee to their mercies
　Whom thou, in terms so bloody and so dear,
　Hast made thine enemies?
Antonio
　　　　　　　　　Orsino, noble sir,
　Be pleas'd that I shake off these names you give me:
　Antonio never yet was thief or pirate, 70
　Though I confess, on base and ground enough,
　Orsino's enemy. A witchcraft drew me hither:
　That most ingrateful boy there by your side
　From the rude sea's enrag'd and foamy mouth
　Did I redeem; a wreck past hope he was. 75
　His life I gave him, and did thereto add
　My love without retention or restraint,
　All his in dedication; for his sake,
　Did I expose myself, pure for his love,
　Into the danger of this adverse town; 80
　Drew to defend him when he was beset;
　Where being apprehended, his false cunning,
　Not meaning to partake with me in danger,
　Taught him to face me out of his acquaintance,
　And grew a twenty years removed thing 85
　While one would wink; denied me mine own purse,
　Which I had recommended to his use
　Not half an hour before.
Viola
　　　　　　　　　How can this be?
Duke
　When came he to this town?

91. *No int'rim* (interim) 'without any break.' ***not a minute's vacancy*** 'without the space of a minute (spent otherwise).'

93–6. These lines bring out very well Orsino's continuing passion for Olivia. She has only to make her appearance, and he turns away momentarily from everything else, as if it had never existed. It is only on second thoughts that he even recollects what Antonio has just been saying. He needs that split-second (between ***fellow*** and ***fellow***) before he can re-apply his attention and see how impossible Antonio's story is.

97–8. *What would my lord . . . seem serviceable?* is no more than a polite way of saying: 'What can I do for you?' ***but that he may not have*** 'except that which he cannot have' – meaning, of course, her love. Her earlier refusal to respond to his suit is now, she believes, strengthened beyond all question, by her newly contracted betrothal to somebody else.

99. What was the arrangement, in fact, with Sebastian – about which Viola can, of course, know nothing?

103. Viola's courtesy towards the Duke is impeccable. She won't answer Olivia simply because Orsino is waiting to say something. ***My duty*** (of deference towards my master) ***hushes me*** keeps me quiet.

104. *aught to the old tune* 'anything like your usual remarks.'

105. *fat and fulsome*. A fine alliterative phrase, both physical and figurative. This is exactly how Olivia feels now about the Duke's over-eloquent addresses.

106. *howling after music*. (Does she have in mind the way music sets some dogs howling?) Courtship from anyone – not just Orsino – will grate on her ears after Sebastian's promises of life-long fidelity.

107–8. *constant . . . to perverseness* implies that Olivia has been consistent (***constant***) only in her stubbornness (***perverseness***). ***uncivil*** discourteous. Olivia is being unnecessarily brutal just now.

109. *ingrate* ungrateful. ***unauspicious*** not responding favourably.

112. How should Olivia say this line? ***become*** suit.

Antonio
> To-day, my lord; and for three months before, 90
> No int'rim, not a minute's vacancy,
> Both day and night did we keep company.

> *[Enter* OLIVIA *and* ATTENDANTS*]*

Duke
> Here comes the Countess; now heaven walks on earth.
> But for thee, fellow – fellow, thy words are madness.
> Three months this youth hath tended upon me— 95
> But more of that anon. Take him aside.

Olivia
> What would my lord, but that he may not have,
> Wherein Olivia may seem serviceable?
> Cesario, you do not keep promise with me.

Viola
> Madam? 100

Duke
> Gracious Olivia—

Olivia
> What do you say, Cesario? Good my lord—

Viola
> My lord would speak; my duty hushes me.

Olivia
> If it be aught to the old tune, my lord,
> It is as fat and fulsome to mine ear 105
> As howling after music.

Duke
>   Still so cruel?

Olivia
> Still so constant, lord.

Duke
> What, to perverseness? You uncivil lady,
> To whose ingrate and unauspicious altars
> My soul the faithfull'st off'rings hath breath'd out 110
> That e'er devotion tender'd! What shall I do?

Olivia
> Even what it please my lord, that shall become him.

113–27. Orsino is so beside himself that he even speaks of murder. Rejecting this (he has not the ***heart to do it***), he directs his anger instead against Viola. He has no doubt now where Olivia's affections lie, and hints at ruthless counter-measures.

114. *Egyptian thief* a robber chief, Thyamis, who, when threatened with capture and probable death himself, attempted to kill one of his captives with whom he had fallen in love, so that they might be re-united in the next life. This was a popular story in Shakespeare's time.

116. *savours nobly* 'has something noble about it.' ***hear me this*** hear this from me.

117. *non-regardance* literally 'the act of not regarding'. To 'regard' someone meant to have a certain opinion about him; and so 'non-regardance' (no opinion at all) implies that someone or something is insignificant. ***faith*** good faith, sincerity (rather than faithfulness). Orsino will naturally resent Olivia's failure to appreciate his sincere offers of love.

118. *instrument* Whom does he mean?

119. *screws* What does his description of his 'rival's' success with Olivia gain by his use of this word? ***my true place*** What does this tell us about Orsino?

120. *Live you* is an imperative. He tells her to go on (***still***) being hard-hearted (***the marble-breasted tyrant***) if she is so indifferent to his own affection.

121. *minion* a scornful term applying to any servile dependant; and most apt if in fact 'Cesario', a mere page, had become Olivia's lover.

122. *tender* regard.

123–4. A loved-one was often spoken of as being 'in the eye of' the lover, as if the lover's eyes gaze so fondly that the other's image becomes permanently fixed there. ***in his master's spite*** in spite of his master.

125. *ripe in* ready for.

127. Olivia's heart is black (like the ***raven***) in contrast with her appearance of innocence (***dove***).

128–9. In spite of his threat to use her cruelly, simply to get his own back on Olivia, Viola has nothing but love and loyalty for her master. ***jocund*** joyful. ***apt*** ready. (Notice the use of the adverb ***willingly*** after the two adjectives.) ***To do*** to cause, give. Orsino's ***rest*** is contrasted with the ***thousand deaths*** Viola is willing to die to bring it about.

ACT 5 SCENE 1

Duke
    Why should I not, had I the heart to do it,
    Like to the Egyptian thief at point of death,
    Kill what I love? – a savage jealousy   115
    That sometime savours nobly. But hear me this:
    Since you to non-regardance cast my faith,
    And that I partly know the instrument
    That screws me from my true place in your favour,
    Live you the marble-breasted tyrant still;   120
    But this your minion, whom I know you love,
    And whom, by heaven I swear, I tender dearly,
    Him will I tear out of that cruel eye
    Where he sits crowned in his master's spite.
    Come, boy, with me; my thoughts are ripe in
        mischief: 125
    I'll sacrifice the lamb that I do love
    To spite a raven's heart within a dove.
Viola
    And I, most jocund, apt, and willingly,
    To do you rest, a thousand deaths would die.
Olivia
    Where goes Cesario?

130. This is Viola's first public affirmation of love for Orsino. But notice how it has come about. Unlike his own carefully thought-out words and occasions, this has come out suddenly, under the pressure of circumstances, with all the more spontaneity, probably, for that reason. (In the same way, Olivia suddenly found herself speaking openly about *her* love for Viola.) And even now, she is ostensibly expressing a young man's affectionate loyalty to his master. This is a most subtle moment – she may not yet be allowing even herself to think of her love for Orsino in any other way. For she is still committed (permanently, she must believe) to this 'sex-less' role, and so her attachment to the Duke may still (even in her own consciousness) be limited and 'de-fused'.
133. *witnesses above* Either 'the stars,' or, more Christianly, 'God and His angels'. The sense is the same – such a gross act of duplicity would simply cry out for divine retribution.
134. *Punish . . .* 'May you punish . . .' *tainting*. True love can be shared with one other person only; otherwise it gets spoiled.
135. *beguil'd* deceived.
137. *Hast thou forgot thyself?* To 'forget oneself' normally means to behave without proper restraint. But here it implies an almost literal forgetfulness of one's very identity. *Is it so long?* Olivia knows exactly when the betrothal took place. The point she is making is that it must be a lot longer ago, if Viola has already forgotten all about it.
138. *Come, away!* This is said to Viola.
139. But Olivia cannot just stand by, silent, and acquiesce in her 'husband's' dismissal. Her actual use of the word brings things at once to a head.
142. *the baseness of thy fear* Olivia implies that 'his' present fear is not worthy of him. But it is a momentary failing she speaks of and not the fatal weakness of character such a phrase would normally signify.
143. *propriety* identity. to *strangle* this, through fear, means to be too diffident to assert oneself.
144. *fortunes* The enhanced status of being married to a Countess seems to be Olivia's meaning in this and the next line.
145. 'Your present greatness will match your previous fear.'
149. *what* that which.

ACT 5 SCENE 1

Viola
                After him I love 130
More than I love these eyes, more than my life,
More, by all mores, than e'er I shall love wife.
If I do feign, you witnesses above
Punish my life for tainting of my love!
Olivia
  Ay me, detested! How am I beguil'd! 135
Viola
  Who does beguile you? Who does do you wrong?
Olivia
  Hast thou forgot thyself? Is it so long?
  Call forth the holy father.
        [Exit an ATTENDANT*]*

Duke
                Come, away!
Olivia
  Whither, my lord? Cesario, husband, stay.
Duke
  Husband?
Olivia
          Ay, husband; can he that deny? 140
Duke
  Her husband, sirrah?
Viola
              No, my lord, not I.
Olivia
  Alas, it is the baseness of thy fear
  That makes thee strangle thy propriety.
  Fear not, Cesario, take thy fortunes up;
  Be that thou know'st thou art, and then thou art 145
  As great as that thou fear'st.
        [Enter PRIEST*]*
              O, welcome, father!
  Father, I charge thee, by thy reverence,
  Here to unfold – though lately we intended
  To keep in darkness what occasion now

150. *ripe* ready. (Olivia refers to their previous plan to keep the betrothal secret till there was a suitable opportunity for the full marriage rite.)

152–7. The priest 'spells out' in order the various parts of the betrothal rite.

153. *joinder* joining.

154. *Attested* Certified. ***close*** union.

157. *Seal'd in my function* 'duly completed by me in my capacity as priest.' ***by my testimony*** Simply to be witness of the betrothal was no small part of the priest's role.

158–9. Very characteristically, the priest thinks in this way of the passage of time.

160–5. Orsino's scathing attack upon Viola would be amply justified if what Olivia and the priest have just said, were true – and there is no reason for him to think otherwise.

161. *grizzle* sprinkling of grey. ***case*** body (that which encloses or 'encases' the soul), or skin (which encloses the body).

163. *trip* false step. Orsino means that Viola's double-dealing will be her own undoing, so that she won't live long enough to have any grey hairs.

164–5. His final scornful dismissal is probably Viola's most painful experience.

166–7. Olivia seems to mean that Viola should not rely upon oaths but upon what ***little faith*** she has in the midst of all her ***fear***.

168. Sir Andrew's entrance, dramatically most opportune, postpones the solving of the puzzle, until full and final capital can be made out of Viola's mistaken identity, with Sir Toby and his cronies, and with Antonio and Sebastian. So Orsino's tirade, and Viola's and Olivia's protests, are 'frozen' – they must live with their torturing uncertainties for a little longer.

169. *presently* at once.

172. *coxcomb*. Normally, this means the jester's cap, designed to resemble a cock's 'comb'. Here it is used facetiously for 'head'.

Reveals before 'tis ripe – what thou dost know 150
Hath newly pass'd between this youth and me.
Priest
A contract of eternal bond of love,
Confirm'd by mutual joinder of your hands,
Attested by the holy close of lips,
Strengthen'd by interchangement of your rings 155
And all the ceremony of this compact
Seal'd in my function, by my testimony;
Since when, my watch hath told me, toward my grave,
I have travell'd but two hours.
Duke
O thou dissembling cub! What wilt thou be, 160
When time hath sow'd a grizzle on thy case?
Or will not else thy craft so quickly grow
That thine own trip shall be thine overthrow?
Farewell, and take her; but direct thy feet
Where thou and I henceforth may never meet. 165
Viola
My lord, I do protest—
Olivia
              O, do not swear!
Hold little faith, though thou hast too much fear.

[Enter SIR ANDREW*]*

Sir Andrew
For the love of God, a surgeon!
Send one presently to Sir Toby.
Olivia
What's the matter? 170
Sir Andrew
Has broke my head across, and has given Sir Toby a
bloody coxcomb too. For the love of God, your help!
I had rather than forty pound I were at home.
Olivia
Who has done this, Sir Andrew?

176. *incardinate*. Sir Andrew thinks he is saying 'incarnate' (='in human form').

178. *Od's lifelings*. This is one of the many oaths we have noted, where the name of God is 'disguised' in reverence. The suffix '-ling' has a diminutive force.

178–9. *for nothing* 'for no good reason, without provocation.'

179–80. *that that I did, I was set on to do't by Sir Toby* Even if there has been something provocative in his behaviour, it was Sir Toby's idea, not his own.

181–3. Viola is naturally baffled by this – she knows about the first part of their encounter but nothing of its violent conclusion. ***bespake you fair*** 'answered you quite reasonably.'

184–8. Sir Andrew's reaction to this is very amusing. We must imagine his aggrieved tone, and, no doubt, some rueful handling of his sore head. ***set nothing by*** 'don't take seriously.' ***tickl'd*** beaten. ***othergates*** otherwise.

190. Sir Toby is never over-deferential. He seems to have gained for himself that degree of licence so often accorded to people of his kind. He is so put out now that he brushes aside Orsino's enquiry almost rudely. ***That's all one*** 'What does it matter?' ***there's th'end on't*** 'That's all there is to it.' How well the contrast between him and Sir Andrew is brought out in their respective comments about their injuries! Sir Andrew almost whines in protest, whereas Sir Toby shows his annoyance by 'biting everyone's head off'. It is rather sad that this is the point at which he takes his leave. There has been a likeable side to him, and he has done as much as anyone in the play to stimulate humour. But it is not easy to remember this now, as he blusters out, insulting his friends and spurning the help that is offered. (Is it perhaps that Shakespeare wishes us never to make the fatal error – he would regard it as such – of giving our final approval to such a rogue?)

191. *Sot* fool. ***Dick Surgeon*** This seems a deliberately unceremonious way of addressing him.

192. *agone* ago.

193. *set* fixed (in a drunken stare).

194. *passy measures pavin* A corruption of the Italian 'passamezzo pavana'. The pavan was a stately dance; Sir Toby prefers the livelier measures.

192. Does he realise that this description of the Surgeon applies better to himself?

ACT 5 SCENE 1

Sir Andrew
The Count's gentleman, one Cesario. We took him for a coward, but he's the very devil incardinate.
Duke
My gentleman, Cesario?
Sir Andrew
Od's lifelings, here he is! You broke my head for nothing; and that that I did, I was set on to do't by Sir Toby.
Viola
Why do you speak to me? I never hurt you.
You drew your sword upon me without cause;
But I bespake you fair and hurt you not.

[Enter SIR TOBY and CLOWN]

Sir Andrew
If a bloody coxcomb be a hurt, you have hurt me; I think you set nothing by a bloody coxcomb. Here comes Sir Toby halting; you shall hear more; but if he had not been in drink, he would have tickl'd you othergates than he did.
Duke
How now, gentleman? How isn't with you?
Sir Toby
That's all one; has hurt me, and there's th' end on't. Sot, didst see Dick Surgeon, sot?
Clown
O, he's drunk, Sir Toby, an hour agone; his eyes were set at eight i' th' morning.
Sir Toby
Then he's a rogue and a passy measures pavin. I hate a drunken rogue.

198–9. The moment of 'disenchantment' does not yet seem to have arrived for Sir Andrew. His offer is in all sincerity, *be dress'd* 'have our wounds dressed.'

200–1. This is ingratitude and callousness at their worst. All these things are true about Sir Andrew; but why should Sir Toby face him with them now? After all, they have provided Sir Toby with his entertainment, and he has, all through the play, carefully nurtured them for this very purpose. Is 'gull' left to the end because Sir Toby despises it most?

203. Sebastian's appearance now, like Sir Andrew's a little earlier, has the effect of switching our attention forward once again. The central reconciliation, which, apart from Malvolio and his fortunes, will bring everything else into line and harmony, can be delayed no longer. Now at last, Viola and her brother come face to face – the first time since their separation in the wreck. Note the continuity: the last thing in everyone's mind has been the unexplained assault upon Sir Toby and Sir Andrew. So Sebastian's first comment is about this; this minor point is to be cleared up first. It is followed by his reconciliation with Antonio; then, keeping, as it were, the best till last, the joyful recognition between brother and sister with a happy ending for both.

205. *with wit and safety* 'if I were to take sensible steps for my own safety.' (He was after all acting in self-defence.)

206. Why in fact did Olivia look 'strangely' (distantly) at him?

208. *for* for the sake of.

209. *so late ago* 'such a little while ago.'

210. *habit* dress. (Why did these have to be the same?)

211. *perspective* an optical instrument which produced a stereoscopic effect. When two pictures were looked at through it, they appeared as one. Orsino describes the sudden appearance together of the twins as a *natural perspective* because its effect is equally fantastic but without artificial aid. *is and is not.* What they see is actually there, and yet it seems an impossibility.

215. *Fear'st thou that . . . ?* From this question, we can deduce that Antonio's first reaction is (quite understandably) to recoil, as one does when confronted by what seems a supernatural event.

216–18. A most effective description of identical twinship.

ACT 5 SCENE 1

Olivia
   Away with him. Who hath made this havoc with
   them?
Sir Andrew
   I'll help you, Sir Toby, because we'll be dress'd
   together.
Sir Toby
   Will you help – an ass-head and a coxcomb and a   200
   knave, a thin fac'd knave, a gull?
Olivia
   Get him to bed, and let his hurt be look'd to.

   [Exeunt CLOWN, FABIAN, SIR TOBY, *and* SIR ANDREW, *Enter*
   SEBASTIAN*]*

Sebastian
   I am sorry, madam, I have hurt your kinsman;
   But, had it been the brother of my blood,
   I must have done no less with wit and safety.   205
   You throw a strange regard upon me, and by that
   I do perceive it hath offended you.
   Pardon me, sweet one, even for the vows
   We made each other but so late ago.
Duke
   One face, one voice, one habit, and two persons!   210
   A natural perspective, that is and is not.
Sebastian
   Antonio, O my dear Antonio!
   How have the hours rack'd and tortur'd me
   Since I have lost thee!
Antonio
   Sebastian are you?
Sebastian
               Fear'st thou that, Antonio?   215
Antonio
   How have you made division of yourself?
   An apple cleft in two is not more twin
   Than these two creatures. Which is Sebastian?

220. *Do I stand there?* Sebastian only now catches sight of his sister.
221–2. *deity . . . here and everywhere* One of the divine attributes is generally held to be 'omnipresence' – being in all places at the same time.
224. *Of charity* 'Out of the goodness of your heart, tell me . . .' Still unsure of what all this means, Sebastian expresses his unconscious need of kindly treatment.
225. *What countryman* 'What country are you from?'
227. *Such a Sebastian* Like the one standing in front of her.
228. *So . . . suited* 'dressed like you.'
226–30. Viola still finds it hard to believe that spirits *can* appear in this way – actually wearing the clothes of a once-living person. Her chief reaction to it is to fear the worst. ***A spirit I am indeed.*** He reassures her, that he *is* a spirit, but a body also – like every other human being.
231. *in that dimension grossly clad. Grossly* because the body was thought of as 'gross' or heavy, dull and base, by comparison with the spirit.
233. *Were you . . .*; 'If you were . . .'; ***as the rest goes even*** 'as the rest of the evidence seems to agree.'

236–42. The next bit of dialogue, with its incomplete lines, catches their mood of excitement and near-certainty.

240. *lively* fresh. (The day of his father's death is still very vivid in Sebastian's memory.)
241. *finished . . . his mortal act* died.
243. *lets* hinders, prevents. 'If nothing stands in the way of our happiness.'
244. *But* except. ***usurp'd*** Male attire is not properly hers.
246. *jump* agree. (What further confirmation can Viola have in mind, apart from allowing her brother to see her in familiar female dress?)

ACT 5 SCENE 1

Olivia
   Most wonderful!
Sebastian
   Do I stand there? I never had a brother;   220
   Nor can there be that deity in my nature
   Of here and everywhere. I had a sister
   Whom the blind waves and surges have devour'd.
   Of charity, what kin are you to me?
   What countryman, what name, what parentage?   225
Viola
   Of Messaline; Sebastian was my father.
   Such a Sebastian was my brother too;
   So went he suited to his watery tomb;
   If spirits can assume both form and suit,
   You come to fright us.
Sebastian
                       A spirit I am indeed,   230
   But am in that dimension grossly clad
   Which from the womb I did participate.
   Were you a woman, as the rest goes even,
   I should my tears let fall upon your cheek,
   And say 'Thrice welcome, drowned Viola!'   235
Viola
   My father had a mole upon his brow.
Sebastian
   And so had mine.
Viola
   And died that day when Viola from her birth
   Had number'd thirteen years.
Sebastian
   O, that record is lively in my soul!   240
   He finished indeed his mortal act
   That day that made my sister thirteen years.
Viola
   If nothing lets to make us happy both
   But this my masculine usurp'd attire,
   Do not embrace me till each circumstance   245
   Of place, time, fortune, do cohere and jump

249. *weeds* clothing.

251. 'All that has happened to me.'

253. *So comes it* . . . 'So it comes about (that) . . .
254–8. Nature, by providing identical twins, male and female, has 'come to the rescue,' and what would have been a disaster has turned out perfectly. Her wooing of the wrong person will have served as a perfectly adequate prelude to her mature love for the right person!
259–61. After his reassurance to the still bewildered Olivia, the Duke says these lines more to himself than anyone else. ***glass*** a reference back to ***perspective*** (line 211).
260. *share in this most happy wreck* The ***wreck*** is indeed producing happiness at last – for Sebastian and Olivia. It may surprise us that Orsino can already see a happy outcome for himself, too. (His rapid detachment from Olivia, and attachment to Viola, is one of the less credible parts of the play. We are, however, somewhat prepared for this: Orsino has always been presented to us as one whose emotions are less deeply involved than he himself claims or believes.)
262. From this, we might infer that Viola's impact upon him has been considerably greater than even he at the time recognised. He has no difficulty in calling her words to mind.
263. Now, for the first time, Viola can voice her feelings for him in full womanly affection, ***overswear*** swear with even greater solemnity and insistence.
264. *as true in soul* 'as wholeheartedly.'
265. *orbed continent* the sun.
269. *upon some action* because of some legal action. (This is the first time we hear of it. What purpose is served in the play by this? Is it simply a link-up with Malvolio, to bring him again into the picture?)
270. *in durance* in custody. ***at Malvolio's suit*** at Malvolio's instigation (in the sense probably that Malvolio took legal action against him).
272. *enlarge* set free. (Compare 'at large'.)
273. *now I remember me* 'now I come to think of it.' (Malvolio's fortunes have been crowded right out of her mind, till this moment.)
274. *distract* distracted. (As we have noticed before, she still has a good deal of feeling left for her steward, even if it is now only pity.)
275. *extracting* drawing away (my thoughts) from everything else. (It seems to take up the idea of ***distract*.**)

That I am Viola; which to confirm,
I'll bring you to a captain in this town,
Where lie my maiden weeds; by whose gentle help
I was preserv'd to serve this noble Count. 250
All the occurrence of my fortune since
Hath been between this lady and this lord.
Sebastian [To OLIVIA*]*
So comes it, lady, you have been mistook;
But nature to her bias drew in that.
You would have been contracted to a maid; 255
Nor are you therein, by my life, deceiv'd;
You are betroth'd both to a maid and man.
Duke
Be not amaz'd; right noble is his blood.
If this be so, as yet the glass seems true,
I shall have share in this most happy wreck. 260
[To VIOLA*]* Boy, thou hast said to me a thousand times
Thou never shouldst love woman like to me.
Viola
And all those sayings will I overswear;
And all those swearings keep as true in soul
As doth that orbed continent the fire 265
That severs day from night.
Duke
                    Give me thy hand;
And let me see thee in thy woman's weeds.
Viola
The captain that did bring me first on shore
Hath my maid's garments. He, upon some action,
Is now in durance, at Malvolio's suit, 270
A gentleman and follower of my lady's.
Olivia
He shall enlarge him. Fetch Malvolio hither;
And yet, alas, now I remember me,
They say, poor gentleman, he's much distract.

    [Re-enter CLOWN, *with a letter, and* FABIAN*]*

A most extracting frenzy of mine own 275

276. *his* his frenzy. (Lines 275–6 could well be an 'aside'.) The arrival of Feste, and Fabian, and the letter, focuses attention still further upon Malvolio.
278. *Belzebub* the Devil's chief assistant, or, perhaps, the Devil himself. ***holds . . . at the stave's end*** 'barely keeps at bay.' (A staff or stave was useful in keeping one's enemies at a distance.) They still think of Malvolio – or pretend to – as being devil-possessed.
There remains now only the clearing up of Malvolio's troubles; everything else is potentially set to rights. The letter he has composed from his 'cell' therefore, re-opens his whole case. Otherwise, like Olivia, we too might have forgotten about him. The play virtually ends with Malvolio's final protest – himself against the whole assembled company – and their verdict upon him. The last words, however, are for the Duke to deliver, as the conventional ending. But these, by themselves, are not enough; the main plot needs to be rounded off a little more smoothly; and this in fact is what is seen to while Malvolio is being fetched.
280–2. *to-day morning* this morning, ***epistles*** and ***gospels*** are the Church names for those parts of Holy Scripture read, one of each, in the Holy Communion Service or Mass, which customarily took place in the early morning. Feste is playing on the two usages of ***epistle*** (Malvolio's letter is an epistle) to provide his facetious excuse for delay. ***it skills not*** 'it makes no difference.'
284. *delivers* 'reads the words of.'
287. *I do but read madness* Is there a hint here at something deeper – a wistful defence of jesting, which exists solely to imitate human foibles, so that the jester's madness is always in that sense our own?
288. *as it ought to be* Madmen's words ought to be delivered madly. It is clear that Feste has begun to read in a really crazy way, perhaps shrieking.
289. *allow vox* allow me to speak. (***vox*** is the Latin for 'voice'.)
290–2. A further quibble on the same point – he must be mentally alert to be able to convey Malvolio's madness through his actual tone of voice and his gestures; ***to read his right wits*** 'to reproduce his true state.'
292. *perpend* consider.
294. *Read it you* 'You read it.'
298. *benefit* natural gift.
300. *semblance* show. (Malvolio refers to the uncharacteristic dress and mannerisms he was tricked into adopting.)
301. *myself much right . . . you much shame* He hopes that when the contents of the letter are divulged, that will clear him, and cause her some shame. (We might have expected 'and' rather than *or*.)
302–3. *I leave my duty a little unthought of* 'I am somewhat neglecting my duty to you.' (He means his duty of due deference to his mistress – he should not speak so frankly to her.)
303. *out of* out of a sense of.

ACT 5 SCENE 1

From my remembrance clearly banish'd his.
How does he, sirrah?
Clown
Truly, madam, he holds Belzebub at the stave's end
as well as a man in his case may do. Has here writ a
letter to you; I should have given't you to-day morning, 280
but as a madman's epistles are no gospels, so it skills
not much when they are deliver'd.
Olivia
Open't, and read it.
Clown
Look then to be well edified when the fool delivers
the madman. *[Reads madly]* 'By the Lord, madam—' 285
Olivia
How now! Art thou mad?
Clown
No, madam, I do but read madness.
An your ladyship will have it as it ought to be, you
must allow vox.
Olivia
Prithee read i' thy right wits. 290
Clown
So I do, Madonna; but to read his right wits is to
read thus; therefore perpend, my Princess, and give
ear.
Olivia [To FABIAN*]*
Read it you, sirrah.
Fabian [Reads]
'By the Lord, madam, you wrong me, and the world 295
shall know it. Though you have put me into darkness
and given your drunken cousin rule over me, yet
have I the benefit of my sense as well as your ladyship. I have your own letter that induced me to the
semblance I put on, with the which I doubt not but 300
to do myself much right or you much shame. Think
of me as you please. I leave my duty a little unthought
of, and speak out of my injury.
     THE MADLY-US'D MALVOLIO.'

306. *savours not much of* 'doesn't sound like.' (Literally 'has no taste of.')

308–18. While Fabian is off-stage, Olivia and Orsino confirm their relationship. This is done briefly, almost perfunctorily. The excitement of the play is all in its tensions and 'impossible' situations – once these are resolved, the drama is virtually exhausted, and there is little to be gained by dwelling on the sequel.
308. *these things further thought on* 'when you have thought more about these things.'
308–9. Olivia will be a sister in view of the union obviously impending between him and the sister of her own Sebastian.
310. *th' alliance* i.e. of herself and Orsino, as 'brother and sister', which will come about when he and Viola are duly joined together. ***on't*** of it.
311. *proper* own. She makes this offer perhaps in Sebastian's name. As Viola's next of kin, he will have some obligation to make this provision for his sister's wedding.
312. *apt* ready.
313. *quits* sets free (from service as his page).
314. *mettle* essential character.
318. Olivia and Viola can freely and happily embrace.

321–37. If anything, Malvolio's stature now is greater than before. There is a dignity, even if a stiff and cold one, and a certain integrity. He is, for better or worse, still himself – disillusioned in the matter of his hoped-for alliance with Olivia, but not broken by his humiliation. He feels his injuries keenly – he makes no secret about that – but he seeks no favours of anyone; his only request is that Olivia shall explain her conduct.

Olivia
  Did he write this?
Clown
  Ay, Madam. 305
Duke
  This savours not much of distraction.
Olivia
  See him deliver'd, Fabian; bring him hither.
             [Exit FABIAN*]*
  My lord, so please you, these things further thought on,
  To think me as well a sister as a wife,
  One day shall crown th' alliance on't, so please you, 310
  Here at my house, and at my proper cost.
Duke
  Madam, I am most apt t'embrace your offer.
  [To VIOLA*]* Your master quits you; and, for your
    service done him,
  So much against the mettle of your sex,
  So far beneath your soft and tender breeding, 315
  And since you call'd me master for so long,
  Here is my hand; you shall from this time be
  Your master's mistress.
Olivia
                A sister! You are she.
      [Re-enter FABIAN, *with* MALVOLIO*]*

Duke
  Is this the madman?
Olivia
              Ay, my lord, this same.
  How now, Malvolio! 320
Malvolio
  Madam, you have done me wrong,
  Notorious wrong.
Olivia
            Have I, Malvolio? No.
Malvolio
  Lady, you have. Pray you peruse that letter.
  You must not now deny it is your hand;

325. **Write from it** 'Write differently.' *in hand or phrase* in actual handwriting or style.

327. **Well, grant it then** Olivia has not recovered herself sufficiently to contradict him, so he assumes that she admits authorship.

328. **modesty** moderation, simple expression.

332. **the lighter people**. How would Sir Toby have reacted to this?

336. **geck** fool.

339. **character** handwriting.

342. **cam'st** Malvolio is the subject of this verb, not Maria.

343–4. **pre-suppose'd Upon thee** 'suggested beforehand, for you to adopt.' **Prithee, be content** Olivia checks in advance a protest Malvolio is obviously about to make at this point.

345. **shrewdly** cruelly. 'What they have done has turned out most cruelly for you.'

346. **grounds** reason.

347. **plaintiff** the injured party who pleads his cause in a court of law.

349. Fabian in a sense speaks for us all. They must not allow the happy atmosphere to be spoiled. To ensure this, he is quite prepared to accept his own share of the blame.

352. **wonder'd at** 'found so wonderful.'

355. **upon** because of. **parts** characteristics.

356. **conceiv'd against him** 'thought him guilty of.'

357. **importance** importunity. (To 'importune' is persistently to urge or pester.)

359. **sportful** playful, good-humoured. (This is intended to take the 'sting' out of **malice**.)

360. **pluck on** induce.

Write from it if you can, in hand or phrase; 325
Or say 'tis not your seal, not your invention;
You can say none of this. Well, grant it then,
And tell me, in the modesty of honour,
Why you have given me such clear lights of favour,
Bade me come smiling and cross-garter'd to you, 330
To put on yellow stockings, and to frown
Upon Sir Toby and the lighter people;
And, acting this in an obedient hope,
Why have you suffer'd me to be imprison'd,
Kept in a dark house, visited by the priest, 335
And made the most notorious geck and gull
That e'er invention play'd on? Tell me why.
Olivia
Alas, Malvolio, this is not my writing,
Though, I confess, much like the character;
But out of question 'tis Maria's hand. 340
And now I do bethink me, it was she
First told me thou wast mad; then cam'st in smiling,
And in such forms which here were pre-suppos'd
Upon thee in the letter. Prithee, be content;
This practice hath most shrewdly pass'd upon thee, 345
But, when we know the grounds and authors of it,
Thou shalt be both the plaintiff and the judge
Of thine own cause.
Fabian
Good madam, hear me speak,
And let no quarrel nor no brawl to come 350
Taint the condition of this present hour,
Which I have wonder'd at. In hope it shall not,
Most freely I confess myself and Toby
Set this device against Malvolio here,
Upon some stubborn and uncourteous parts 355
We had conceiv'd against him. Maria writ
The letter, at Sir Toby's great importance,
In recompense whereof he hath married her.
How with a sportful malice it was follow'd
May rather pluck on laughter than revenge, 360

361–2. There have been faults on both sides, and Fabian asks that they be fairly weighed. Fabian has been given some very significant lines to deliver. He has to strike a sober note, and hint at a larger justice than has frequently been evident. What he says is some justification in effect of the whole play. He does it with dignity and a certain finality. He brings in a sanity which helps to offset Feste's unbridled sneers and Malvolio's savage reply.

363. baffl'd brought to public ridicule.

364–70. Fabian has spoken fairly, Olivia pityingly, but Feste positively taunts his victim. In this he serves two purposes. There are, in every audience, those for whom a subtle revenge is not enough, and who insist that every possible advantage shall be taken of the 'villain' once he is down. Such are delighted when Feste throws Malvolio's earlier strictures (almost perfectly remembered) back in his face. They have been waiting for just such a moment, and would feel cheated without it. Feste's words also have their necessary part in the working out of the 'Humours' element, which presents us with stereotyped characters, and an equally fixed scale of punishment and reward. Created as such, Malvolio must, for his unmitigated self-love, receive and carry away with him the full weight of scorn and ridicule. But because *Twelfth Night* is only partly a 'Comedy of Humours', we are spared the spectacle, at the end, of wholesale condemnation of him. Instead, Feste's unholy glee, while catering for certain elements in the audience – perhaps in each one of us – is relieved by a more enlightened humaneness from other quarters. To hold these two distinctive concepts in balance is one of the play's greatest achievements.

365. thrown. The original letter said **thrust**.

366. interlude a short play within the main one.

366–7. that's all one Compare line 190.

370. whirligig a spinning top. The idea is that just as any one point on a rotating object is bound to come round again to where it started, so, if one waits long enough, all wrong-doing will meet with its proper punishment. (It is the same as 'the wheel coming full circle', a fairly familiar image.) The clown's function, as we have noticed, was to stand back from events, from time to time, and comment shrewdly, even cynically, but always to good effect. This line of his makes some amends for the personal invective preceding it.

371. So Malvolio finally leaves us, indifferent to affection and offering none, neither giving nor seeking forgiveness.

If that the injuries be justly weigh'd
That have on both sides pass'd.
Olivia
Alas, poor fool, how have they baffl'd thee!
Clown
Why, 'Some are born great, some achieve greatness, and some have greatness thrown upon them'. I was one, sir, in this interlude – one Sir Topas, sir; but that's all one. 'By the Lord, fool, I am not mad!' But do you remember – 'Madam, why laugh you at such a barren rascal? An you smile not, he's gagg'd'? And thus the whirligig of time brings in his revenges. 365

370

Malvolio
I'll be reveng'd on the whole pack of you.

[Exit]

372–3. But, in welcome contrast, both Olivia and Orsino are prepared to receive him back into the 'family circle'. ***notoriously abus'd*** disgracefully ill-treated.

373. *entreat him to a peace* 'try to persuade him to make friends.'

374. We hope this is not Orsino's only reason for wanting Malvolio calmed down!

375. *golden time*. An interesting and very Shakespearean phrase. 'The occasion that will crown all that has gone before with happy fulfilment.' ***convents*** either, 'summons': or 'is convenient'.

376. *solemn combination*. This is probably kept deliberately vague to include both the actual marriages and the closer relationship between all four that will result.

377. *souls* selves.

380. *habits* clothes.

381. *fancy's queen* because she receives the full homage of his love *fancy* = love.)

382–401. This kind of ending was quite familiar on the Elizabethan stage, and is not without its counterpart in modern entertainment. Music has played a significant part in *Twelfth Night*, and the songs have contributed in their own right to the mood and action. This concluding piece, addressed to the audience, and most likely accompanied by a little dance, is an odd mixture of doggerel and shrewd insight. It captures the wistfulness that haunts so much of the clown's more obvious banter and crudeness. In it, Feste traces step by step the frustrations of his own mean existence, from boyhood to old age, its futility brought out in each second and fourth line, where wind and rain keep up their burden of sublime indifference. But the song does no more than hint gently at this. The ending of the piece, however, brings us back to the business of the moment. The world will go on as it always has, but the play is over; and the clown, on behalf of the whole company, hopes we have enjoyed it.

382. *and* This is superfluous; it may have been inserted by a playhouse musician.

384. The child's only experience then of the folly of life was through his playthings.

388. *knaves and thieves* Feste seems to put himself before us as a rogue, on the 'wrong side of the law'. (In spite of the plurals here, and further on, Feste is speaking of himself throughout, at least ostensibly.)

390. *to wive* to be married.

394–7. This clumsy stanza seems to suggest that the singer and his wife always went to bed drunk. (***toss-pots*** drunkards.)

Olivia
   He hath been most notoriously abus'd.
Duke
   Pursue him, and entreat him to a peace;
   He hath not told us of the captain yet.
   When that is known, and golden time convents,   375
   A solemn combination shall be made
   Of our dear souls. Meantime, sweet sister,
   We will not part from hence. Cesario, come;
   For so you shall be while you are a man;
   But when in other habits you are seen,   380
   Orsino's mistress, and his fancy's queen.

        [Exeunt all but the CLOWN*]*
        *[*CLOWN *sings]*

   When that I was and a little tiny boy,
      With hey, ho, the wind and the rain,
   A foolish thing was but a toy,
      For the rain it raineth every day.   385

   But when I came to man's estate,
      With hey, ho, the wind and the rain,
   'Gainst knaves and thieves men shut their gate,
      For the rain it raineth every day.

   But when I came, alas! to wive,   390
      With hey, ho, the wind and the rain,
   By swaggering could I never thrive,
      For the rain it raineth every day.

   But when I came unto my beds,
      With hey, ho, the wind and the rain,   395
   With toss-pots still had drunken heads,
      For the rain it raineth every day.

   A great while ago the world begun,
      With hey, ho, the wind and the rain,
   But that's all one, our play is done,   400
      And we'll strive to please you every day.

        [Exit]